The Alcaic Metre
in the English Imagination

Also available from Bloomsbury

Reading Poetry, Writing Genre edited by Silvio Bär and Emily Hauser
Sappho and Catullus in Twentieth-Century Italian and North American Poetry
by Cecilia Piantanida
Victorian Horace by Stephen Harrison

The Alcaic Metre
in the English Imagination

John Talbot

BLOOMSBURY ACADEMIC
LONDON • NEW YORK • OXFORD • NEW DELHI • SYDNEY

BLOOMSBURY ACADEMIC
Bloomsbury Publishing Plc
50 Bedford Square, London, WC1B 3DP, UK
1385 Broadway, New York, NY 10018, USA
29 Earlsfort Terrace, Dublin 2, Ireland

BLOOMSBURY, BLOOMSBURY ACADEMIC and the Diana logo are
trademarks of Bloomsbury Publishing Plc

First published in Great Britain 2022
Paperback edition published 2024

Cover design: Terry Woodley
Cover image © Chronicle / Alamy Stock Photo (Sappho) and Pictorial Press Ltd / Alamy
Stock Photo (W. H. Auden)

A catalogue record for this book is available from the British Library.

Library of Congress Cataloging-in-Publication Data
Names: Talbot, John, 1966- author.
Title: The Alcaic metre in the English imagination / John Talbot. Description: London;
New York : Bloomsbury Academic, 2022. | Includes bibliographical references and index.
Identifiers: LCCN 2022004151 | ISBN 9781350232495 (hardback) | ISBN 9781350232532
(paperback) | ISBN 9781350232501 (ebook) | ISBN 9781350232518 (epub) |
ISBN 9781350232525 Subjects: LCSH: English poetry–History and criticism. |
English language–Versification. | English literature–Classical influences. | Latin
language–Metrics and rhythmics. | Greek language–Metrics and rhythmics. | Classical
languages–Influence on English. Classification: LCC PR508.V45 T35 2022 |
DDC 821/.04–dc23/eng/20220331
LC record available at https://lccn.loc.gov/2022004151

ISBN: HB: 978-1-3502-3249-5
         PB: 978-1-3502-3253-2
         ePDF: 978-1-3502-3250-1
         eBook: 978-1-3502-3251-8

Typeset by RefineCatch Limited, Bungay, Suffolk

To find out more about our authors and books visit www.bloomsbury.com
and sign up for our newsletters.

uxori carissimae

Contents

Permissions

Acknowledgements

I am grateful to many colleagues and students – among them both scholars and poets – who have contributed in various ways to this book. I thank my university for generous support, and the editors of *Studies in Philology*, *Classical Journal*, *The International Journal of the Classical Tradition* and Cambridge University Press for permission to adapt some portions of my work that originally appeared in their pages. Any study of the alcaic strophe in English must acknowledge the seminal work of Rosanna Warren, to whom I am grateful also for enlightening conversations. Editors Alice Wright and Lily Mac Mahon have offered unstinting and expert advice and support. During the writing of this book, my appreciation of both Latin and English poetry has been enriched and quickened by many conversations with Victoria Moul.

By far my greatest debt is to Sandy Talbot.

Preface

'Curious prosodic fauna'

There's a rueful provocation within W. H. Auden's fantasy of his ideal audience: 'Every poet has his dream reader: mine keeps a lookout for curious prosodic fauna like bacchics and choriambs.'[1] Rueful, because what poet could expect modern readers to meet him on such terms as these? How many readers know or care that a choriamb is a dipping cadence – two short syllables sandwiched between two long ones (– u u –), or that a bacchic (u – –) rather steeply rises from a single short to two longs?[2] One very good critic has called Auden's preoccupation with metre 'irritatingly reductive', since there is so much more to poetry than formal technique, let alone such exotic material specimens as bacchics and choriambs.[3] What poet, however formidable his poetic powers, could seriously wish to attract the admiration of the metrical equivalent of bird-watchers or train-spotters? Auden could be suspected of reducing his poetry to a faintly snobbish game, on something like the level of finishing the *Times* cryptic crossword before rising from the breakfast table. What's worse, Auden's notion of his ideal reader flies in the face of his own concession, sixteen years earlier, that his 'dream reader' was increasingly unlikely to exist. 'We have to accept as an accomplished fact', he had written in 1948, 'that the educated man of today can read neither Latin nor Greek.'[4] Your dream reader, a connoisseur of choriambs? In these days of very small Latin and almost no Greek? Dream on, Wystan.

Provocative, though, in that anticipating just such objections, Auden insists on the power of ancient Greek and Latin metres on the English poetic imagination. And not just classical metres generally, but specifically (because bacchics and choriambs belong to this class) lyric poetry, the most metrically intricate sort of classical verse, the kind most alien – in its formal aspects – to English poetry. You could dismiss Auden's remark as characteristically flip, in the manner of the impish schoolmaster he sometimes affected. Already by the mid-twentieth century (and how much more so now, in the twenty-first), to compose poems with obscure Greek metres in mind was becoming an eccentricity. It is asking too much of today's readers even to recognize classical metres, let alone appreciate them.

But I take Auden's point seriously, and in this book take up the challenge of behaving like one of his dream readers, keeping my eye peeled for classical prosodic flora like bacchics and choriambs, not only in Auden's own poems (where they abound) but throughout poetry in English. The test will be whether I can show that such interest serves greater ends than the gratification of pedants, and that by 'curious prosodic fauna' Auden meant something more than mere curiosities. If it proved true that the elements of Greek and Latin metre in English verse were charged with feeling and meaning, then to identify them, and flesh out their critical implications, would be to recover a dimension of poetic expressiveness that increasingly eludes even intelligent readers.

What kinds of expressiveness tend to get lost, and what kind of nuances can be recovered? I need a handle with which to pick up that large bundle, and in this book focus on one verse form: the alcaic strophe or stanza, an ancient metre, devised by a Greek poet, modified and perfected by a Roman poet, and passed down through many generations of modern neo-Latin poets and versifiers.[5] It has for five hundred years exerted pressure on the sonic and visual contours of English verse, and because its relation to English literature is unusual, it offers a particularly useful way of exploring the effects of classical metres in English poetry.

Before coming to alcaics, though, I propose, as a test case, a poem of Robert Frost's, written in a different classical metre. It's a useful way in, since it will immediately reward our keeping a lookout for those curious prosodic fauna, choriambs.

'To tease the metrists': Robert Frost and an ancient metre

Robert Frost first published one of his most celebrated lyrics, 'For Once, Then, Something', in the July 1920 issue of *Harper's Magazine*. It is an account of a failed epiphany: the speaker's inability to see beyond the superficial or material realm into whatever may lie beyond. A lofty theme, but developed, characteristically, through humble quotidian particulars: the speaker kneels at a well, gazing into the water with the hope of seeing through to the bottom. Just at the moment when he thinks he has caught a glimpse of something beneath the surface – maybe a pebble, a glimpse of which may betoken the flash of some ultimate insight – a droplet of water from an overhanging fern falls into the well, scrambles the image, breaks the spell, and jarringly returns the speaker's vision to the superficial plane.

Others taunt me with having knelt at well-curbs
Always wrong to the light, so never seeing
Deeper down in the well than where the water
Gives me back in a shining surface picture
Me myself in the summer heaven godlike
Looking out of a wreath of fern and cloud puffs.
Once, while trying with chin against a well-curb
I discerned, as I thought, beyond the picture,
Through the picture, a something, white, uncertain,
Something more of the depths – and then I lost it.
Water came to rebuke the too clear water.
One drop fell from the fern, and lo, a ripple
Shook whatever it was lay there at bottom,
Blurred it, blotted it out. What was that whiteness?
Truth? A pebble of quartz? For once, then, something.[6]

The poem is rich in classical reference, but one could be forgiven for not noticing. Frost has taken care to avoid obvious classical elements. Here are no Graeco-Roman stage properties such as Milton's 'woful Shepherds' weeping for Lycidas, or Keats's 'marble men and maidens overwrought'. True, when the speaker sees himself in his reflection 'godlike / Looking out of a wreath of fern', that's a picture of a classical poet crowned with a wreath, but the image is fleeting, its classical reference underplayed. The tone, too, is self-deprecating. The speaker's posture – gazing at his own reflection – unflatteringly recalls Ovid's Narcissus. This is classical reception with the lightest of touch.

It takes an Audenesque eye – keeping a lookout for curious prosodic fauna like bacchics and choriambs – to see into the depths of this poem, which impishly protests its own shallowness. Choriambs are, in fact, precisely at issue. That is because the poem is composed in an accentual-syllabic approximation of the ancient Greek and Roman metre known as the phalaecean hendecasyllabic, whose metrical pattern can be represented like this: – – – u u – u – u – u. The first, second, and final syllables are variable, but among the fixed syllables, there's the choriamb, right in the middle: syllables three through six. The remaining part of the line, syllables seven through eleven, takes on an iambic movement whose very familiarity to anglophone ears is likely to mislead readers about the metre of the poem as a whole. English-speakers are acculturated to listen for the alternation of stressed and unstressed syllables out of which iambic verse is formed, and that expectation can blind readers, or I should say deafen them, to the choriambic core of these lines. Adjusting their aural expectations, though – keeping a lookout for the choriambs – readers can not only feel the movement of the choriambs, but notice how often they coincide with particularly relevant sense-units: the speaker's predicament ('wrong to the light'), the object of his gaze ('down in the well'), his deepening questioning ('more of the depths'), the sequence of events that thwart him ('came to rebuke', 'fell from the fern', 'blotted it out'), and the final, equivocal sense of what he may or may not have glimpsed ('pebble of quartz?'). The choriambic lilt is not only classical, and not only graceful in itself: it is also an organizing element of Frost's thought, a ripple (in a poem with a significant and vexing ripple) in what might have been the familiar iambic pattern that too many critics have mistaken it for. To feel that choriambic ripple is to enter into the metrical texture of the poem. This sort of experience, of the distinct metrical textures of classical lyric verse forms as they make themselves felt in the alien context of English poetry, will be a pervasive concern of this book.

Important as those local metrical effects are, the classical metre in Frost's poem generates wider contextual resonances. As an instance of classical reception, this is all the more striking because it is the only poem Frost ever composed in imitation of a classical metre. He was himself preoccupied with its metrical aspect. One afternoon in 1917, Frost had been tutoring his schoolgirl daughter Lesley in the rhythms of Latin metres. To help her master the hendecasyllabic, Frost challenged her to a contest: father and daughter would try their hand at composing a poem in English hendecasyllabics. The result was the germ of 'For Once, Then, Something' – my point is that the poem emerged from the metre, not the other way round.[7] Two years later Frost was still tinkering with that tricky verse form. 'I've been trying Hen Dekker syllables,' he reported in a letter to Lesley, 'but without much luck lately.'[8] Bad luck or not, he was enjoying experimenting with the metre: 'Between you and me,' he confided to a friend that same month, 'I am having a lot of fun with *Hen Dekker* syllables.'[9]

Frost's choice of this exotic classical metre is exactly the kind of literary move that motivates this book. But his is a surprising choice, given his commitment to the English iambic line. 'In our language,' Frost wrote in a preface to his *Collected Poems*, 'there are virtually but two [metres], strict and loose iambic.'[10] 'Virtually all his verse is iambically based', a leading metrist confirms.[11] More to the point, Frost criticized poets such as Robert Bridges who – as we will see in Chapter 5 of this book – sought to reproduce in English the quantitative measures of classical verse. 'Vowels [in English] have length there is no denying,' Frost conceded. 'But the accent of sense supersedes all other accent[,] overrides and sweeps it away.'[12] He congratulated himself for resisting the temptation to go so far in his emulation of Virgil's *Eclogues* as to try to reproduce its metre – dactylic hexameters – in his own English.[13] So why did a poet so deeply committed to the iambic ('Tell them Iamb, Jehovah said, and meant it'),[14] and so suspicious of attempts to imitate classical metres in English, depart from his usual practice in this single instance?

If you wanted an answer to such a question – if you were curious about that curious ancient metre and wanted to understand its relevance to a modern American poem – you'd find much to mislead you in the critical literature. There, Frost's metre is often ignored, and sometimes even misidentified. As recently as 2001, a distinguished Frost scholar referred to the poem – with its fifteen lines of eleven syllables – as a sonnet.[15] Other commentators do recognize the phalaecean hendecasyllabic, but, the label once affixed, fail to account for the presence of this exotic form in a modern American poem. One critic duly identifies the metre, but without any consideration of what it contributes to the poem, except for the observation that the feminine line-endings enforce a sense of inconclusiveness.[16] (To which the obvious rejoinder would be that feminine line-endings can be arranged in the case of any number of English metres, including iambics.) Another scholar, an astute reader of both English and Latin verse, rightly brings up the Roman poet Catullus, who used the phalaecean hendecasyllabic so often and so memorably that we tend to associate the metre with him. True enough, but why Frost should wish to bring in Catullus' metre, just this once, in this particular poem, we're not told.[17] A recent study of Frost's prosody teems with insights into the poet's metrical subtlety, but when it comes to 'For Once, Then, Something,' it has nothing to say, except to label the verses 'classical Phalaecean hendecasyllabic' and pass on to other poems.[18] I mention these oversights not out of spite or hostility, but in sympathy: it is easy to overlook the presence of classical metres in English, especially now, when the study of Greek and Latin, once central, has now receded to the margins of literary culture. It is sympathy with earnest readers, professional scholars or not, who may be missing this dimension of English verse, that leads me to write this book.

Poets themselves are sometimes less than helpful on this point. Frost wanted readers to notice his classical hendecasyllabics too, but he was characteristically coy about it. Writing to a friend in 1920, the year of its publication, roguish Frost boasted that the poem was 'calculated to tease the metrists,' but there are perhaps fewer metrists among his readers than Frost might have hoped, and the rich implications of Frost's use of the ancient metre have been missed or ignored. In that sense Frost joins Auden as an example of a poet who dreams, mostly in vain, of readers prepared to spot and savour exotic classical metres in their English verse.

What Frost hoped his readers would tease out is his poem's teasing resonances with the ancient poet most widely associated with the phalaecean hendecasyllabic. Forty-three of Catullus' 116 surviving poems are written in hendecasyllabics, among them some of his most widely known. The most famous of them, the poem that begins *vivamus mea Lesbia atque amemus*, 'Let us live, my Lesbia, and let us love' (c. 5), is a standard text in schools and has in itself cemented, in the minds of generations of schoolchildren, the association of phalaecean hendecasyllabic with the name of Catullus. It is his signature metre.[19] For a modern poet of Frost's generation to write in hendecasyllabics is to invoke Catullus, just as to write in *terza rima* or in the In Memoriam stanza was once to conjure the ghosts of Dante or Tennyson. (That the same is now no longer quite true is one of the themes of this book.) Frost's affection for Catullus is one of the strongest currents in his literary life. In a feature article in the *Chicago Tribune* in the last decade of his life, he listed Catullus' volume among the three 'Books That Have Meant the Most' to him.[20] He names and quotes Catullus in his own poems,[21] and refers to him frequently and with approval throughout his letters and speeches. To an audience at a reading in 1962, he confessed that when he was 'bothered' with modern problems and needed the remedy of perspective, it was to Catullus he would regularly turn.[22]

What does the presence of Catullus' metre contribute to Frost's poem? After all, 'For Once, Then, Something' is a philosophical poem about the possibility, or impossibility, of seeing beyond the confines of the material world into some kind of transcendent reality. It would be hard to find in Catullus, whose supremely this-worldly poems centre on his passion for his mistress, his delight in his northern Italian hometown, his scathing attacks on various contemporary louts, and his despair at his brother's death – it would be hard to find many traces of metaphysical contemplation of the kind we have in Frost's poem. In Lucretius, maybe, or Virgil, both of whom mattered to Frost, but not Catullus.

The poem's occasion is the key. 'For Once, Then, Something' is a riposte to those among Frost's contemporary critics who had complained of what they took to be his philosophical shallowness and evasiveness, his 'enigmatical reserve' and 'failure to achieve a final, comprehensive vision'.[23] A survey of press reviews of Frost's early books shows how common this line of criticism had become by 1920. Even when Frost received favourable notices, reviewers tended to fault the poetry for what they took to be its philosophical superficiality, naivete, or inconclusiveness. A reviewer in the *Times Literary Supplement* in 1913 was among the first to characterize Frost's verses as naive.[24] Two months later another English reviewer referred to 'the simple woodland philosophy of Mr Frost'.[25] The perception of the poet as a rustic hayseed piping his woodnotes wild still has popular currency, and has not altogether vanished from among scholars. Moreover, some early reviewers who did acknowledge the sophistication of Frost's lyrics nevertheless complained – in this case with greater justification – of a certain elusiveness or reserve, an unwillingness to come down conclusively on any side. Among them is Lascelles Abercrombie in *The Nation*, for whom Frost's 'exceptionally sly and elusive' treatment of his themes was bound to frustrate even 'the most analytically disposed reader'.[26] Abercrombie was an ally whose reservations, though, were quite as strong as those of a later critic who would object to Frost's 'wistfulness, ambivalence, and theological uncertainty'.[27] It is just this critical attitude that precipitated the theme of 'For Once, Then, Something': the poem is a retort, an expression of 'irritation with those critics who doubt the seriousness of his efforts'[28] and his apparent 'refusal to assert or deny theology'.[29] The word 'rebuke' in line 11 ('Water came to rebuke the too clear water') deserves critical emphasis, since the poem not only describes that rebuke, but itself becomes one: 'Just as the droplet of water came as a rebuke to *me* for thinking myself entitled to some transcendent vision, so this poem comes as a rebuke to you "others" who have demanded such insight of my poetry.' To put it another way: critical discussion of the poem has tended to miss the significance of its implied occasion. It is a philosophical poem, yes, but couched as a rebuttal, belonging to the genre of a response to hostile critics.[30]

Under this aspect, the meaning of Frost's use of an exotic Latin metre starts to become clear. For one of Catullus' characteristic modes is that of rebuttal: a number of his most memorable poems involve firing back at those who have criticized, harmed, or misunderstood him. Significantly, he tended to use phalaecean hendecasyllabics as the vehicle for such rebuttals. When some unknown thief makes off with Catullus' writing tablets, he responds to the affront by summoning, to carry out his revenge, his preferred metre: his hendecasyllabics (*adeste, hendecasyllabi*, 'Come on, my hendecasyllabics'), like a pack of trusted attack-dogs. So too in poem after poem. The pinching of a napkin will bring upon the thief a slew of avenging hendecasyllabics (c. 12.10). With hendecasyllabics he teasingly rebukes Calvus for the gift of an anthology of bad poetry, and threatens retaliation (c. 14). And even in poems which themselves are not principally retorts, there often come strokes of rebuttal, as when the poet in his most famous hendecasyllabic poem rebukes the censorious old men who would disprove his love for Lesbia (c. 5.2) and others who would give the couple the evil eye (5.11–13).

This coincidence of metre and matter has not gone unnoticed. More than a century ago, Robinson Ellis, author of the leading English commentary on

Catullus at the time Frost wrote 'For Once, Then, Something', declared the hendecasyllabic the 'proper rhythm' for a rebuke.[31] If that word 'proper' strikes us as overconfident or even dogmatic, we should bear in mind that metrical propriety, the notion that a given metre is fit for certain topics or attitudes, but not for others, has never been as strong in English literary culture, was considerably weakened by the Romantic revolution, and today may be thought nearly to have vanished. The very versatility of the sonnet form, for instance, has undermined its traditional association with love-poetry. Only with the lowly limerick form, still strongly associated with nonsense and bawdy, do we find consensus on the question of metrical propriety. (My own experience as a teacher tells me that the sonnet and the limerick are the only two received metrical forms which the typical non-specialist reader is likely to recognize in the early twenty-first century.) The ancients, though, were much more comfortable with the notion of associating this or that metre with a particular genre or attitude. Ellis's claim is backed up by many classicists, including one who holds that hendecasyllabics 'were on the whole selected for light-hearted abuse' (as against iambs which Catullus reserved for harsher attacks).[32] Another commentator goes a touch further, and sees Catullus' hendecasyllabics as appropriating something of the invective force normally associated with iambics.[33] The point is not that Frost will have been acquainted with and influenced by scholarly opinions on the generic propriety of hendecasyllabics (though he would have had access to Ellis's 1898 commentary), but that it would not be hard for any sensitive reader of Catullus to perceive the association between the hendecasyllabic metre and a particular rhetorical stance, a kind of vivacious and teasing retort to critics and other offenders.

There is a particular hendecasyllabic poem of Catullus which especially resonates with 'For Once, Then, Something'. In c. 16, Catullus responds to the charge of his friends Furius and Aurelius that his racy verses are themselves evidence of the poet's immorality. To misjudge the poems, in this case, is to misjudge the poet's character. 'You have falsely assumed', Catullus effectively tells his friends, 'that because my poetry is immodest, I myself must be immodest too.' Frost's poem is apposite: his critics, he says, claim that his poems fail to plumb the depths of reality, that they reflect only the image of 'me myself' (l. 5). The implication is that Frost is not only narcissistic, but a modern embodiment of Narcissus himself, gazing into the water to find only his own face reflected on the surface. Shallowness of poetry implies shallowness of the poet. Both poets, then, wield a particular metre, the phalaecean hendecasyllabic, to defend themselves against not just any old sort of abuse, but specifically criticism of their poems and, by extension, their character.

Frost's poem signals affinity with Catullus' brand of wit. The Roman poet responds to the charge of obscenity by (ironically) heaping obscenities on his critics.[34] The poem begins and ends with the phrase 'Pedicabo ego vos et irrumabo,' that is, a threat of sexual assault meant to underscore the active rather than passive role. The obscenity is meant to be both alarming and witty. 'My verses are immodest, you say? Well then, *pedicabo ego vos*', and so on. It is true that Catullus does not *merely* respond with the obscenities his critics had complained of, since the offending phrases he uses are meant to assert a masculinity that Furius and Aurelius had denied him; and it is also the case that part of Catullus' argument is that the supposed indecency of his verses is not to be taken seriously, but as a dash of colour, the 'wit and spice' (l. 7) of urbane light verse. But advancing such a disclaimer involves the irony of writing obscene verses to defend your poetry against the charge of obscenity.

'For Once, Then, Something' involves a similar, if much milder, sort of shrewdness. Where his critics had charged him with philosophical inconclusiveness, Frost responds by being conclusively inconclusive. To those critics who complained of Frost's lack of a 'final, comprehensive vision', Frost replies with a poem whose subject is exactly his lack of a final, comprehensive vision. His poem is as complex, both philosophically and technically, as any critic could wish, and in purporting to have no more insight than any other rural well-gazer, Frost produced a work of great sophistication. Not least because to respond to critics of your poetry, and to do so by seeming to give them a double dose of what they were criticizing you for in the first place, is to perform a particularly Catullan kind of poetic sophistication. Especially (and this for Frost was the clincher) if you do it all in phalaecean hendecasyllabics.

The contrast with Catullus is also significant. Frost's retort, unlike Catullus', is deceptively gentle, and infused with such diffidence ('as I thought'), irony ('and lo'; 'Truth? A pebble of quartz?'), and self-deprecation ('and then I lost it') as to seem, not a triumphant riposte, but a concession that his critics were mostly right. That hapless tone is feigning: Frost is in complete control, roundly defeating his critics. But the evidence of his triumph lies largely in his handling of the Catullan metre. Its association with scathing Catullan invective creates a counterpoint to the apparent geniality of his tone – his retort to his critics is rather more fiercely pointed than its tone implies, because through its metre it is allied with Catullus' brand of vehemence. Frost's poem conceals rather than flaunts its erudition, thus compounding the ironies. 'For Once, Then, Something' is doubly sophisticated in pretending to be ignorant and hapless.

If Auden had wanted to justify his interest in 'curious metrical fauna' as critically important, rather than as pedant's hobby-horse, Frost's poem would have served as a fine instance. But because Frost's poem does not advertise its metre, and because the metre itself, in its seventh through eleventh syllables, takes on an iambic motion, English readers who can't see what Auden's dream reader keeps an eye out for – the curious prosodic fauna that is the phalaecean hendecasyllabic – will miss whole dimensions of its meaning. My purpose is to recover as much meaning as possible from English poems whose amplest reading depends on perceiving and understanding the movements of ancient metres.

'Carminibus stupens': The lyric metres of Sappho and Alcaeus

I propose nothing like a survey of the various classical metres which, for five hundred years, poets have been striving to bring over into English. These would include dactylic hexameters, the measure of Homer and dozens of other classical poets. There is also its slightly clipped variant, the elegiac couplet – the conventional form for epitaphs, yes, but flexible enough also to serve poets as various as Archilochus and Solon, Plato and Propertius, Catullus and Ovid, as well as legion anonymous epigrammatists. Or the dazzlingly complex choral metres of poets such as Pindar and the Attic dramatists, set to music and performed by troupes of dancers. English verse has felt the impress of all these metres, and I will have something to say in passing about some of them. I will also return briefly to Catullan hendecasyllabics, both in Chapter 1 and again at the very end of this book, where we will find Auden himself using them. Amid such variety of metres, though, severe selection is called for. This book takes a single metre, the alcaic strophe, as its subject. Even still, before I quite come to the alcaic itself, I want to introduce it in relation to another metrical form, the sapphic, since it is in conjunction that those two metres have made their generative presence felt in Western literature.

Their namesakes, the poets Sappho and Alcaeus, apparently developed those metres in the late seventh- and early sixth-century BCE on the Aegean island of Lesbos, crafting song after song in the genre now known as lyric monody: songs composed for solo voice performance, accompanied by a stringed instrument.[35] That portion of their art which involves the singing voice and its musical accompaniment is almost wholly lost to us,[36] and of the lyric texts themselves only fragments survive, in the form of mutilated manuscripts or as quotations in the works of later authors. The remnants nevertheless continue to fascinate, especially the surviving verses of Sappho who, since the eighteenth century, when she began to appear regularly in English translation, has enjoyed an increasing prestige among English poets and readers. (Certain Romantic or sub-Romantic notions about the aesthetic of ruins have sometimes made a virtue of the tantalizingly ruinous condition of the texts.)

One element of the art of Sappho and Alcaeus that has more or less escaped time's ravages is their metres. Even a fragment of a poem is usually enough to establish the overall metrical pattern, which in most cases can be confirmed in the intact works of later imitators. (The Roman poet Horace, who will come to be a central figure in this book, is the chief example.) Of the various metres in which Sappho and Alcaeus composed their songs, two stand out. The metrical pattern of the sapphic strophe can be represented like this, where 'x' stands for *anceps*, a syllable that may be either long or short:

```
– u – x – u u – u – x
– u – x – u u – u – x
– u – x – u u – u – x
   – u u – u
```

It matters very much that in all four lines of the sapphic lurks one of those curious metrical features, the choriamb, that Auden hoped his readers would keep a lookout for. Alcaics, too, are built around choriambs. The metrical movement of that strophe as used by Alcaeus and Sappho is complicated, and I will discuss it in depth in Chapter 2. For now, this quick glimpse of the schema will do:

```
x – u – x – u u – u –
x – u – x – u u – u –
   x – u – x – u – x
      – u u – u u – u – x
```

Horace, writing in Latin, altered the metre, regularizing the fifth syllable as long, and following that syllable with a fixed caesura. Hence we speak of Greek alcaics and Latin or Horatian alcaics.

To write poems in these metres probably constitutes the longest formal lyric tradition in Western poetry. They have survived for twenty-six centuries not only in Greek and Latin, but also in the modern vernacular literatures. They continue to shape the aural imagination of English poets writing today. This is odd, since most other ancient metrical patterns have failed to survive in English.

So far as I know, there is no longer a robust living tradition of English poets composing original verse on the model of (say) ancient Greek dactylic hexameters, the metre of the Homeric epic. And even when, in the nineteenth century, a brief vogue emerged of English poets trying to find a convincing way of writing English hexameters, the experience was fraught with contention, uncertainty, and, in most critics' mind, failure.[37] Attempts to create English versions of other classical metres (such as the elegiac or indeed the phalaecean hendecasyllabic) have been merely sporadic. But when it comes to the metres of Sappho and Alcaeus, a tradition not only persists, but flourishes.

Odder still, given that English poets in the twenty-first century have jettisoned much of the classical tradition, and so may be expected either to ignore or despise such arcane metrical schemes as sapphics and alcaics. The extent of classical learning is at a low ebb, not just among readers but also poets, for whom knowledge of Latin and Greek is no longer thought an essential literary credential. I would go further and say that now a poet schooled in the ancient languages cannot be assured of any cachet attached to such learning, and in fact risks the opprobrium of critics and readers who think learned poetry must also be pedantic or culturally oppressive. In any case anglophone poets casting about for formal models now have, in English literature, nearly a millennium's worth of metrical templates of every kind, including countless nonce forms and (what was not in practice available to the ancients) the option of that other formal challenge, free verse. Modern alternatives to the sapphic and alcaic stanza are legion. Yet poets continue to turn to that pair of ancient metres, renewing them in the form of English verse, and so in part renewing English verse.

I speak of the sapphic and alcaic metres as a pair because history and convention have linked them, and their eponymous authors, again and again. The two poets themselves were contemporaries and compatriots. A red-figure Attic vase of the fifth century BCE depicts Alcaeus singing, as he strums his *barbitos* or lyre, to Sappho herself, who stands listening beside him, her own instrument in hand. There is a fragmentary lyric, often attributed to Sappho, featuring a dialogue between unnamed speakers; Aristotle (*Rhetoric* 1367a) asserts that the interlocutors are none other than Alcaeus and Sappho themselves. (Rilke in a 1907 letter to his wife interpreted the vase as a depiction of the lyric dialogue.)[38] Their greatest emulator, Horace, writing six centuries later and in Latin, composed dozens of poems in the sapphic and alcaic metres, making them the two dominant lyric forms in his four books of *Odes*, the single most influential collection of ancient lyric verse. He further reinforced the association of Alcaeus and Sappho by producing, at the beginning of his second book of

Odes, a sequence of poems of which the first is alcaic, the second sapphic, and so on, alternating through no fewer than seventeen consecutive odes. A metrical tour-de-force, yes, but also an act of implicit literary criticism, suggesting the primacy of Sappho and Alcaeus among lyric poets, inviting consideration of the different qualities of those two metres, and above all establishing Horace as their literary heir, in whom the excellences of both Greek poets are combined and made new. In one of those poems, moreover, he conjures the ghosts (literally) of Sappho and Alcaeus by imagining their departed shades performing for the spirits of the dead in the afterlife. Even Cerberus, the hundred-headed hound of hell, is entranced and momentarily 'placated' by the sapphic and alcaic 'songs' (carminibus stupens, *Odes* 2.13.21–8). And though many modern poets have written sapphics and alcaics in the various European vernaculars, it's a nice irony that the first major poet to write English poems in Sappho's metre (a man) was so closely related to the first major poet (a woman) to write alcaics in English. For Sir Philip Sidney and Mary Sidney Herbert, Countess of Pembroke, were brother and sister.[39]

'The grandest of all measures'

In the end, though, I focus on the alcaic. One reason is aesthetic. There is a particular fascination in the alcaic strophe itself. Its structure is more complex and rhythmically various than the sapphic's: its beauty and intricacy warrant critical attention. I myself am drawn to it as the most attractive and bewitching of all lyric metres, but I am not alone: Alfred Tennyson called it 'the grandest of all measures',[40] and laboured for decades to find ways of introducing into his own poems something like the cadences of the alcaic, its tempo-shifting complex of suspensions and responsions, so unlike anything in 'native' English prosody. For this reason, the alcaic offers a particularly revealing lens through which to study the ways in which classical metrics can complicate, enrich, and renew English verse.

Another reason: the appeal of the underdog. The trajectory of the English alcaic's history, especially when contrasted with the sapphic's, is revealing. For though Sappho and Alcaeus are linked in the Western imagination, it is a curious feature of their English afterlives that their metres have followed separate and unequal careers. Sapphics have proliferated: no ancient lyric metre has so often found its way into English verse. From Sidney and Greville in the sixteenth century to Geoffrey Hill in the twenty-first, English poetry offers scores upon scores of sapphics, employed with such variety of effects as to produce vivid incongruities. Swinburne's 'Sapphics' (1866), for instance, with its languorously erotic evocation of Sappho herself, contrasts almost shockingly with the sapphics into which Isaac Watts, in the previous century, had cast his vision of the Christian apocalypse in the hymn 'The Day of Judgment'. A vogue for sapphics in late twentieth-century America meant that an accomplished poet, Timothy Steele, could confidently address a post-classical readership with a book called *Sapphics and Uncertainties* (1995), a very rare instance of a volume's title calling attention to the metrical form of its poems. The prestige of Sappho herself, especially since the nineteenth century, has helped to keep poets and readers interested in the stanza-form that bears her name, and poets writing in English continue to tune their music to her lyre. Already in 1582, the Anglo-Irish poet and metrical theorist Richard Stanyhurst, in the introduction to his translation of the *Aeneid* into quantitative English hexameters, acknowledged the preeminence of the sapphic over all other classical metres in English verse.[41] In short: the sapphic stanza in English is well-known – you might almost say famous. Though the book on English sapphics is yet to be written (and this is not that book), its author, whoever it turns out to be, will find no shortage of primary sources.

The English alcaic presents the opposite case. Though it was Horace's most frequent choice of metre, English versions of the alcaic are few compared to the sapphic, and have suffered the relative neglect of critics and scholars. The metre languishes in the shadow of its sapphic counterpart, whose relative familiarity and prestige has obscured the contributions of the alcaic to English poetry. To take just two examples of this asymmetry. In 2009, four leading scholars of Elizabethan verse published an excellent and much-needed edition of the Sidney psalter, that metrically various collection of English verse paraphrases of the psalms by the siblings Philip and Mary Sidney.[42] Her translation of Psalm 120 is apparently the first instance of the alcaic metre in English – a superb poem to which I will return in Chapter 3. In their general introduction and in notes to the individual poems, the editors point out several of the other English adaptations of classical metres, but curiously omit to mention the alcaic. A second instance: in 2016 J. Alison Rosenblitt brought to light, for the first time, a juvenile manuscript of E. E. Cummings, which she dates to *c.* 1916, when he was a Harvard undergraduate. It contains two verse quatrains, the first of which reads:

> O muse, my blessing, source of my confidence,
> Arise and hasten! Leave thy far native land!
> Inspire this breast, thou bless'd of ages!
> Aid thy found servant, – this once do his will![43]

The budding poet was composing alcaic verses in English, a fact which alone raises questions about the role it may have played in his poetic formation. Laying that aside, and laying aside, too, any number of observations that may be made about his handling of the form, I note that at roughly the same time, Cummings had also ventured a poem in 'Sapphics', which he first published in *The Harvard Monthly*. Later that poem found a permanent place in Cummings's *Complete Poems*.[44] Here again: the English sapphic gets the attention, and the English alcaic languishes for a century in the archives. Of course I bring up both of these instances facetiously – nobody is setting out to suppress the English alcaic. But the two cases are consistent with the way the alcaic has yet to emerge from the sapphic's shadow.

A third reason for the book involves the English alcaic's character as a late bloomer. Whereas sapphics have been written consistently in English over five centuries, the English alcaic has fared much more unevenly, and has only recently come into its own as a naturalized English metre. Its tardy reception into English could not have been predicted from the popularity of alcaics written in Latin in Europe, Britain, and America in the modern period. Alcaics in Latin are among the notable achievements of John Milton, George Herbert, and Samuel Johnson. To write in that metre as a schoolboy exercise was a regular part of a poet's formation on both sides of the Atlantic, and to produce alcaics into adulthood (for instance, as occasions for gentlemanly compliment or satirical riposte) remained a feature of literary culture right up to the nineteenth century.[45] One might have expected to find poets trying their hand at producing English versions of the alcaic metre, as so often they did with sapphics. But until the nineteenth century, they almost never did. From the late sixteenth century to the mid-nineteenth, some loose approximations of the alcaic form can be found: significant ones, but few. The mid-nineteenth century, though, saw a remarkable development: a kind of renaissance of the English alcaic, sparked in part by contemporary debates about vernacular metres and their relation to the classics. The twentieth century saw an even greater flourishing, of which the leading exponent was to be W. H. Auden himself, whose admirers, especially in North America, later developed and refined the English alcaic. Even more remarkably, now, in the twenty-first century, each year finds new poems appearing in alcaics from all over the English-speaking world.

When, in a 2009 volume of essays on Horatian receptions, I first identified and described this 'late flowering of English alcaics',[46] it was clear that what reviewers (such as Charles Martindale in *TLS* and Jonathan Wallis in *Bryn Mawr Classical Review*) found most striking was not just the belatedness of the alcaic's emergence into English, but an irony bound up in the cultural context of its emergence.[47] For the rise of the alcaic in English coincides, paradoxically, with the gradual but definitive disestablishment of the classics in the schools and universities of Britain and America during the twentieth century. This inverse relation between the decline of classical studies on the one hand, and the proliferation of English poems composed in that most complex of fixed classical lyric metres, naturally complicates the interpretation of alcaic poems written in the last hundred years. But it also touches on a wider question of classical and English literary relations: that is, what to make of English works inspired by the classics in an age when most educated participants in literary culture (not only readers, but also critics, scholars, and indeed the writers themselves) have no acquaintance with classical literature in the original languages. The very belatedness of the emergence of alcaics as a popular metre in English poetry makes it particularly relevant to the study of the survival of classical reception in the twenty-first century, the first century since the renaissance in which neither poets nor their readers can be expected to have first-hand experience with Latin or Greek, let alone with the complex quantitative metres of Latin and Greek poetry.

This book emerges from that 2009 chapter on modern alcaics. Restricted to a chapter's length, I had to leave too many things unsaid: here I find scope for saying them. The lapse in time has allowed me to reconsider my earlier positions: not only to develop them but (as it has turned out) to correct some of them where I think I had gone wrong. Moreover, in the intervening decade several studies (most notably those of Hannibal Hamlin, Richard Hillyer, Meredith Martin, Llewelyn Morgan, Victoria Moul, Juan Christian Pellicer, J. Alison Rosenblitt and Elizabeth Vandiver) have appeared or are about to appear which, in various ways, are relevant to my topic. Taking them into account has enriched my thinking. The book has also offered me the opportunity to revisit, rethink, and substantially revise ideas about alcaics I have written about elsewhere.

I think this is the first book to focus on the English alcaic strophe. Until now, almost all critical attention to the English alcaic has come in passing, as tangential to some other subject. The great majority of critical observations on English alcaics are isolated from one another: for instance, a comment on a Victorian poet's alcaics is made in the context of Victorian studies, with no reference to Elizabethan alcaics or modernist versions of the stanza. The alcaic deserves its own book: as an art form of intricate beauty, for its extraordinary durability, for its mostly unacknowledged role in English poetry, for the part it plays in continuing to shape the imagination of English poets today, and for what it can reveal about the force of poetic metre generally.

I ought to make clear what I think this book is not. Above all, it is not a history of the alcaic, either in its classical or English forms. It is selective, proposing instead a mere handful of test cases, each one an impetus for thinking about a particular aspect of the relation of the alcaic to English poetry. It is far from exhaustive: a number of English alcaics by significant writers I have left on the cutting-room floor. Robert Louis Stevenson and Edward Arlington Robinson are just two examples; a more painful one is the alcaic poem of E. E. Cummings I quoted above. There are many English alcaics, and even more near-alcaics, of historical significance by lesser writers, especially Victorian translators (Lord Lytton's are the preeminent example, but there are many more), which I would like to have included. With reluctant decency I omit mention of the alcaics among my own volumes of poetry. And there is room for only the briefest acknowledgement of alcaics in other vernacular languages, notably Italian and Russian but especially German, which offered models to English versifiers from the nineteenth century onwards.[48]

The book is not a literary history, and does not pretend that its implications call for a radical reconsideration of literary history. The more modest truth is that the story of the alcaic in English poetry is one strand in the history of English literature that has not yet been adequately acknowledged or traced. Merely to study it is to expose subterranean connections between writers not hitherto linked in literary history. My account brings in, and sometimes surprisingly unites, major poets from across five centuries, including Mary Sidney, John Milton, Andrew Marvell, Arthur Hugh Clough, Alfred Tennyson, Edward FitzGerald, Robert Bridges, Wilfred Owen, W. H. Auden, Marianne Moore, John Hollander, Donald Hall, Robert Bly and others, while constantly referring to lyric poets of antiquity, above all Horace. Critical accounts of English poetry (except when the sonnet is involved) ordinarily obscure the metrical continuities between otherwise dissimilar poets.

Finally, though much concerned with metrical form, both its textual contours and its contextual resonances, this book does not propose any radical reconsideration of metrical theory. I am particularly sensitive on this point, given the remarkable recent ferment among scholars of poetic metre in English poetry of the nineteenth and early twentieth centuries. They have succeeded not only in making clear the 'unstable' character of metrical theory in those periods, and the ferocity of the theoretical debates around metre, but have also tried to recover, through various acts of historical reconstruction, some sense of the underlying assumptions of various 'metrical communities'.[49] Against such thoroughly historicized and theorized accounts of prosody, my own readings of

Arthur Hugh Clough, Alfred Tennyson, and Robert Bridges (himself a veteran of the prosody wars) find me treating their metres in more conventional terms, as the approach that makes the best sense of their classically influenced prosody.

This book's beginning is preposterous in the etymological sense, since it postpones what notionally ought to come first (an introductory discussion of the alcaic strophe) until the second chapter. The point of departure instead is a case study, juxtaposing a twentieth-century classic, Wilfred Owen's 'Dulce Et Decorum Est', with a twenty-first century poem in English alcaics by the American poet John Hollander. It is odd to begin in this way, since Owen's case is in no way straightforward. The point is to show that the alcaic presence in English can manifest itself as powerfully by its absence as by its presence: in Owen's poem, the alcaic is erased through an act of metrical misquotation, an erasure that Hollander, in his own alcaics a century later, acknowledges and partially restores. Both poems raise questions about the relation of classical metres to childhood nostalgia. The chapter is doubly preposterous in taking 'preposterousness' itself (the literary preposterousness of reading poets in reverse historical order) as one of its subjects, and as characteristic of English classical reception after the disestablishment of classics from the curriculum.

Having opened the door to some of the implications of studying English alcaics, I turn, belatedly, in Chapter 2, to a critical description of the alcaic's metrical form itself, both in its Greek and Latin forms. Horace naturally comes in for special attention, as his particular handling of the verse form, and its prominence in his work, make him the greatest exponent of the alcaic in any period. After some very close readings of Horace's metrical technique, the chapter ends by acknowledging the tradition of post-classical alcaics in Latin.

There follow three chapters dedicated to specific case-studies of the alcaic's fortunes as an English metre. The point of Chapter 3 is to show how alcaics can be brought into English verse, and how the effort of transplanting the ancient metre into English soil spurred the creation of several new English metrical forms. The chapter is bookended by Mary Sidney and Alfred Tennyson, whose long preoccupation with the alcaic was the impetus for the invention of several new metrical forms. In that way the alcaic is revealed as an important contribution to the culture of metrical innovation in the Victorian period.

Chapter 4 finds me reading Tennyson's *In Memoriam* in light of its metrical connections (or so I contend) to the alcaic strophe, connections enriched and complicated by its relations to the metre of FitzGerald's *Rubáiyát of Omar Khayyám* and by the translations of Charles Stuart Calverley. The point is to propose that the alcaic can be felt as a residual presence in certain English metrical forms to which it is related, and to suggest that some of the pressing questions of *In Memoriam*, having to do with persistence and mutability, manifest themselves at the level of poetic form. The end of the chapter raises questions about the tension between the visual and auditory aspects of poetry, an issue that recurs and is developed in the following chapter.

Two poets, Robert Bridges and W. H. Auden, pose for the diptych that is Chapter 5. The point is to show how alcaics found a place in the changing milieu of twentieth-century English verse. Auden emerges as the leading exponent of the English alcaic, but my account of his success is troubled by Auden's sense of disquiet about the relation of his alcaics to the culture's increasingly apathetic attitude to the classical tradition. That unease persists in my Afterword, whose point is to propose that the paradoxical flourishing of alcaics in the postmodern world may be a sign not of continuity but of cultural disinheritance.

I do not conceive of the chapters as discrete. Each chapter refers to earlier ones (even Chapter 1 refers to my discussion of Frost above, and on the last page of the book I return to hendecasyllabics). There is a recursive quality to my thought that readers may find irksome but imparts a sort of unity to the whole. In a sense, all the preceding chapters merely supply the context for the Afterword, the slenderest and least temperate part of the book, but possibly the most suggestive. The cumulative thesis is perhaps a little tenuous but it may be most clearly felt in the Afterword.

My aims are those of a literary critic more than a scholar or theorist. Scholarship underpins this book: often my own scholarship, still oftener the superior work of others. But this is chiefly a work of literary criticism and, for all its insistence on attending to the sounds and cadences of ancient poets' actual Greek and Latin words – what Robert Frost called 'the untranslated classics' [50] – it is as much a meditation on English receptions of classical verse as on classical verse itself. That emphasis ought not repel classicists, who increasingly acknowledge not only a linear but also a reciprocal relationship between modern literature and its ancient sources, and have, in the past three decades, increasingly welcomed the study of classical receptions. [51] I hope this book will interest classicists as much as those principally interested in English studies. Balancing the interests of both audiences is tricky. I will be grateful for the patience of professional classicists who suffer through passages intended to explicate some point of Latin or Greek for intelligent readers who happen to be unfamiliar with those languages. It is for such readers, too, that I have transliterated passages from the Greek of Alcaeus into the Roman alphabet, allowing them to sound out the words and perceive the metrical patterns of the stanzas. I hope English scholars will countenance similar impositions in the opposite direction. (Readers without Latin and Greek may find their patience tested especially in Chapter 2, which necessarily enters into some technical discussions of the alcaic metre as used in the ancient languages.) It is good for students of modern and classical literatures to keep in touch with each others' worlds. Many recent studies in the classical tradition demonstrate it is possible to address both audiences, and that is the pitch I seek.

'An irreducibly literary project'

Every critic has his or her dream readers. As for my own, what would unite them is curiosity about poems themselves as (above all) works of art made of words and rhythms. My ideal readers are interested in poems as built things, and eager to figure out how those things tick. From his chair as Oxford Professor of Poetry, Auden revealed that his first question when reading a poem was always, 'Here is a verbal contraption. How does it work?'[52] Though I could quarrel with that word 'contraption', I approve his priorities. They have not been the priorities of academic criticism of the last few decades, which has tended to slight questions of form and metre in particular, and evaluative artistic judgment in general, in favour of the now-familiar range of contextual and theoretical methods. I mention this not out of contempt – those methods have yielded rich results – but only to signal this book's differing emphasis, and so to give some sense of its relation to literary studies broadly.

I hope for it a modest place among recent books that suggest a return to an interest in the aesthetic, formal, and (in the case of poetry) metrical aspects of literature that have for some time been unfashionable. 'The *Zeitgeist* is changing', one scholar has recently written; academics, he thinks, are increasingly returning to critical approaches that are 'alert to the distinctiveness of literature', as against those that 'dissolve literary studies into a minor branch of cultural history', and in which 'the distinct existence of the poem as poem is dissolved'.[53] It matters that this prognostication of a return to the study of form comes from Derek Attridge, who for forty years, against prevailing fashions, has been conveying, in his articles and monographs on English prosody, the 'exhilarating discovery' that comes of showing 'how a string of words conforms to [metrical] patterns that pervade the verse tradition'.[54]

But the approach to literature Attridge has in mind goes beyond his own close study of metrics, and I can think of scholars in whom I sense fellow feeling, though they write on very different topics. I have already mentioned the movement among students of nineteenth-century prosody. I could point also, though, to slightly different approaches: for instance, the programmatic determination of Gillian Woods, in her book-length study of Shakespeare and residual post-Reformation Catholicism, to focus *primarily* on the poet's art, as against art's cultural, historical, and material contingencies. 'This is an irreducibly literary project', she announces confidently. 'Its questions are not primarily biographical, historical, or theological, but rather creative: what is the imaginative function of Catholicism in Shakespeare's drama.'[55] Without disapproving of interdisciplinary adventures, she nevertheless wonders whether too much blurring of boundaries between literature and (say) social history may have resulted in an unsatisfactory treatment of both; she hopes that 'by returning to some of its aesthetic and formal principles, literary criticism might help rather than hinder interdisciplinary debate'.

Alongside which may be set the example of Peter McDonald – no less a poet than a scholar – in his recent study of rhyme in nineteenth-century verse. Like Wood, he presses the need for artistic discrimination and sensitivity to stylistic nuance, as against 'the dispassionate, stylistically unjudgmental, perspective of a modern academic critic'.[56] A purely contextual or theoretical approach 'fails to do justice to the literature of the past', he avers, 'by refraining from the kinds of evaluation to which, once, it was entitled'.[57] McDonald calls his own approach 'stylistic criticism'. His method is finding champions, such as Ross Wilson, who was moved to praise it, in *TLS*, as refreshingly working in opposition to 'literary history and (implicitly) to literary theory – without, on the one hand, blithely reopening the theory wars of yesteryear'. Moreover, and more provocatively, Wilson defends McDonald by asserting a currently unpopular principle: that a close critical account of the minutiae of poetic form can be 'as theoretically significant as any professedly theoretical statement'.[58]

Just so my own hopes for this book. Simply as matter of inclination and aptitude I align myself with McDonald in offering my work as 'stylistic criticism'; with Woods, as 'an irreducibly literary project'; and with Ross, in the conviction that the details of verse technique are as important as theoretical formulations. McDonald's book provoked Wilson to say that its emphasis on poetic form and technique (such as rhyme) is not just worthy but also, and by accident, timely. If my own book, which may not seem to be of topical relevance, can at all be called 'timely', it is in that sense – that it shares in a small, though I hope growing, feeling that the time is right for the pendulum of criticism to swing back towards the poem as a work of art, its words, its sounds, its rhythm, and its value. It's just that even to put it that way implies that such an approach is either traditional (in needing to be returned to) or new (in constituting a break from recent trends).

In fact it is neither old nor new, but perennial, and has been practised without abatement by a handful of scholars and critics who seem never to have felt the pressure of conforming to academic fashions. I mention two of them as models. The late D. S. Carne-Ross, through his books, but perhaps most importantly in his scores of articles and reviews, lifted the veil on the creative energies in the minute verbal, metrical, and formal subtleties of poets in English, Spanish, Italian, Latin, and Greek. His perceptions were especially lucid when he wrote on translation, a field in which questions of technique rise to the fore. 'The greatest critic of literary translation since Matthew Arnold,' he has been called,[59] though he was also, more broadly, as George Steiner asserted, one of the greatest critics ever.[60] And Christopher Ricks has for more than half a century steadily and unperturbedly been writing 'stylistic criticism', whose 'questions are not primarily biographical, historical, or theological, but rather creative'. No critic of English poetry in our time can register the expressive power of the minutest verbal and formal nuance, and communicate his perceptions in prose so adroit, pregnant, witty and often itself moving. The greatest stylistic critic of our time is himself a great prose stylist. I court folly by mentioning Carne-Ross and Ricks, as my own book can only suffer by comparison. I think of them, though, and those they write for, as my own dream readers.

And then there's the fact that Ricks neatly brings us back to where this preface began, to Auden's dream of his ideal audience. For his verbal acuity, his sensitivity to formal craft, his attention to details such as 'curious prosodic fauna' and much else, Auden called Christopher Ricks 'exactly the kind of critic every writer dreams of finding.'

1

Coming Late to Latin

Wilfred Owen, John Hollander

It is odd, maybe, to begin a discussion of the alcaic in English with a poem in which the alcaic does not appear. On the other hand it may be telling. The alcaic strophe in English may sometimes be felt forcefully by its absence.

That is the case with Wilfred Owen's most famous poem, especially since it involves perhaps the most famous single moment of classical reception in modern literature, the quotation of the Horatian tag 'dulce et decorum est pro patria mori', a line that Horace composed according to the alcaic metre. As such it is precisely at issue whether that metre figures in the English poem or not. That very matter was taken up nearly a century later when the American poet John Hollander, with Wilfred Owen in mind, composed a poem which, very pointedly, *is* in English alcaics. In 'To An Old Latin Teacher', Hollander belatedly (that is the operative term) addresses the fact of the alcaic's non-appearance in 'Dulce Et Decorum Est', and brings to the fore ideas central to this chapter: what it means to come late to Latin (in adulthood rather than childhood), and to approach the classics anachronistically (by coming to them through and after English literature, rather than the other way round). I propose Hollander's poem not only as a superb instance of classical reception – taking in both Horace and Wilfred Owen's reception of Horace – but also as an eloquent articulation of what classical reception of a poetic form means in a post-classical, postmodern world. All turns on a moment of metrical misquotation of the alcaic metre in 'Dulce Et Decorum Est'. To illustrate the idea of metrical misquotation, consider an instance from T. S. Eliot's 'The Waste Land'.

Metrical misquotation

Eliot's originality lies in part in his way with other people's words. The shrewdness, for instance, in his not only quoting another writer, but in also, and at the same time, misquoting him. The passage in question finds a woman (she works as a typist) in the aftermath of an assault by a dinner-guest in her own bed-sit apartment. The assailant has taken his leave, and his victim tries to put the incident out of her mind.

> When lovely woman stoops to folly and
> Paces about her room again, alone,
> She smoothes her hair with automatic hand
> And puts a record on the gramophone.[1]

The first line of this passage is, famously, a quotation from Oliver Goldsmith's *The Vicar of Wakefield*, but it is also a kind of misquotation. Not that Eliot misquotes Goldsmith's *words*, for there they are, all seven of them, in the same order: 'When lovely woman stoops to folly and'. The quotation is faithful in respect of lexis and syntax. The divergence is instead metrical. Eliot's quotation is unfaithful in respect of metre and lineation, for what Goldsmith actually wrote was this:

> When lovely woman stoops to folly
> And learns too late that men betray,
> What charm can soothe her melancholy,
> What art can wash her guilt away?[2]

Eliot lifts the seven words in question out of their original metrical setting, iambic tetrameter, and conforms them to the pentameter measure of his own poem. A minute adjustment, but consequences follow like tumbling dominoes.

To pick up just six of them: first, *disruption*. In Eliot, the expected line-break after 'folly' strikingly fails to arrive. Goldsmith's poem is meant to convey an uncomfortable situation's distress, but Eliot's disruption of the line-break brings to his version a far more palpable sense of something amiss. Second, and similarly, *belatedness*. Goldsmith's verses can merely speak of it ('and learns *too late* that men betray'), but Eliot's rearrangement does better, because it enacts belatedness by postponing the line-break. That tardy beat comes heavy with (third) a sense of *lassitude* befitting the complacent response of the typist in the poem, and the indifference of the young man who has assaulted her. 'Assault' is not quite the word for the liberties Eliot takes with Goldsmith's metre. But he does tamper with it, and tampering brings in (fourth) a hint of *violation*: the earlier poem has been handled, manhandled, made to conform to Eliot's own metrical designs. The alteration plays havoc with *rhyme*, and this fifth point has many ramifications. 'Folly' is demoted from its emphatic position at line's end.

This precipitates not just the evaporation of the rhyme 'folly / melancholy', but with it the moral resonance between the two words. In rhyme's reasoning, 'melancholy' follows from 'folly' almost as surely as 'tomb' must succeed 'womb': the neatness with which Goldsmith brings the two words, in that sequence, into rhyming relation implies both a morality and an uncomplicated attitude towards it. All of which Eliot undoes with a stroke. In his revision, the 'folly / melancholy' rhyme evaporates, and with it the assertion of cause-and-effect. Instead, a new rhyme-word, the menacingly bland 'and', reaches after an answering 'hand', that 'automatic hand' with which the violated typist smoothes her hair. Empty gesture – as if it were not messy, the messy episode with the young man. Eliot's rhyme too is an empty gesture. 'And / hand' – a rhyme amounting to what? Not the consciousness of guilt, in the way that 'melancholy' duly catches up to 'folly' in Goldsmith's quatrain, for the consciousness of her folly is exactly what the typist refuses to touch, or be touched by, as she lifts her hand to smooth her hair. Eliot effects this moral reversal of Goldsmith with the lightest touch on the rudder, the postponement of a line break for the space of a single monosyllable. Then there's the sixth consequence, the *isolation* and *dangling* of the conjunction at the line's brink. It is more than a matter of rhetorical suspension (the way that, in conversation, a pause after 'and' leaves you hanging). It's the abrupt vacancy that follows 'and', through which vacancy we float until the equally abrupt trochaic substitution 'Páces' (/ u) lands us, with a thud, into the next line. Already a rhyme-word nearly empty of meaning, 'and' idles, lonely and isolated, on the brink of an emptiness.

This relation between two texts, in which one poet faithfully reproduces an earlier poet's words while distorting his metre, deserves a name: call it 'metrical misquotation'. In Eliot, who practised it often, it can be, as in this instance, a means by which language is, as he put it, dislocated into meaning. More generally, metrical misquotation demonstrates what is often ignored: how much of a poem's power resides not only in the choice of words, but in metrical minutiae and the placing of line-breaks. Eliot's originality in quoting and misquoting is a matter not of choosing words but of minute judgments of timing.

I raise the example of Eliot because the point of departure I have in mind for this book involves a similar instance of metrical misquotation in a great English poet. Five years before Eliot published 'The Waste Land', Wilfred Owen began composing a poem, now famous as few English poems are, whose energies derive in large part from his use of an earlier writer's words – exactly seven words, as it happens, just as in Eliot's case – which is at once a quotation (in respect of semantics) and a misquotation (in respect of metre and lineation). The difference, though, is that Owen was quoting not English words, but Latin, and the metres involved were not just 'English' metres, but also the alcaic strophe.

'Occasional metrical outrages'

[….] My friend, you would not tell with such high zest
To children ardent for some desperate glory
The old Lie: Dulce et decorum est
Pro patria mori.[3]

'The old Lie': those three monosyllables are meant to torpedo the venerable maxim out of Horace, which supplied Wilfred Owen with the title and conclusion of his most famous poem. But in 'Dulce Et Decorum Est', Owen makes himself the author of – not exactly a *new* lie, but a new unfaithfulness, doubly provocative for coming under the cover of apparent fidelity. For it is not true that Horace wrote, as Owen has it, 'Dulce et decorum est / Pro patria mori', but instead 'Dulce et decorum est pro patria mori.' The stanza in which Horace's phrase originally appears (*Odes* 3.2.13–16) looks like this:

dulce et decorum est pro patria mori.
mors et fugacem persequitur virum,
   nec parcit imbellis iuventae
      poplitibus timidove tergo.

It is a sweet and fitting thing to die for one's country. Death hunts down the man who runs away, and has no mercy on the hamstrings of the unwarlike youth and his cowardly back.[4]

This is the alcaic strophe. (For a rough metrical scheme of the stanza, see the Preface; a detailed discussion of this complex stanza follows in the next chapter.) In Owen's poem, what's at issue is only the first line of the alcaic stanza, which, because of its eleven syllables, is referred to as the hendecasyllabic line: – – u – – – u u – u – . Looking at Horace's poem on the printed page, what the eye immediately picks out is that the seven words in question, *dulce et decorum est pro patria mori*, coincide neatly with the first line of the alcaic strophe. A further detail, which the eye cannot pick out because it is a matter for the ear to hear, involves elision. There are thirteen syllables in the line. But it is a convention of Latin versification that a terminal vowel followed by an initial vowel produces elision; a word ending in '–um' likewise elides with the following word when it begins with a vowel. Strikingly, both conditions obtain in

Horace's line. 'Dulce' elides with 'et' to produce the sound 'dulcet', and 'decorum' with 'est' to produce the sound 'decorumst' or 'decorest'. The result is that the thirteen syllables are made to fit into the eleven-syllable template: 'Dulc(e) et decor(um) est pro patria mori.' Double elision here makes the coincidence of sense and line-unit uncommonly snug.

That coincidence matters. Horace in his odes is generous with enjambment; to resist it here, to frame the maxim to coincide exactly with the line, contributes to its gnomic force and suggests inevitability. The sentiment is literally 'fitting'. There is a further neatness in the relation of the sentence structure to the metre. One of the features of Horace's alcaics is the way his hendecasyllabic lines are made to break, in almost every instance, after the fifth syllable.[5] In this case, that caesura, appearing between 'est' and 'pro', effects a special clarity: a neat division between grammatical subject ('it is a sweet and fitting thing') and predicate ('to die for one's country'). That's to say: not only is the entire sentence trimly framed within the line-unit, but the two grammatical halves of the sentence themselves conform to the conventional metrical boundaries. All this lends the phrase the weight and finish of an epigram, quotable and easily detachable from its context (as Owen's poem demonstrates). These metrical features, too, embody an attitude of composure and authority.

Owen's handling of the quotation is destructive of just these qualities. In the first place, it fractures into two a line that in Horace had been stoutly integral. Owen's way of quoting it makes it unstable: to spill over the line-break brings in a flickering sense of contingency, of slippage, which is absent from the line as Horace arranged it. More strikingly, the second part of Horace's maxim, the predicate 'pro patria mori', is in Owen not only sundered from its subject clause but abandoned, isolated – the spent tail-end of the poem. It does not, as in Horace, so much round out an epigram as sputter, puffing its last. It has a dying fall.

The fracturing of Horace's line affords Owen scope for grotesquerie born of rhyming. There is a high incongruousness in rhyming 'high zest' with the distinctly nondescript word 'est'. But even that is as nothing to the perversely brilliant stroke that brings 'desperate glory' to rhyme with 'mori'. In Owen's poem, in which death could hardly be less glorious, to rhyme 'glory' with the Latin for 'to die' is to force together the two ideas that the poem itself goes to such lengths to divorce. Yoking them in rhyme is an abrasive irony; its energy is that of mutual revulsion, such as fills the room when two estranged spouses are forced to share it. In Owen's way of thinking, the concepts behind 'glory' and 'mori' pointedly do not rhyme, though in his version of the line, the Latin and English are made awkwardly to do so.

Not only does Owen leave Horace's line shivered, but he travesties Horace's metre in a second way. Owen's poem unfolds in flexible but strongly-marked iambic verse, a measure that will not accommodate a metrical quotation of so complex a line as the alcaic hendecasyllabic. Yet Owen compels just that accommodation. It requires suppressing the elisions of 'dulce' with 'et' and 'decorum' with 'est'. Only in that way can the Latin be read as conforming to the iambic movement of the English: 'The **old** Lie: **Dul**ce **et** decorum **est**.'[6] The price, then, of getting Horace's Latin into the English poem's measure is to wrest it out of its original alcaic metre. The weight and movement of the line are greatly altered. Contrast the gravity of the Latin '**dulc**(e) **et** de**cor**(um) **est**', with its four long syllables out of five, as against the alternation of stressed and unstressed syllables when the line is grafted into the English metre. Recasting Horace's alcaics into an iambic pentameter poem compounds the loneliness of the severed portion, 'pro patria mori', since it becomes the only line in the poem that is metrically defective. It gives us six syllables and three feet; but we wait in vain for the remaining four syllables and two feet. In Horace, 'pro patria mori' had neatly rounded out the cadence of a metrical unit; Owen's 'pro patria mori' leads into a metrical vacuum. It's a loud silence; it's a double amputation.

One of Owen's earliest and most distinguished readers fastened on the capacity of his prosody to ruffle propriety. Robert Graves had seen a draft of Owen's poem 'Disabled', and wrote, in October 1917, to express his general approval, with the following caveat:

> So good the general sound and weight of the words that the occasional metrical outrages are most surprising. [.…] Owen, you've seen things; you're a poet; but you're a very careless one at present. One can't put too many syllables into a line & say 'Oh, it's all right. That's my way of writing poetry.' One has to follow the rules of the metre one adopts. Make new metres, by all means, but one must observe the rules where they are laid down by the custom of centuries.[7]

Though it refers to another poem, this judgment is apposite to the passage from Horace in 'Dulce Et Decorum Est'. It *is* a kind of outrage to treat Horace's metre as Owen does; he does *literally* both 'put too many syllables into a line', and so flouts metrical 'rules where they are laid down by the custom of centuries'. But though Graves puts down to 'carelessness' Owen's metrical irregularities, the disregard of metrical decorum in 'Dulce Et Decorum Est' is expressive, intentionally or otherwise.[8] It enacts a contentious relationship with the Latin line that is particularly subtle and unnerving.

The violence done to Horace's metre is likely to go unnoticed because it is overshadowed by two other, more overt, kinds of vehemence. The first of these, obvious to any reader, Latinless or not, is that with which Owen deplores the violence of war. The second kind of vehemence is curiously literary: the ferocity of Owen's repudiation not of war only, but of other people's *poems* about war. When, after eight lines of elegant, not to say delicate, rhetorical suspension, Owen suddenly rounds upon 'My friend', he is famously directing his animus against a contemporary poet, Jessie Pope, whose verses, such as her 1914 pro-war poem 'The Call', regularly appeared in the newspapers and were meant to cajole and shame reluctant young men into enlisting:

> Who's for the trench –
> > Are you, my laddie?
> Who'll follow the French –
> > Will you, my laddie?
> Who's fretting to begin,
> Who's going out to win?
> And who wants to save his skin –
> > Do you, my laddie?[9]

In early drafts of 'Dulce Et Decorum Est' he had satirically dedicated his poem 'To a certain Poetess' and (at once more specifically and more generally) 'To Jessie Pope etc'.[10] By '*etc*' [*sic*] he meant not only Jessie Pope, but all those of her ilk (and there were a great many) who published poems, tracts, or sermons quoting Horace's 'dulce et decorum est' in the interest of drumming up enlistments.[11] This abrupt departure into literary disagreements, from what hitherto had been a report of a battle scene, emerges as a surprise. It is one thing to depict the horror of war; it's another thing to attack writers.[12] 'Dulce Et Decorum Est' is not just a war poem, but a kind of literary quarrel.

There is a third kind of vehemence that takes that literary quarrel further: Owen's distorting of the alcaic metre, the violence done to Horace's metrical voice. That element of violence needs recovering by a study such as this, since recognizing it requires a kind of literary training that has mostly vanished. It is not noticed even by critics who emphasize what they take to be Owen's tendency to reject revered elements of the classical tradition.[13] It may, however, be the most important kind of violence in the poem. His undoing of Horace's alcaic rhythm may be construed as a particularly nasty twist of the knife.[14] It is the subtlest and deepest kind of violence in the poem, for reasons that have to do with a complex relation between Latin metres, childhood, and nostalgia.

Coming late to Latin

Wilfred Owen was appalled at the notion of a grown man coming late to Latin: 'Nothing gave me the creeps more surely than the sight of old Kemp, trying to learn Latin Conjugations at 24! Is any scene in George Eliot more piercing-sorrowful than Baldassare the scholar failing to read a paragraph?'[15] Owen himself had just turned 21 and was working as an English teacher in Bordeaux when he confided, in a letter to his mother, Susan Owen, this memory of one A. G. Saxleby-Kemp. Owen had known Kemp while working as a fellow assistant to the vicar of Dunstan from 1911 to 1913. While in the vicar's employ, both young men had struggled, in their spare time, to study and revise: Kemp aiming to qualify for a theological post, Owen preparing for an exam required for matriculation for an external degree at London University. During that time Owen had won a Bible Society prize for Latin Translation,[16] but Kemp seems to have been a latecomer to Latin, a fact which alarmed Owen. Pitiful old Kemp, wrestling with Latin conjugations at the ripe old age of twenty-four! 'Gave me the creeps' – as one might marvel at a grown man only just learning to tie his shoes. The letter is dated 24 May 1914. One month later, the Archduke Ferdinand was dead, and three years later, Owen would be composing 'Dulce Et Decorum Est', a poem which, as we shall see, cannot be disentangled from the matter of learning, or failing to learn, Latin in childhood.

Owen's reaction to Kemp was not the condescension of a privileged élite. Owen was not upper-class, and his own Latin education had been spotty. In his early teens he had studied Latin (but not Greek) at Birkenhead Institute. His Latin education was interrupted, though, when his family moved to Shrewsbury and enrolled the boy in the Shrewsbury Technical Institute, where no classical languages were offered. He was no longer on the approved path to university, and as for Latin, Owen was thereafter on his own. Between leaving school and his enlisting in the army, he struggled for years to find time to support himself on the one hand, while boning up on his Latin and other subjects, in hope of matriculating at London University and, later, at the University of Reading. In the same paragraph in which he reported feeling 'the creeps' at the sight of Kemp, his senior by three years, trying to learn Latin, he lamented that his own hopes of passing his matriculation exams now seem 'less and less probable'.[17] Later that year, still in Bordeaux, and even as 'Zeppelins were careering across the channel', he took a position as a tutor to a pair of English boys, and wrote to his mother that the subjects he was teaching them might stimulate his own exam revisions, 'especially Latin'.[18] But it was not to be: Owen never made it to university, and that disappointment was linked to his sense that his Latin remained (as he put it to his mother in 1912), 'tarnished'.[19] It must have stung when, later, Siegfried Sassoon had to point out that the title Owen had devised for his poem 'Apologia pro poema mea' ought correctly to read 'pro poemate meo'. The mistake is understandable, since 'poema' resembles a first-declension feminine Latin noun.[20] Sassoon, a Marlborough boy and a Cambridge man, would have known that 'poema' is a neuter Greek loan-word and as such declines differently. In short: learning Latin was a constant source of anxiety and aspiration for Owen. The interruption of his childhood study of Latin hobbled him and helped to thwart his university ambitions. No wonder he shuddered at the even more unfortunate Kemp, 'trying to learn his conjugations at 24!' He shared with Kemp the predicament of too little Latin, too late.

What is at stake in coming late to Latin? It is the link between classics and nostalgia for childhood. That connection is harder for us to grasp, now that few learn Latin at all, and even among those who do, many learn it late, as university undergraduates. In the nineteenth century, though, when classical education from childhood was far more common, the effects of early exposure to Latin were clearer.[21] They can be inferred, for instance, from Thomas Babington Macaulay's essay on Milton. Why, he asks, are the classical allusions in *Paradise Lost* so moving? Not so much because of their literary logic (in bringing Milton's own narrative into meaningful relation with a classical text) as for their nostalgic power. They waken recollections of the reader's own childhood, when, in the schoolroom, the relevant Greek or Latin first entered his consciousness. A classical allusion in a passage of English poetry is 'the first link in a long line of associated ideas'. The associations Macaulay has in mind are personal rather than strictly intellectual: 'the dear classical recollections of childhood, the schoolroom, the dog-eared Virgil, the holiday, the prize'. There is no separating childhood from the classics, and a Latin reference is a ticket to travel back through time. A classical allusion in Milton is 'like the dwelling place of our infancy revisited in manhood'.[22] No need to track the references down: their power lies in their general nostalgic evocation of the reader's childhood encounters with Latin and Greek.

No such nostalgic transport at all, though, is available to us whose childhood was not saturated with memories of plugging away at the classical languages. We can pillage encyclopaedias to discover the meaning of learned references. We can acquire, as adults, an expert command of Latin and Greek. We may even come to apprehend classical allusions with refined sensibility, but our apprehension will belong to the adult consciousness. We will never know the peculiar emotive force of classical allusions as effortless, unbidden, intimate remembrance of 'the dwelling place of our infancy'. Our infancy was spent elsewhere. What's at issue is not whether we eventually learnt Greek or Latin, but whether we came to Greek and Latin early. Poor us, like poor 'Old Kemp, trying to learn Latin conjugations at 24' – too late to experience the mystique of classical reminiscence that Macaulay celebrates.[23]

Wilfred Owen compared 'old Kemp' to George Eliot's Baldassare, the former professor of classics struggling pathetically to re-learn Greek and Latin from scratch in middle age. I would adduce another character of Eliot's, this time from the third chapter of *The Mill on the Floss*, as evidence of the nineteenth-century understanding of the power of half-forgotten childhood Latin to linger in and haunt the adult imagination. Eliot's Mr Riley is not the sort of public schoolboy Macaulay had in mind: for that very reason he has something more in common with Owen, who had to settle for a second-tier school. But even Mr Riley's inferior Latin education has created a mental atmosphere that he still inhabits:

> [. . .] though Mr Riley had received a tincture of the classics at the great Mudport Free School, and had a sense of understanding Latin generally, his comprehension of any particular Latin was not ready. Doubtless there remained a subtle aroma from his juvenile contact with the 'De Senectute' and the Fourth Book of the 'Æneid', but it had ceased to be distinctly recognizable as classical, and was only perceived in the higher finish and force of his auctioneering style.[24]

The cinching words are 'tincture' and 'aroma'. With them Eliot neatly distinguishes mere intellectual knowledge of Latin from another kind of understanding, the apprehension of Latin as a *feeling* analogous to the experience of colour or smell. Mr Riley's mind remains coloured by his schoolboy Cicero and Virgil, though he never quite mastered them: the 'tincture of the classics' is something other, and (significantly) more durable, than competence in Latin. The special quality of Eliot's use of 'tincture' is residual: it is not the colouring of the mind that attends the competent study of Latin, but that weathered and distressed tincture that remains after the Latin is properly forgotten. As for 'aroma': to characterize a vestigial feel for forgotten knowledge as a smell is especially apt, given the Proustian capacity of smells to evoke the past, and childhood memories in particular. Eliot's bit of teasing – that Mr Riley's apprehension of classical style survives 'only in the higher force and finish of his auctioneering style' – is a nice bit of comedy, and so is her jibe that Mr Riley's 'sense of understanding Latin generally' did not happen to include the ability to actually translate 'any particular Latin'. This is tantamount to saying that he was on familiar terms with Latin but could not translate a word of it. It would not at all cancel the force of Eliot's satire to claim that Mr Riley's 'sense of understanding Latin generally' is something more than just a euphemism for incompetence. The consciousness produced by such colourations and atmospheres of forgotten knowledge is a complex and subtle thing.

The feeling that 'classical antiquity and one's childhood were inevitably linked'[25] was still strong in the early twentieth century. It was, for instance, taken for granted that readers of *The Times* would recognize that feeling in a poem that appeared in its pages on 14 December 1914, as the first Christmas of the Great War was approaching. Its author, the Eton headmaster C. A. Alington, sought to assure British soldiers abroad that 'We don't forget – while in the dark December / We sit in schoolrooms that you know so well', and that 'Through all of it, the same old Greek and Latin, / You know we don't forget.'[26] The implication is that Old Etonians of all ages, not just those then fighting the war, would have been transported by the very mention of Greek and Latin, as would any who had enjoyed a public-school education.[27]

A similar attitude had attended the inauguration, in 1911, of the Loeb Classical Library, that series of Greek and Latin classics, uniformly bound with facing English translations. To whom were these affordable bilingual editions meant to appeal? Not, chiefly, to the learned, who would despise both the presence of the English translations and the absence of full apparatus; nor to readers without classical training who, except for the most determined autodidacts, could make no use of the Greek and Latin on the left-hand page. But there remained a third class of readers: those who, having studied at least Latin, had forgotten some or even most of it: those for whom the classics were a memory. To just such readers a 1912 advertisement in the *Times Literary Supplement* is addressed, promising that 'the Loeb Classical Library will be welcomed by those to whom their classics are at best a pleasant reminiscence.'[28] The advertising men demonstrated a shrewd grasp of Macaulay's notion of the power of classical nostalgia. The advert attests to the number of readers for whom what remained of schoolboy studies was not the knowledge of Latin, but the memory of once *having known* it. Virginia Woolf, writing in *TLS* (five months before Owen wrote 'Dulce Et Decorum Est'), imagined that she and her fellow readers of the Loeb volumes would seem 'not so much to read as to recollect what we had heard in some other life.'[29] To read the Loebs was not so much to read the classics as to remember them from childhood study. Reviewing the Loeb volume that included that standard schoolroom author Catullus, classicist John Henry Fowler confidently put his finger on the pulse of the audience most likely to appreciate the bilingual format:

> Many an old public school boy who has forgotten most of his classics, and who
> never read more than a few of the poet's lyrics, cherishes throughout life a real
> affection for the graceful and musical lines in which Catullus, at an age in which
> he might still have been a public school boy himself, immortalized the memory
> of his gallant yacht, the dainty lilt of the lines to Lesbia's sparrow, the joyous ring
> of the Epithalamion of Mallius.[30]

'Many an old public schoolboy who has *forgotten* most of his classics.'
Fowler takes for granted that in 1913 (four years before Owen would write 'Dulce
Et Decorum Est') the experience of Latin literature is inseparable from schoolboy
reminiscence. His notion of Catullus as composing poems while 'he might still
have been a public school boy himself' presses the association close to the point
of comedy, and yet it would be wise to take Fowler's larger point in earnest.

The liveliest apprehension of 'Dulce Et Decorum Est', then, would entail not
only the knowledge of Horace's Latin, but the childhood memory of it.
Latecomers to Latin can acquire the one but not the other. In this respect, Owen's
use of the word 'children' exerts pressure on, and clarifies his use of 'old', as
including the sense 'long familiar': 'You would not tell with such high zest / To
children ardent for some desperate glory /The old Lie'.[31] The manuscripts show
that Owen had considered an alternative – 'To young men ardent for some
desperate glory' – only later to cancel 'young men' and restore 'children'.[32] That
restoration is vital. It need not preclude interpreting 'children' as evocation of
young men of enlistment age, tragically young and, like children, susceptible to
the jingoistic blandishments of a Jessie Pope. But the poet's insistence on 'children'
brings in the association, so alien to our time but so typical of Owen's, of
childhood and the classics.

My point is that the special power of Owen's poem lies deeper than in a mere
repudiation of Horace's ideology. It resides in Owen's tampering with the
formative experience of his putative readers, for whom memory, nostalgia, and
childhood are bound up with the experience of reading Horace. I say 'tampering'
because Owen's quotation of Horace involves tampering with his metre.

Classical metres and childhood

But were classical *metres*, specifically, also the stuff of nostalgia for men of
Wilfred Owen's generation? They were. The 'musical lines' of the classical poets,
and in particular the 'dainty lilt' of Catullus, transports Fowler back to his
childhood, and he knows that many a grown man who has forgotten the words

of his schoolboy Latin will not have forgotten the 'lilt' – the metrical cadence – of Latin verses. One of the poems Fowler recalls, the second poem of Catullus (c. 2), addressed to the pet sparrow of the poet's mistress, begins with this line: 'passer, deliciae meae puellae' (Sparrow, the favourite plaything of my mistress). By referring to its 'dainty lilt', Fowler refers to the energies that animate the movements of the line's words through its metrical template. This is none other than the phalaecean hendecasyllabic (– – – u u – u – u – u), the very metre, as noted in the Preface of this book, adopted by Robert Frost for his poem 'For Once, Then, Something'. (Given that Fowler associates this metre with the schoolroom, it is fitting that Frost's own poem had its genesis in his daughter's schoolgirl efforts at learning the phalaecean hendecasyllabic.)

The 'lilt' Fowler names may be felt in the third through sixth syllables, which taken together form, yet again, the choriamb (– u u –), the metrical foot Auden hopes readers will keep an eye out for, and which appears in its different way within the alcaic strophe. Here in the phalaecean hendecasyllabic, the choriamb functions as a kind of hinge between the two long (and so slower) syllables which precede it, and the alternation of long and short syllables that follows. There's a jaunty quickening in that choriambic dip – 'dainty' is not the term I would reach for, but 'lilting' certainly. None of which needs explaining to Fowler's 1912 *TLS* audience. He assumed his readers would simply remember, with 'real affection', the phalaecean hendecasyllabics as a feature of their upbringing. Such an assumption has been impossible since the middle of the twentieth century. Today's readers cannot be assumed even to have studied Latin, but the gulf is even wider than that. Even if they studied English poetry at school, they are unlikely to have done so with much attention to metre. Metrically incompetent poets now regularly achieve acclaim, or what passes for acclaim in the poetry world. Even professional literary people, including academics and critics, often reveal, implicitly and sometimes openly, indifference or insensitivity to the critical implications of metrical nuance.

That this had long been otherwise is everywhere evident. The Greek and Latin poems, in classical metres, of John Milton and George Herbert and Samuel Johnson are the fruits of intense and conventional schoolboy training in classical verse composition. Andrew Marvell's 'The Garden' and 'Hortus', which generate complex interrelations between an English and a Latin version of the 'same' poem, are mature manifestations of the schoolboy exercise of translating English verses into Latin, and vice-versa – with strict attention to the classical metres. So Alfred Tennyson's metrical *jeu d'esprit*, 'Hendecasyllabics', depends, for its effect, on the reader's catching the whiff of the schoolroom, and memories of drill in classical metres:

O you chorus of indolent reviewers,
Irresponsible, indolent reviewers,
Look, I come to the test: a tiny poem
All composed in the metre of Catullus,
All in quantity, careful of my motion,
Like a skater on ice that hardly bears him,
Lest I fall unawares before the people,
Waking laughter in indolent reviewers.
Should I flounder a while without a tumble
Through this metrification of Catullus,
They should speak to me not without a welcome,
All that chorus of indolent reviewers.
Hard, hard, hard it is not to tumble,
So fantastical is this dainty metre.
Wherefore, slight me not wholly, nor believe me
Too presumptuous, indolent reviewers.
O blatant Magazines, regard me rather –
Since I blush to belaud myself a moment –
As some rare little rose, a piece of inmost
Horticultural art, or half coquette-like
Maiden, not to be greeted unbenignly.[33]

Here is the same metre (– – – – u u – u – u – u) which, Fowler thought, a public schoolboy would 'cherish throughout life with real affection'. Tennyson's poem turns on just such recognition: the poem, as he published it in *Cornhill* magazine in 1863, comes without gloss on the metre or on Catullus. Prior acquaintance is assumed. The poem is meant to evoke experience of having oneself written metrical exercises at school. In its self-deprecation, its puckishness, it reads as a parody of schoolboy metrical exercises. Defending his skill at versification against his critics, Tennyson plays the schoolboy aiming to satisfy a demanding schoolmaster: 'Look, I come to the test, a tiny poem / All composed in the metre of Catullus, / All in quantity, careful of my motion.' Did Fowler know this poem? His putative public schoolboy cherishes the lilt of Catullus' metre because it is 'dainty'. Tennyson: 'So fantastical is this *dainty* metre'.

Footnotes and 'the implication of forgotten knowledge'

Were he alive today, it may have given Wilfred Owen the creeps to discover that in the twenty-first century, most readers of his poem are, with respect to Latin, even worse off than old Kemp. They have not even come late to Latin – they have not come at all. Macaulay's world of schoolboy classical reminiscence is all but extinct. The disestablishment of the classics from the school curriculum has been chronicled elsewhere, but I note 1960 as a watershed.[34] That was the year Cambridge University abolished Latin as a condition of matriculation. It amounted to a formal acknowledgement of a revolution in literary culture: for the first time in centuries, acquaintance with the ancient languages was no longer assumed of the highly educated élite. The dislocation of classics occurred at more or less the same time in America and throughout the Anglophone world. With each decade, then, ever more of Owen's readers have come to 'Dulce Et Decorum Est' as strangers to Latin and foreigners to that shared hinterland of classical nostalgia.

For most readers today, editorial intervention is part of the experience of the poem. Reading it means having to turn away from the poem's ardour to the inert lumber of a footnote: helpful maybe, but tending to break the spell. And even if helpful, then only up to a point. The typical footnote will translate the Latin, attribute it to a Roman poet called Horace (65–14 BCE) and, in the case of ampler glosses, offer some brief indication of the literary, social, or historical context of the poem. All very well, but a footnote cannot retroactively supply a reader with the experience of a childhood of which a Horatian tag will trigger the memory.

If footnotes cannot make up for the memory of childhood Latin, imagination may – in part. To imagine experiences we have never had is, after all, part of the experience of reading. Poets can do much to impute to readers knowledge they did not acquire in childhood. When, in the final act of *The Merchant of Venice*, Jessica and Lorenzo compare themselves to four pairs of classical lovers (Cressida and Troilus, Thisbe and Pyramus, Dido and Aeneas, Medea and Jason), Shakespeare imputes to his audience long familiarity with those amorous couples. Modern readers, unfamiliar with the allusions, may nevertheless respond to the imputation of familiarity and, through the imagination, 'feel' the resonances of a familiarity they do not themselves possess, but can imagine others possessing. Similarly, the vulnerability of Eve, unaware of her imminent abduction, leads Milton to an allusion of exactly the kind that, in Macaulay's view, is meant to waken schoolboy memories of classical study:

Not that fair field

Of Enna, where Prosérpine gath'ring flow'rs
Herself a fairer flow'r by gloomy Dis
Was gathered, which cost Ceres all that pain
To see her through the world;[35]

Even if I am not one of Macaulay's classically-trained schoolboys, I might nevertheless infer, without the aid of notes, the portentousness of the backstory Milton concentrates into the single word 'that': not just '*that* fair field', but especially 'all *that* pain'. The force of the adjective is not so much demonstrative or deictic as confidential. 'All *that* pain' draws me into an intimacy: the company of those in the know, those who have *long* known, of Ceres' pain, and whose sympathies have been formed in part by it. So even those of Owen's readers who come late to Latin, or never at all, may, by picking up on 'the implication of forgotten memory',[36] make that which is previously unknown to them – a sequence of seven Latin words – seem not unknown but 'merely forgotten'.[37] How many readers of 'Dulce Et Decorum Est', rather than recognizing the Horatian tag, might have *imagined* the feeling of recognizing it?

When it comes to classical metres, though, we begin to run up against the limits of what readers may reasonably be expected to do in order to compensate for having come late, or never, to the classics. No editor, however helpful on the other aspects of Wilfred Owen's debt to Horace, has ever supplied a footnote explaining how 'Dulce Et Decorum Est' recalls, but then undoes, the alcaic metre of Horace's poem. Metrical allusions defy the capacity of readers to imagine remembering what they never knew. Shakespeare and Milton, by their powers of suggestion, can go some way towards 'making the unknown seem merely forgotten'. But what could Tennyson or (more pointedly) Frost do to imply a long history of associations and memories connected with the phalaecean hendecasyllabic?

Doubly so for Owen in 'Dulce Et Decorum Est'. Owen's allusion consists not in reproducing a classical metre, as Tennyson and Frost had done, but in *avoiding* writing in a classical metre. Quoting Horace's words only, he misquotes the alcaic metre, wrests the words from their Latin metrical template and sets them marching to the beat of his English iambs. The ancient metre is felt by its absence, not its presence. Owen's shoehorning of Horace's Latin into accentual iambics turns the apparently straightforward act of quotation into an erasure of the alcaic metre, the form in which those Latin words have their original vitality. That erasure comports marvellously with the poem's spirit of repudiation. Those of Owen's readers who (in Fowler's words) 'cherished through-out life' the 'graceful and musical' classical metres they learnt as children will have been able to feel, and be scandalized by, Owen's 'metrical outrage', the distortion of the alcaic line. For the rest of us, though, the erasure itself is invisible, and it requires the work of a critic to reveal to us the spectral presence of the alcaic at the end of Owen's poem. In that sense it is a kind of emblem for the ways the presence of the alcaic strophe in English literature can be overlooked. It catches something of the alcaic's significant, but curiously oblique, relation to English literature.

John Hollander's preposterous alcaics

There is nothing oblique, though, about my next instance, a poem in English which not only overtly embraces the alcaic strophe, but even picks up the final lines of Wilfred Owen's poem and translates them – metrically – back into an alcaic template, as if to restore the metre that Owen had so suggestively undone. This new poem brings us to the twenty-first century, and so anticipates a major concern of this book: that the alcaic's influence in English verse has been most widely felt in the past half-century, just when the classics have been disestablished from the curriculum in the English-speaking world, and when poets and readers have been more likely than ever to come to adulthood, as 'old Kemp' had done, without Latin or Greek, and (unlike Kemp), unlikely ever to learn them.

Hollander's 'To an Old Latin Teacher', published in the 2004 collection *Picture Window*, brings together (1) Horace generally, (2) the alcaic strophe, (3) Horace's line 'dulce et decorum est / pro patria mori', (4) Owen's 'Dulce Et Decorum Est', (5) questions of metrical misquotation, and (6) the issue of coming late to Latin. Hollander's ways of inviting and resisting the influence of the alcaic are so different from Owen's as to demonstrate, as a point of departure for my study, the range of uses to which the alcaic in English may be put. 'To an Old Latin Teacher' begins with the power of a snowfall to make us see a familiar landscape afresh:

> Snow fell all night and suddenly there was morning:
> a startling vision from a familiar window,
> while yet an ordinary sight: a
> neighboring hill had become itself more
>
> completely, thrusting forward in all that sunlight
> as having donned a secular alb with which to
> set out along the gleaming paths of
> vision extending in all directions
>
> and so what one had always been quite aware of
> had shown a new significance now – or merely
> revealed what it had always meant (this
> must have been slowly accumulating).[38]

These three stanzas are also a familiar *literary* landscape seen afresh, since they refer to the opening lines of one of Horace's best-known odes (1.9) – written in alcaics, and the first alcaic poem to appear in Horace's first book of odes – in which the poet calls attention to the view from his house to distant Mount Soracte clad with snow. As if to make the allusion doubly clear, the poems in *Picture Window* are ordered so that 'To an Old Latin Teacher' immediately follows Hollander's own translation of *Odes* 1.9, which begins like this:

> See how Soracte, glistening, stands out high in
> its cape of snow, how laboring woods let go of
>   their load, and all the streams are frozen
>   over completely with sharpest cold now.[39]

Both poems are composed in a metre closely based on the alcaic strophe. (Hollander's version of the alcaic adds an extra syllable in the first two lines of the stanza.) So: 'To an Old Latin Teacher' begins in Horatian reminiscence, imitating both the theme and the alcaic metre of Horace's Soracte ode. Lest the reader suppose, though, that Hollander has known Horace's Latin poems from childhood, the poem turns on a confession: Hollander has come late to Latin (very late indeed by Wilfred Owen's standards), and for most of his life had had only a knowledge about, but not firsthand acquaintance with, Horace:

> I know this keeps on happening all the time with
> what one has lived with knowledge *about* but never,
>   until now only, knowledge *of,* then
>   suddenly seeing it one bright morning...
>
> as if, like some Chocorua or Monadnock
> I'd left for others to climb, I saw the
>   hill as a text I'd only known in
>   pieces; and such was my understanding
>
> of Horace. Never having him as a schoolboy,
> for I'd come late to Latin in any case; since
>   an introduction back in the sixth grade,
>   nothing amounted to more than hearsay.

The difference between Latin acquired earlier or later, and the special privilege of having had Latin 'as a schoolboy', matters in 'To an Old Latin Teacher', just as in 'Dulce Et Decorum Est'.

One difference, though, is that in Owen's poem, the same issue is only implied. Owen is explicit about coming late to Latin, not in the poem itself, but in that letter to his mother about Kemp. In Hollander's poem, however, the experience of coming late to Latin becomes the very subject of the poem, and the next verses trace the career of the speaker's remedial classical education undertaken in adulthood:

> Then I acquired some more later on, not yet in
> an overheated classroom some winter morning
>   but rather, warm in bed, beside you
>   clasped by the Latin you'd always loved, in
>
> the way we're told vernaculars best are studied,
> in undemanding, intimate pedagogy,
>   you answered all the simple questions,
>   sending me back to old Suetonius
>
> and Robert Graves and others for all the raunchy
> and easily retold imperial scandals,
>   and all the while the scraps of grammar,
>   stories of syntax – a kind of folklore –
>
> that barely got me started on all those decades'
> unearned and poor and ignorant use of Latin,
>   Catullus holding my attention,
>   Ovid then coming to claim his own; and
>
> then it was Milton led me at last to Virgil
> and finally, delighting in the *Aeneid*,
>   which, most preposterously through this
>   mode of progression, I came to live with.

Lucky John Hollander, tutored by his special someone in a cosy bed. 'Intimate pedagogy' shows Hollander feelingly alert to the link, so important in Owen's poem, between education and the affections, though in his case the affectionate memories of learning will be different from the schoolboy kind. Instead he gets at schoolboy experience via this loved one, who is no latecomer but who has 'always loved' Latin. Through this teacher Hollander comes to a knowledge of those bits of schoolboy lore – those 'scraps of grammar, / stories of syntax' – which are transmitted from generation to generation of students. He means mnemonic devices, for instance, or *amo-amas-amat*, or metrical templates (*dum dum dum, dee-dee dum dee dum dee dum-dum*, as one might perform the alcaic hendecasyllabic line), or first lines of famous poems ('*nunc est bibendum*'). These are the small change of the classical schoolboy and schoolgirl tradition. They are shibboleths; to recognize them is to be a classical insider. 'A kind of folklore' indeed. Hollander is initiated, late, into schoolboy culture, and documents his initiation with the alertness of an anthropologist.

What's most to seize on, though, is Hollander's phrase 'most preposterously'. In a poem about reactivating his dormant Latin, Hollander unpreposterously reactivates the Latin sense of *pre-post-erous*, 'first-last; proper order reversed'. Coming late to Latin, for Hollander, means inverting the 'proper' sequence of literary inheritance, in which Homer bequeaths his riches to Virgil, who passes on the compounded interest to a receptive Milton, and so on. To come to the *Aeneid* by way of *Paradise Lost* is to make the journey in the 'wrong' direction. This is normative now – most of us now come to Horace, for instance, through modern poets, such as Wilfred Owen. It requires some effort of imagination, when reading Horace's ode and coming to the phrase 'dulce et decorum est pro patria mori', to suppress the voice of Wilfred Owen, and the literally preposterous sensation that the Roman poet is quoting the English one. For me, there is a corner of that Roman ode that is forever English.

Hollander's next stanzas track his effort to override the effects of his own preposterous reading. The idea is to take stock of all those Horatian phrases that have entered Anglophone culture as familiar quotations, decontextualized, and restore them to their original Latin contexts. Here Horace, that most quotable of poets, comes to the fore, whose swarm of maxims hovered about Hollander's childhood, but torn from the poems in which they originally appeared:

> What scraps of Horace hovered about my childhood,
> though? '*Integer vitae scelerisque purus*',
>   my father sang, in its contracted
>   setting from Germany, shorn of all those
>
> last words of loving Lalage, softly laughing
> and chattering, and thus undoing what Horace
>   was up to, then the *carpe diem*
>   coming, of course, when I got older,
>
> enough to guess what all that might have to do with
> the growing bed of flowers I'd want to pluck from:
>   *eheu fugaces*, with its Roman
>   sigh that a friend informed me had been

> pronounced at his St. Grottlesex school to rhyme with
> 'give me the *key*, Hugh' (rather than – what? – forget
>   and poets all are doomed in being
>   ever Postumous, in any case); then
>
> *odi profanum vulgus* at just the time I
> began to feel a bit of all that myself, seemed
>   like pure high modernism to a
>   celebrant aetat sixteen, who'd later
>
> believe *beatus ille qui procul* – parents?
> *negotiis* of all the nineteen fifties? –
>   it rang a bell and who could say the
>   wrong one? Then *nunc est bibendum* and all
>
> (and any undergraduate yahoo knew what
> the gist of that was, sans any word of Latin),
>   and then the quite indifferent foot of
>   *Pallida Mors*, which to think of causes
>
> a simple form of shuddering in us, rather
> than any sense of fairness. . .and all those other
>   old rags of tags that the English language
>   made seem its own like the tough *aes triplex.*

Hollander sets off in italics no fewer than eight Horatian phrases – 'old rags of tags' – which an educated English-speaker without Latin can only experience preposterously, because they have become familiar in English long before one discovers their source poems, if ever. The English language has made them 'seem its own'. They are Latin analogues to what 'skin of my teeth' is to those unacquainted with the Bible, or 'one fell swoop' to those who have used the phrase a hundred times before coming upon it, to their surprise, in *Macbeth*. Each of the Latin phrases Hollander quotes lives an afterlife in English literature (in Herrick, in Marvell, in Tennyson, in Pope), but for most people now those tags are the beforelife, and the original Latin context is the afterlife.

But even when those Latin phrases are quoted verbatim, their use in a modern context often amounts to 'undoing what Horace / was up to.' Wilfred Owen, wittingly or not, was undoing what Horace was up to when he made a new lie out of 'The old Lie: dulce et decorum est / Pro patria mori' by altering the context, and hence the implications, of the familiar Latin tag. Of which Hollander – most significantly – is mindful:

What Wilfred Owen called 'the old lie'[40] of *dulce et*
decorum est pro patria mori (what could
    you mean by *patria* to make this
       true? Later on we would come to wonder).

I finally came to pick up the pieces, putting
these tags and all the others where they belonged and
    when raised from later dead allusion
       quickened in far-reaching strophic vigor.

In these crucial stanzas Hollander's poem apprehends what no critic has hitherto pointed out: that Owen's metrical misquotation makes of Horace's tag not just allusion, but a 'dead allusion', because the words are stripped of their original *metrical* force, their 'strophic vigor'. The poem embodies that point, since the very poem in which he raises the issue is itself written in the very metre that Owen, 'undoing what Horace was up to', had eschewed. Hollander takes up what in Owen had been 'a dead allusion' and quickens it by restoring it to an alcaic metric setting, restoring its strophic vigour.

That metrical restoration, though, involves some innovative twists. Since Hollander is already writing in a near-equivalent to the alcaic strophe, the obvious thing to have done would be to contrive that Horace's Latin tag should coincide exactly with the beginning of a line. For instance:

      . . . what Wilfred Owen called 'the old lie of
  "*dulce et decorum est pro patria mori*"'

That arrangement would have restored Horace's seven words to their corresponding metrical pattern. Hollander could have quoted Horace's exact words in their exact order, while also preserving the Roman poem's original metre. But he does not. Instead, Hollander follows Owen in breaking up the Latin metrical template. He ignores the elisions *dulc(e) et* and *decor(um) est*, and allows the line to be fractured across a line-break, though his fracture falls in a different place from Owen's:

What Wilfred Owen called 'the old lie' of *dulce et*
decorum est pro patria mori[41]

This is shrewd and suggestive. Hollander neither arranges for the Latin words to correspond exactly with the original alcaic pattern, even though that option was easily available. The implication is that Owen's metrical misquotation of this famous line of verse is now itself a part of the classical tradition, and a part of the history of the alcaic strophe. Hollander may have at last got back to Horace, but he got there *via* Owen, and Owen's undoing of the alcaic line is not a mistake that now needs to be undone itself. The point of the classical tradition – the study of it (as in a monograph) or the practice of it (as in a poem) is not to follow the thread of later writings back to the pure, uncontaminated original. The successor works have become part of a living whole that includes the original work: in this case Horace *Odes* 3.3. Yet even though associations of Owen's poem cling to it, in Hollander's poem the Horatian tag is *partially* restored by being released from Owen's iambics and getting back into the swim of alcaics – the freshly quickened English alcaics of a later (and this time, fully sympathetic) poet.

Hollander takes this metrical alchemy a step further. Reconsider this earlier stanza, in which Hollander remembers his immigrant father singing a musical setting of one of Horace's odes:

> What scraps of Horace hovered about my childhood,
> though? '*Integer vitae scelerisque purus*',
>   my father sang, in its contracted
>   setting from Germany, shorn of all those
>
> last words of losing Lalage, softy laughing . . .

The poem in question is *Odes* 1.22,[42] whose opening stanza, at least to modern ears, sounds something like the boast of Tennyson's Galahad, that his strength is as the strength of ten because his heart is pure:

> integer vitae scelerisque purus
> non eget Mauris iaculis neque arcu
> nec venenatis gravida sagittis
>   Fusce, pharetra,

(1–4)

> The man of unblemished life who is unstained by crime has no need of Moorish javelin or blow, or a quiver full of poisoned arrows, Fuscus

Because it sounds like a declaration of lofty morals, this introductory stanza has often been detached from the rest of the poem. One of the last century's great Latin scholars, Eduard Fraenkel, reminisced that 'not very long ago' – he was writing in 1957 – 'it was the custom at many German schools to have the first stanza sung at funeral services in Hall, to a tune not distinguishable from that of an ordinary church hymn; the tempo, needless to say, was *molto adagio*'.[43] It is in just this form – set to music and sung by his immigrant father – that John Hollander, as a child, and before learning Latin, came to know this 'scrap of Horace'. Hollander's poem is about 'finally' discovering the original contexts of such familiar scraps of Horace and 'putting / these tags and all the others where they belonged'. When you restore that edifying quotation from Horace to its original context – that is, when you read on beyond the first stanza – what you discover is an increasingly whimsical tone that nearly cancels the force of Horace's claim, that moral virtue protects a man from physical harm. It turns out that Horace, wandering through the Sabine woods and singing about his *inamorata* Lalage, had encountered a ferocious wolf who nevertheless 'fled from me, though I had no weapons'. Horace is really boasting that his miraculous immunity derives not from his moral purity, but the intensity of his love for the beautiful Lalage, 'with her sweet laughter and her sweet talk'. Horace's ode turns out to be gleefully facetious, not at all the solemn thing its first stanza leads the unwary reader to believe.[44] You can set the detached first stanza to organ music and sing it, *molto adagio*, at funerals, but that requires missing the point of a poem which, as the great classicist Wilamowitz drily joked, can only be sung at a graveside by somebody who doesn't understand it.[45] Hollander has corrected that misapprehension by discovering that the solemn Latin lyrics that he had heard his father sing were in fact the ironical beginning of a Horatian ode that is not solemn at all, but breezily erotic: his father's truncated version had been 'shorn of all those / last words of losing Lalage, softly laughing'.

In this very act of restoring a familiar Horatian quotation to its proper context, Hollander nevertheless performs an act of metrical misquotation akin to Owen's. For the Horatian ode that begins with '*Integer vitae*' is not composed in alcaics at all, but in that metre's sibling, the sapphic stanza. Yet Hollander makes Horace's sapphic line conform to the pattern of his English alcaics. Like Owen, he is quoting Horace's exact words in their exact order, but fitting them into the pattern of a different metre.

Hollander's conflation of metres, then, is an ingenious way of remembering Owen's conflation of metres in 'Dulce Et Decorum Est'. What's even more remarkable is that it is also Horatian, since Horace himself had done something very similar. Near the end of the second ode of Book 4, he had incorporated into that poem, written in the sapphic metre, a five-word interjection ('o Sol pulcher, o laudande') written in a very different metrical pattern. The stanza in question finds Horace imagining himself acclaiming an Augustus returning in military triumph to Rome (*Odes* 4.2.45–8):

tum meae, si quid loquar audiendum
vocis accedet bona pars, et, 'o Sol
pulcher! o laudande!' canam, recepto
    Caesare felix.

Then, if I have anything to say that is worth hearing, I shall join in to the best of my ability, singing, 'O glorious day, O worthy of all praise!' in my joy at Caesar's return.

Those five words that Horace imagines himself singing, 'o Sol / pulcher! o laudande', are part of a conventional exclamation, which the classicist Richard Thomas has called the equivalent of 'hip hip hooray'.[46] Though written in the metrical pattern known as *versus quadratus*, Horace has nevertheless managed to fit them into his stanza in just such a position as to conform, simultaneously, with the very different metrical pattern of the sapphic.[47] Both Owen and Hollander, then, share Horace's capacity for absorbing lines of other poet's verse and making them conform to the metrical pattern of their own poems. Hollander's unique move is to take a line that Owen had already transformed from Latin alcaics into English iambics, and to give it a new and 'far-reaching strophic vigor' by restoring the line to an alcaic measure – though a slightly altered alcaic measure of his own devising. Hollander's metrical misquotation imitates Owen's, but as it turns out, Horace himself engages in productive metrical misquotation.

'To an Old Latin Teacher', then, is more than just a very good instance of the persistence of the ancient alcaic metre into the twenty-first century. It explicitly sets itself up in creative relation to Owen's 'Dulce Et Decorum Est', and so reveals how differently the same ancient metre – indeed the same line of Latin poetry – can be received in English literature. Where Owen's engagement with the alcaic is covert, making the metre felt through its absence, Hollander openly reinvents the alcaic strophe in English. Owen undoes Horace's alcaics, as part of a repudiation of Horace's words, or others' appropriation of them. Hollander restores Horace's Latin words to a familiar metrical context as part of a wider and welcome rediscovery of Horace's poetry. Because Owen's distortion of the alcaic is negative, the erasure of the alcaic in his poem is available only to those who know Latin. Since, further, in Owen's day Latin was usually learnt in childhood or not at all, and because the poem complains of the deceiving of 'children', a vital part of the poem's emotional power turns on the question of having known (or not) Latin from childhood. Hollander's poem itself acknowledges his lack of childhood Latin, and narrates his attempt to find out how much feeling for Horace can be recovered in coming to Latin late and preposterously – indeed, from coming to 'dulce et decorum est pro patria mori' first through Owen's poem, and only later coming to know the line in its ancient context. His reinvention of the alcaic strophe in 'To an Old Latin Teacher' holds all of these complex ideas together.

Most of these issues will return, under a different aspect, in the late chapters of this book. Now, though, it is time to turn – preposterously – from English to the classical languages, to examine the character of the alcaic strophe itself, in the form of the actual ancient metre that the English poets have inherited.

2

'A Marvel of Metrical Disruptions'

The Alcaic Strophe Itself

The aesthetic of a metrical scheme

Who could be expected to be stirred by the sight of a mere diagram such as I give below? It is a metrical schema, a mapping of the pattern of long and short syllables – x standing for a syllable that may be either long or short – that make up the metrical pattern of the alcaic strophe:

```
x – u – x – u u – u –
x – u – x – u u – u –
   x – u – x – u – x
      – u u – u u – u – x[1]
```

It happens, though, that this mere abstract template has moved critics to admiration, as if aesthetic qualities inhered in the pattern itself. In the mind's eye of the classicist L. P. Wilkinson, for example, the design of the alcaic stanza took on the shape and motion of surf. He pictured 'the gathering wave of the first two lines, the thundering of the third, and the rapid backwash of the fourth'.[2] Somewhat less concretely, another classicist, Gilbert Murray, perceived an elaborate metrical 'progress', again in three stages. 'There is symmetry', he began dryly enough, 'between [lines] 1 and 2, a symmetry between 3 and 4, but' (and here his pulse begins to quicken) 'but in 4 is the perfect rhythm, smooth and untroubled, of which 3 is an approximation or "attempt", and to which all three verses lead by a kind of progress.' One passes through a variety of rhythms, only to arrive, at last, at the 'perfect rhythm' of the fourth line. The notion is almost teleological, and dramatic, too, since for Murray the satisfying resolution of the fourth line 'would be nothing in particular if it were not reached by a struggle'.[3]

One can see what they meant. In their differing ways, both Wilkinson and Murray were inferring a kind of miniature metrical drama in three acts. Act I would go something like this: the first two lines unfurl themselves massively and memorably. They are the longest lines in the stanza, stretching out to eleven syllables (so: 'hendecasyllabics'). But when Wilkinson speaks of the 'gathering wave', he must have had in mind not only their uncoiling extension, but also a sense of massiveness, especially when, as often, the indeterminate first and fifth syllables are long: – – u – – – u u – u – . This version of the line, in which five of the first six syllables are long, suits expressions of stateliness and forcefulness. That graceful metrical flourish – the choriamb in syllables six through nine – adds a dash of acceleration without enfeeblement, given that the line ends with a stressed syllable, and especially since line 2 repeats line 1, so both seem to coalesce into a bloc. This opening couplet, then, with its repetition of a complex and assertive rhythm, cuts a metrical figure that resembles what a composer does in announcing a theme. It is propositional (like the octet in a Petrarchan sonnet) and crescent: it sets something big in motion.

That motion rises to a culmination in Act II. This is expressed in the third line's interruption of the pattern established in the opening couplet. The first five syllables of line 3 may follow the pattern of the hendecasyllabics, and for a moment the reader may assume that line 3 will simply repeat them. But then an invariably long syllable in the eighth position prohibits a repetition of the choriamb that is a fixture of lines 1 and 2. After which the line comes to an end after just nine syllables (hence 'enneasyllabic'). That curtailment, that drop from eleven to nine syllables, constitutes a second departure from the initial couplet. A further difference: the enneasyllabic line can (and often does) end with a short syllable, producing for the first time in the stanza a feminine ending, a dying fall which contrasts with the rising finish (u –) of the hendecasyllabic lines. So when a poet arranges a line whose first and last syllables are short, but whose fifth is long (u – u – – – u – u), one can sense the rising motion of the beginning of the line, the cresting of the three long central syllables, and, in the last three, a falling-off. The total effect is of lines 1 and 2 rising to a culmination in line 3 – especially when the fifth syllable is long.

Whereupon Act III: the rapid falling rhythms of the fourth (decasyllabic) line, with its twin rippling dactyls (– u u – u u – u – x). When that last syllable is short, the dactyls seem to peter off into a curtailed version of themselves, a double trochee (– u – u). The movement is rapid. Where line 3 is (in Wilkinson's term) a metrical 'struggle', working its way up to a mid-line peak, the headlong plunge of line 4 is all release and resolution. It's a resumption, too, if you hear the first four syllables of line 4 as a choriamb, which picks up the choriambs of lines 1 and 2, in a kind of return to the tonic key.

As 'metrical contraptions' go (to recall Auden's phrase), the alcaic, even in the abstract, is among the most intricate combinations of patterned responsions, pauses and accelerations, repetitions, asymmetries and recoveries ever devised. A thrilling sense of metrical diversity, of progressing through a choriambic rhythm (1–2) to a roughly iambic rhythm (3) that runs on into dactyls (4), is counterbalanced by a feeling of unity, in the sense that the choriambic element can be detected in the fourth line, and as such echoes the first two lines, producing a sense of resolution. Beside the alcaic, our familiar 'English' lyric quatrains (four lines of iambic pentameter, or of tetrameter alternating with trimeter) seem unadventurous and tame. The alcaic is not only far more complex than typical English metres, it is at once more delicate and more dynamic, precariously in danger of losing control. 'A marvel of metrical disruptions delicately resolved,' writes the poet Rosanna Warren in a precise formulation of the stanza's dynamics, attending to the way that, in 'modulating' from the first two lines, in its third line 'the stanza loses its balance ... to recover it only in the final breath: it is a form that celebrates the marriage of order and disorder as the figurative soul of art'.[4]

'The current unfashionability of metrics'

The judgments of Murray and Wilkinson ought to detain us for a moment as worthy of historical framing, because they cast light on the vagaries of scholarly and critical fashions. A critic today could envy the confidence with which Murray, writing in 1927, and Wilkinson, as late as 1945, could propose, as a matter of serious classical scholarship, an aesthetic response to the alcaic strophe's metrical schema. Their approach could be criticized as essentialist or impressionistic or decontextualized, but one could still be impressed by bravura of their critical judgments. They imply a readership interested in, and receptive to, personal responses to the expressiveness of metrical minutiae – a fact almost as interesting, from a historical perspective, as the judgments themselves.

That is because after Wilkinson, scholars and critics of both Alcaeus and Horace rarely had anything to say about the aesthetic qualities of the alcaic. Roughly from mid-century, classicists largely restricted themselves to documenting the technical aspects of the stanza, often for the purpose of generating tables of statistical data as evidence for the dating of individual poems.[5] Far less attention was given to the critical implications of the stanza form. Major commentaries on Horace had little to say about metre as a feature of style and expressiveness.[6] Classicists, on very rare occasions, lamented this omission,[7] but the gap was not filled even by scholars who had begun to approach Horace's *Odes* with the kind of attention to poetic metre that New Critics, then ascendant, had been applying to the formal aspects of English poetry.[8] If Auden in the early 1970s had consulted scholarship to see what was being said about curious prosodic fauna such as bacchics and choriambs, he would have found that the only classicists paying attention to them at all were chiefly interested in documenting their existence and frequency, rather than thinking about what effects they might produce in sensitive readers of poetry. He might have inferred that classical scholars thought it rather bad form to write about the aesthetic properties of metre.

The exceptions to this rule are almost comically rare. It was only in passing, in a single sentence, that the Greek scholar D. A. Campbell, in 1985, spoke of Alcaeus' 'cunning use' of his eponymous metre in one particular stanza, because it suggested the movement of the storm-tossed ship it was describing.[9] 'Cunning use' is a provocative assertion. It calls to mind a swarm of questions: how could the poet have handled the form differently? Can other examples of the 'cunning use' of the alcaic strophe be pointed to? Answering these questions would require a more systematic application of the critical intelligence that produced Campbell's fleeting observation.

Then there is the tantalizing instance of Richard Heinze who, in a 1959 monograph concerned with a purely technical account of Horace's lyric metres, momentarily focuses on these lines from the Delius ode:

> omnium
> versatur urna serius ocius
>   sors exitura et nos in aeturnum
>   exsilium impositura cumbae.

(2.3.25–8)

> For all alike is the lot shaken in the urn; sooner or later, out it will come, and put us aboard the skiff for eternal exile.[10]

Heinze duly notes the outstanding metrical features: caesura bridged by elision, consecutive monosyllables, synaloepha. But then, in an uncharacteristic move, he ventures an insight into the poetical impact of the metrical features he has just named: 'Diese sich häufenden Hemmungen des Rhythmus sind beabsichtigt: sie sollen den Todensgedanken wie mit wuchtigen Schlägen in stoßweis artikulierter Rede einhämmern.' (These increasing inhibitions of the rhythm are intentional: they are intended to hammer in the thought of death as if with powerful blows, in bursts of articulated speech.)[11] This superb judgment, as elegant as it is accurate, shows what might be gained if those who know metre best would more often consider the effects of metre on the character and quality of the poetry. Suppose Heinze had applied the same critical acumen to all of Horace's odes, noting any instance in which the handling of the metre responded to some larger aspect of the poetry. We have no such book. Heinze's insight was a brief moment of critical illumination in a treatise crammed mostly with something else: exacting, if somewhat arid, learning.

But things have begun to change. Towards the end of the twentieth century, and in the first two decades of the twenty-first, there has been some quickening of interest in the artistic qualities of the alcaic. One aesthetically sensitive commentator, David West, devoted a page to what he called the 'Alcaic effect' – that bracing contrast in tempo between the slower enneasyllabic third line and the rapid decasyllabic line that follows it.[12] That was in 1998, and West's brief instance of metrical criticism might be thought of as having broken more than a decade of silence from prominent classicists about the Latin alcaic strophe as a vehicle for poetic imagination, and as an accomplishment of the poetic imagination in itself. Two years earlier, though, Rosanna Warren, a classically trained poet of great metrical sensitivity, had broken the silence on English alcaics with a brief and illuminating reading of W. H. Auden's elegy to Sigmund Freud.[13] In 2001 she published a second essay, even briefer but just as suggestive, containing the elegant critical formulation I have quoted above. Hers was perhaps the first extended discussion of the alcaic's literary value since Wilkinson. In that same year, 2001, I began writing about alcaics, and went on to publish, on and off over the course of several years, three articles on the critical implications of Greek, Latin, and English alcaics, whose various insights I am trying to unite and develop in this book. In 2012 Andrew S. Becker published a dense and searching article on the classical alcaic which focused, refreshingly, on the musical and acoustic qualities of the stanza.[14] I am happy that Becker draws on some of my own observations on both Latin and English alcaics, and happier still to refer readers to his indispensable article, with its unequalled attention to the minute technical details of the Latin alcaic. Classicists are beginning to discover, or rediscover, the artistic significance of the alcaic.

The term 'alcaic effect' has been picked up again in Llewellyn Morgan's 2010 study *Musa Pedestris: Metre and Meaning in Roman Verse*.[15] This lively book, which presents itself as resisting 'the current unfashionability of metrics,'[16] comes in for special mention, though not because it is much concerned with alcaics themselves. The few but insightful pages Morgan gives to that metre come, as so often in discussions of the alcaic, as tangential to a longer discussion of the alcaic's more famous sibling, the sapphic.[17] It is a broader concern of Morgan's study, though, that I signal here: his anxiety to justify the very idea of studying the expressive dimension of classical metres at all:

> When I argue that metres are more than the inert forms of poetic composition and carry their own meaning, I have the impression that many classicists think I am suffering from some kind of critical synaesthesia, asking questions of the metre of a poem which are appropriate only to its language. But all I can say is, that if there is something pathological about how I experience metrical form, I am fully satisfied that I share the condition with Roman writers and readers of poetry.[18]

Granted: writing about poetic metre is a slippery business, doubly complicated when the language in question is both foreign and ancient. But for Morgan, sixty-five years after Wilkinson, to feel the need to defend his claim that classical metres are 'more than the inert forms of poetic composition' is evidence of remarkably persistent critical indifference to the ways that metrical forms can mean and move. What Morgan calls 'the current unfashionability of metrics' has lasted rather longer than that generous turn of phrase implies. Metrical tone-deafness among scholars and readers is now sufficiently entrenched as to require Morgan to defend his decision to write an entire book on the literary value of classical metres. The accounts of Murray and Wilkinson are evidence that it was not always so: they drew out the critical aesthetic quality of metrical patterns, and assumed a similar confidence in their readers.

A sample of Greek alcaics

If so much can be claimed for the mere abstract pattern, what can be said about actual alcaic poems? The place to begin is with Alcaeus himself, the nominal inventor of the stanza-form.[19] The ruinous condition even of the few scraps of lyrics that have come down to us means that we can say far less about his own alcaic verses than Horace's, which survive abundantly and unmutilated. Yet here is a telling stanza, one of two that survive intact from a single fragment. 'I fail to understand the direction of the winds', says its storm-tossed seafaring speaker, 'one wave rolls in from this side, another from that, and we in the middle are carried along in company with our black ship.'[20] The Greek stanza reads like this:

ἀσυν<v>έτημμι τὼν ἀνέμων στάσιν·
τὸ μὲν γὰρ ἔνθεν κῦμα κυλίνδεται,

τὸ δ' ἔνθεν, ἄμμες δ' ὂν τὸ μέσσον
νᾶϊ φορήμ<μ>εθα σὺν μελαίνᾳ

asun<n>etēmmi tōn anemōn stasin:
to men gar enthen kuma kulindetai,
to d' enthen, ammes d' on to messon
nai forēm<m>etha sun melainai

(1–4)

No stanza more literally realizes Wilkinson's conception of the alcaic as the gathering, cresting, and backwash of a wave. The sense of building comes from the way that, in line 2, a long syllable occupies the fifth position, where in line 1 that fifth position had been short. The second line ('one wave rolls in from this side') is, fittingly, more massive. Then 'the jerky rhythm of the third line is followed by the rapid movement of the fourth in illustration of the headlong rush of the ship'.[21] Those are the words of D. A. Campbell, whom we find practising – like Richard Heinze, for the space of only one sentence – metrical criticism, registering an aesthetic response to the movement of the alcaic strophe. By 'jerky rhythm of the third line', Campbell must mean that the iambic pattern established in the first four syllables is interrupted by the intrusion of a long syllable in the fifth, which arrests the line's momentum and makes it pause, teetering for a moment, before it plunges back into its iambic motion, followed by the still more rapid dactyls of line four.

It will not be the case (it need not be the case) that every alcaic stanza achieve such plainly mimetic effects. Nor should we put claims for the expressiveness of fixed metres beyond the reach of scepticism: few tactics could be more damaging to the critical study of metre than to find metrical meaning everywhere. But if it came to mounting a rebuttal to those critics who find Llewelyn Morgan 'pathologically' sensitive to poetic form because he detects meaning in metre, this stanza would be a good place to start. Some will dismiss Wilkinson's characterization of the alcaic ('gathering wave, cresting, rapid backwash') as the indulgent impressionism of an age long gone. But it is not so easy to get such a charge to stick to Campbell, who was writing in 1985, and not as some dreamy literary critic, but one of the twentieth century's leading editors of Greek lyric.

The ruinous condition of the Greek lyric corpus allows only glimpses, like the one above, of what Alcaeus and Sappho could do with the metre. For an ample sense of what the metre can do in the hands of a master, we must turn to Horace. When Wilfred Owen and John Hollander, in their different but overlapping ways, engage with alcaics, it's chiefly Horace they have got in their sights; for them, as for most English poets, Alcaeus is not on the radar. So what kind of metrical contraption is Horace's version of the alcaic?

Horace's reimagined alcaics

When, in the final decades of the first century BCE, Horace set about composing his first three books of *Odes*, he was reaching back through the centuries to find metrical models in the lyrics of the two great Lesbian monodists. That's to say he was reviving a metrical tradition more remote in time to himself than the Tudors to us, and with the further removes of a foreign language and culture. Their revival involved, moreover, the technical problem of transposing song lyrics into a cognate but distinct art form: poetry composed chiefly to be read, not sung.[22] Exactly that achievement is among Horace's boldest claims to greatness: to have recreated the suave and subtle metrical patterns of Alcaeus and Sappho in the relatively chunky and unsupple Latin language. The feat was akin to getting German to move with the legato, *cantabile* ease of Italian. Within this larger accomplishment, Horace's handling of the alcaic was a particular achievement, not only as a matter of quality but also of primacy.[23] For while Horace claims to have been the first such innovator, in fact the sapphic stanza had already been brought over into Latin by no less a poet than Catullus (c. 11 and 51). But the alcaic – that verse form had not existed in Latin until Horace created it.

Or rather re-created it, since he altered the alcaic's movement slightly, just enough to impart his own personal touches. First, he introduced a greater proportion of long syllables. While Alcaeus had allowed the option of a long or short syllable in eight of the stanza's 41 positions, Horace makes the fifth syllable of lines 1–3 invariably long. The remaining 38 syllables he makes long much more often than Alcaeus had done. The effect of those changes is to make Horace's alcaics always more regular, and often slower, than Greek alcaics.[24] One can feel the contrast by considering the metrical pattern of the first two lines of the stanza of Alcaeus fragment 208 quoted above:

```
u – u – u – u u – u –
u – u – – – u u – u –
```

In the first line, the two available free positions (syllables 1 and 5) are short. In the second line, the first position remains short, but the fifth becomes long – a variation that slows down the movement of the line right in the middle. That slight *rallentando* is just enough to suggest the instability of the turbulent seas

Alcaeus is describing. When Horace writes his own account of a storm-tossed ship, his metrical alterations produce a different effect:

> non est meum, si mugiat Africis
> malus procellis, ad miseras preces
>   decurrere

(3.29.57–9)

It is not my way, if the mast creaks in an African gale, to resort to piteous prayers

In the first two lines of the stanza, Horace characteristically makes the four open positions (syllables 1 and 5 in both lines) long in every case (– – u – – – u u – u –). The result is weightier lines. What they lose in sprightliness, they gain in gravity. Gravity befitting the moralizing declaration of the speaker as he nears the end of a long, philosophically complex poem? Probably, but in any case, the far greater proportion of long syllables is typical of Horace's style of alcaics. A Horatian alcaic very rarely moves with the rhythm of, say, this enneasyllabic line from Alcaeus – θνάτοι]σι θεοσύλαισι πάντων (thnatoi]si theosulaisi pantōn, Campbell 298, l. 18) – where iambs take over the first half of the line. The speaker is referring to the rape of Cassandra by Ajax in the Trojan temple of Athena, 'who of all the blessed gods is most terrible to sacrilegious mortals' (ἃ θέων / θνάτοι]σι θεοσύλαισι πάντων / αἰνο]τάτα μακάρων πέφυκε, 17–19). The crucial fifth syllable, which Alcaeus makes short, falls, tellingly, in the middle of the word for 'sacrilegious'. That's the syllable which gives the line a freer movement than the more staid rhythm Horace favoured.

Horace's 'pivot syllable'

Casual readers could be forgiven for thinking Horace's minute alterations to Alcaeus's rhythms too nice a distinction to matter. But that would run counter to the testimony of formidable witnesses, including Alfred Tennyson. When he published English poems modelled on the alcaic stanza (they are the subject of the third chapter of this book), Tennyson went out of his way to signal their deviation from the 'Greek' alcaic, in which he heard 'a much freer and lighter movement' than in Horace's, with its greater number of long syllables and graver gait.[25] Wilkinson, too, felt the difference: for him, the decisive feature is Horace's decision to fix a single syllable: to make the fifth syllable of the enneasyllabic line invariably long. Those three successive long syllables in the middle of the third line strengthen the impression of progression towards a metrical climax, followed by a falling-off (u – u | – – – | u – u) . Wilkinson indicated the contrast between Greek levity and Horatian gravity by pointing to this stanza from one of the most famous fragments of Alcaeus, which finds the poet urging preparations for a winter-time drinking party (Campbell 338.5–8):

κάββαλλε τὸν χείμων᾿, ἐπὶ μὲν τίθεις
πῦρ, ἐν δὲ κέρναις οἶνον ἀφειδέως
μέλιχρον, αὐτὰρ ἀμφὶ κόρσα
μόλθακον ἀμφι<βάλων> γνόφαλλον

kabballe ton xeimōn᾿, epi men titheis
pur, en de kernais oinon apheideōs
melichron, autar amphi korsai
molthakon amphi<balōn> gnophallon

Down with the storm! Stoke up the fire, mix the honeysweet wine unsparingly, and put a soft fillet round your brows

What's to notice is the fifth syllable in the third line, which, because it is short rather than long, ensures a jaunty iambic rhythm. As against the very different movement of a Horatian alcaic such as this one (*Odes* 3.1.5–8):

regum timendorum in proprios greges,
reges in ipsos imperium est Iovis,
    clari Giganteo triumpho,
        cuncta supercilio moventis.

Dreaded monarchs have power over their own flocks; monarchs themselves are under the power of Jove, who in the glory of his triumphs over the Giants moves the whole universe with the nod of his brow.

This is all rather grander than the passage from Alcaeus, and not just because of the semantic content of the words. The rhythm of the third line (u – u | – – – | u – –) is key. 'There is all the difference in the world', says Wilkinson, between the tripping movement of the Greek line and the stately progress of the Latin one. What exactly is the difference Wilkinson perceives? Horace's line builds up to the majestic, indeed slightly menacing, three longs that correspond, expressively, with the adjective Gigāntēō. His enneasyllabic lines often ascend to a plateau of three successive long syllables, whose drag and spaciousness can lend weight and majesty to the words themselves. The effect occurs again and again throughout the *Odes*, often for dramatic effect, especially when, as in the literally gigantic instance above, Horace contrives to make those three long syllables correspond with a significant word. So when, in a bit of imperial flattery, he predicts that Augustus will take his place among the company of the gods, the emperor's name corresponds exactly to those three climactic syllables ('quos inter Augustus recumbens', 3.3.11). When Augustus' Egyptian rival, Cleopatra, is shown fastening the fatal asps to her breast, the Latin word for serpents dramatically occupies the same metrical position ('tractare sērpēntīs, ut atram', 1.37.27). Or, when irony calls for grandiloquence instead of grandeur: 'regina, sūblīmī flagello', (3.26.11) where Horace's persona, an ageing lothario, melodramatically calls on Venus to raise her whip 'on high' (sublimi) against the girl who ignores him. In this instance, the correspondence of 'sublimi' with the three long syllables adds a touch of sublime comedy.

For its role in creating these climactic three long syllables, and for its central place within them, Wilkinson called the fifth position in the alcaic enneasyllabic line the 'pivot syllable', and he seems to have been the first to notice that 'in 307 cases out of 317, by my reckoning .... what I have called the pivot syllable is reinforced by bearing an accent'.[26] That's to say: not only do the three long syllables constitute a metrical climax of the stanza, but within those three syllables the middle one, because almost always it is not only long, but accented, constitutes the peak of that climax. So when Horace, in the Soracte ode, describes the winter woods as 'straining' (laborantes) under the burden of snow, that crucial word comes in middle of the third line, and the accent within that word is made to coincide with the fifth syllable, at the very centre of those three long syllables: 'silvae la|borántes, |geluque' (*Odes* 1.9.3). Later in the same poem, middle-age Horace urges his young interlocutor not to miss out on 'sweet love and dancing while you are still a lad', and a great deal of the speaker's rueful vehemence comes from the way that the word for 'sweet' (dulces) is positioned at the climactic point in the third line, and the accented syllable of that word in the fifth position, the pivot syllable: 'appone, nec dúlcis amores' (*Odes* 1.9.15).

The establishment of norms enabled special effects to be contrived by aberrations. Thus in 1.29.11, one of the ten exceptions mentioned above, 'quis neget arduis / **pronos relabi posse rivos** / montibus....?' (10–12), 'the rhythm changes and we feel the river turn from gliding down to mounting up'.[27] The poem in question finds Horace marvelling that the effete scholar Iccius, against all likelihood, has abandoned his study and decided to try his fortunes as a soldier. Given that reversal, what other improbabilities must be true? Or, as the passage above puts it, 'Who would deny that **down-rushing rivers can flow back up** steep mountains?' Wilkinson zooms in on a minute but vital metrical abnormality: that in the third line, *pronos relabi posse rivos*, the Horatian norm (that the fifth syllable should coincide with the stressed syllable of the given word) is violated. The Latin *relábi* (glide up) is accented on its second syllable, but here Horace has allowed the unstressed third syllable of the word to occupy the pivot position of the line. That slight reversal of his accustomed metre prompted Wilkinson to 'feel the river turn from gliding down to mounting up.' There must be some readers who will think that Wilkinson's response to the merest of metrical nuances a case of ingenious hypersensitivity. But there are other, purely formal, aspects of that passage which, had he pointed them out, would have buttressed his claim that the metrical anomaly suggests abrupt reversal. To take just one example: the syntax of Horace's sentence embodies the topsy-turvy world it posits. There is the elaborate syntax, by which the adjective 'steep' (arduis) is separated from 'mountains' (montibus) by four intervening words and two intervening lines, and 'down-rushing' (pronos) is separated by two words from 'rivers' (rivos), which sits at the opposite end of the line. All four words are arranged in an extremely artful pattern, by which the two adjectives precede, and the two nouns follow, the central placement of the verb 'posse' and its complementary infinitive 'relabi'. The distribution of the nouns and adjectives is, moreover, chiastic. We could express the unusual syntax: *a1 a2 v2 v1 n2 n1*. To disrupt normal word-order for expressive effects is one of the pillars of Horace's art. In this instance it coincides, expressively, with a disruption of a metrical norm Horace himself had established. Wilkinson was right to feel moved by it.

If Tennyson was right, that the Greek alcaic enjoys 'a much freer and lighter movement' than Horace's, it does not follow that the relative rigidity of the Horatian alcaic makes it less expressive. The opposite is true. Horace's fixing the length of the fifth syllable in lines 1–3 creates an abstract boundary which, alternately honoured or ignored, can yield expressive effects. It's precisely the expectation that the 'pivot syllable' in line three should be both long and bear the accent that makes an exceptional instance ('pronos relabi posse rivos') both striking and expressive.

Poetic punctuation: Horace's fixed caesura

One of Horace's metrical innovations in particular bears out this principle: his imposition of a fixed caesura between the fifth and sixth syllables of lines 1 and 2 of his alcaic. Wouldn't regularizing that feature make the stanza more rigid? So one might think, but artists love limitations, and in Horace's hands the regular caesura creates a boundary against which the poet can play on the teasing interrelationship between constraint and freedom.

Readers of Horace's alcaics become accustomed to the cadence of this dependable caesura. The pause is often very strong, clearly separating distinct syntactic units:

> Nunc est bibendum, | nunc pede libero
>
> *(Odes* 1.37.1)

> Now let the drinking begin! | Now with unfettered feet (let us thump the ground)

> di me tuentur, | dis pietas mea
> et Musa cordi est. | hic tibi copia
>
> *(Odes* 1.17.13–14)

> The gods watch over me; | the gods are pleased with my devotion and my Muse.
> | Here in your honour Plenty (will flow)

The ear comes to expect the first five syllables to constitute a unit. (No such expectation obtains for the freer Greek alcaics.) By regularizing the caesura, Horace creates, within the stanza, a metrical boundary whose observance or transgression can generate all kinds of meanings. Take the idea of transgressing the boundary of the caesura. For the reader habituated to the caesura's regular appearance, its sudden absence breaks in with something like the disjointed force of syncopation in music. As when Horace famously describes the defeat of Cleopatra's ships by Octavian at the battle of Actium. The Egyptian queen, Horace writes, was set on bringing Rome down, 'but her frenzy was sobered by the survival of scarcely one ship from the flames; and her mind, crazed with Mareotic wine, was brought down by Caesar to face real terror'. Or so a prose translation would have it; in the Latin, though, something is afoot metrically which no prose version can reveal (Odes 1.37.12–16):

> sed minuit furorem
>
> vix una sospes | navis ab ignibus
> mentemque **lympha|tam** Mareotico
> redegit in veros timores   15
> Caesar

Lines 13 and 14 enact a metrical contrast. In 13, the expected Horatian caesura, between the fifth and sixth syllables, is duly observed. But in 14, where the words refer to Cleopatra's crazed drunkenness, the very word for 'crazed' (lymphatam) spills over the metrical boundary in a prosodic counterpart to the queen's own impudence. From this slight variation of his metrical norm, Horace creates a strong feeling: 'furorem' in line 12 is a strong enough word: 'frenzy'. But the metrical transgression in 14 goes beyond referring to recklessness: it physically enacts it, by tumbling recklessly over the caesura. This is one of only five times, out of 634 hendecasyllabic lines in the Horatian corpus, in which the caesura is violated.

Earlier in the same poem, there's another violation of the Horatian caesura, this time not connected directly to Cleopatra. Until her defeat, Horace had noted, strict discipline was called for at Rome: 'Before this it was sacrilege to bring the Caecuban [wine] out from our fathers' cellars' (5–6):

> antehac nefas **de|promere** Caecubum
> cellis avitis

The power of 'nefas' (sacrilege) lies in its lexical meaning. Very well, but what's more powerful is the way that Horace causes the word 'depromere' (bring out) to enact the meaning of 'nefas' by doing what is ordinarily forbidden in a Horatian alcaic: to spill over the metrical boundary. Given the poem's concern with drunkenness (Cleopatra and her band are both literally drunk and drunk with malign ambition; the Romans are allowed to break out the wine only after observing the sobriety necessary to defeat their enemies), it is fitting that two of the five exceptions to the Horatian caesura rule should occur within it. Those two instances of metrical irregularity link the references to the Roman Caecuban wine and the specifically Egyptian Mareotic, pointing up the restraint and continence of the Romans, as against the transgressive indulgence of Cleopatra.[28]

The destructive force of anger is the ostensible object of another of Horace's odes. Having rehearsed a conventional list of disasters to which anger may eventually lead, the poet works up to the most drastic of consequences, the overthrow of whole cities. 'Anger', he warns, 'is the chief reason why lofty cities have been utterly levelled, and arrogant armies have gouged their walls with a hostile ploughshare. Control your emotions. I too, in my sweet youth, was afflicted with a hot temper' (1.16.19–24):

> cur perirent
> > funditus imprimeretque muris

> hostile aratrum **ex|ercitus** insolens.
> compesce mentem: | me quoque pectoris
> > temptavit in dulci iuventa
> > > fervor

Just as the exulting army runs the plough over the defeated city's walls, the very word for 'army' ('exercitus') is made to overrun the metrical barrier Horace has established in his alcaic. That enacted violence appears in sharp relief against the next line, whose first two words, by stark contrast, neatly coincide with the Horatian caesura. Most expressively: for 'compesce mentem' means 'control your anger', and by keeping snugly within the boundary of the caesura, the words themselves enact metrically the restraint they enjoin. At that moment, the transgressive phrasing recovers its metrical decorum, just in time to urge moral decorum.

The fixed caesura gives Horace the power to make certain words glow with special emphasis. Words positioned on either side of the caesura demand greater attention, and acquire something of the emphatic force normally reserved for words at the beginning or end of a line. This is obvious when the word-break corresponds with a new sense-unit, as in the passage I've just quoted above, 'compesce mentem: | me quoque', where its placement immediately after the caesura throws strong emphasis onto the first-person pronoun 'me': the sense is 'I fully admit that *I myself*, when I was young, was just as given to temper-tantrums *as anyone else*.' The effect is subtler, though, when the emphatic word comes in the middle of a clause rather than at the beginning or end. Unless, for instance, readers attend to Horace's particular way with the alcaic strophe, they may miss the emphasis given to 'nunc' (now) in this stanza (*Odes* 1.29.1–4):

> Icci, beatis **nunc** | Arabum invides
> gazis, et acrem militiam paras
>   non ante devictis Sabaeae
>   regibus . . . . ?

What **now**, Iccius? Have you got your eye on the rich treasure of the Arabs? Are you preparing a fierce campaign against the as yet unconquered princes of Sheba . . . ?

Here the humour depends on savouring the contrast between the novice soldier's only very recently abandoned philosophical indifference to riches. In terms of prose sense, *nunc* is the least conspicuous word in the line; in terms of metrics, it is the essential word, showcased in the emphatic position just before the caesura. The metre makes the joke.

Elsewhere, Horace urges a certain Valgius to desist from mourning overmuch the death of a friend. Let me remind you, Horace insists, that the Homeric hero Nestor, 'the old man who lived three generations', did not bewail his beloved Antilochus *forever* (*Odes* 2.9.13–15):

at non ter aevo functus amabilem
ploravit **omnis** | Antilochum senex
    annos

Yet the old man who lived three generations did not spend **all** his years grieving
for his dear Antilochus

A proper voicing of the translation would lay the main stress on 'all'. The emphasis
that Horace imparts metrically can, in English prose, be brought out only by
italicizing the adjective or the use of bold typeface. In another ode Horace,
deploring the recent Roman civil wars, grimly asks 'what plain has not been
enriched with Latin blood' (*Odes* 2.1.29–30). What's not at all clear from that
prose translation is the emphasis created by Horace's metric, where the word for
'Latin' occupies a special position at the caesura: 'quis non **Latino** | sanguine
pinguior / campus'. The nuance is crucial: 'we have been done in not by our
enemies, but by ourselves'. Or again: when Horace reassures Phidyle, a country
girl of modest means, that the gods will accept her sacrifice even if it is 'not made
more persuasive by an expensive victim' (*Odes* 3.23.18), the crucial word,
'sumptuosa' (expensive), occupies the same metrical position: 'non **sumptuosa** |
blandior hostia'.

That Horace's odes often involve striking antithesis will be clear enough to
any reader. What's easy to miss, though, is the role his handling of the alcaic
metre plays in making antithesis so striking. Again and again Horace deploys his
antitheses against the fixed caesura. As in the Soracte ode (a poem which turns
on antitheses: age and youth, winter and summer), where the ageing speaker
exhorts his young friend to enjoy the pleasures of youth while 'your **green** age is
free from peevish **whiteness**' (1.9.17–18)

donec **virenti** | **canities** abest
morosa.

It is not enough to note, as most commentators do, the striking chromatic
juxtaposition of green ('vierenti') and white ('canities'), but also that those
opposing words take up their positions on either side of the caesura. They are
thus not only brought together (by syntax), but also separated (by metre). The
caesura, by dividing 'virenti' from 'cantities', calls attention to the separateness of
youth and age, and adds piquancy to the speaker's later description, in the final
two stanzas, of the delights of youth. To the literal meaning of the words, the
caesura adds the authority of its own demonstrated restraint: it vouches for the
resigned wisdom of the speaker, by refusing foolishly to confound the categories

of youth and age. Horace has combined antithetical words, but in such a way as to ensure that the caesura keeps them, simultaneously, separate.

When, in another ode, Horace intervenes to break up a brawl that has erupted during a symposium, he reminds those caught up in the kerfuffle that drinking parties and weapons do not mix (*Odes* 1.27.5–6):

vino et lucernis | Medus acinaces
immane quantum discrepat:

Where there is wine and lamplight, a Persian dagger is utterly out of place

Here things Roman and Persian uncomfortably jostle. To the left of the caesura in line 5: the civilized trappings of the symposium, wine and lamps ('vino et lucernis'). To the right: outlandish oriental weapons, Persian daggers ('Medus acinaces)'. These incongruous categories are juxtaposed within the line – but also neatly separated by the caesura. The effect is consonant with the mock-horror of the speaker's imprecation. There is, after all, no real danger of Persian daggers mixing with wine and lamps: no fight breaks out after all, and the poem ends with some jovial jesting. Weapons and drinks keep to opposite sides of the word-break. Too tidy to carry any sense of threat, the metrical separation harmonizes with the comic grandiloquence that critics have detected in the poem.[29]

Horace works the expressive structure of his alcaic caesuras on even larger scales. He can build whole blocks of sense within the boundaries of the caesuras; as such they become in his hands a means of regulating the shape and pace of expression across several stanzas of a poem. As in these three alcaic stanzas (1.17.17–28) which find Horace trying to woo his beloved Tyndaris to the seclusion of his country retreat – and out of the hands of his jealous and violent rival, Cyrus:

hic in reducta | valle Caniculae
vitabis aestus | **et** fide Teia
   dices laborantis in uno
      Penelopen vitreamque Circen: 20

hic innocentis | pocula Lesbii
duces sub umbra, | **nec** Semeleius
   cum Marte confundet Thyoneus
      proelia, nec metues protervum

suspecta Cyrum, | **ne** male dispari   25
incontentis | iniciat manus

> et scindat haerentem coronam
> crinibus immeritamque vestem.

Here in my secluded valley you will escape the heat of the Dog [Star], **and** with Teian lyre sing of Penelope and glass-green Circe, who were lovesick for the same man. Here in the shade you will drink cups of innocuous Lesbian [wine], the son of Semele Thyone will **not** combine with Mars to stir up a fight; and you will not have to worry **in case** the lustful Cyrus, in a fit of jealous suspicion, lay his wild hands on one who is ill-equipped to stand up to him, tearing the garland you have on your head and also your unoffending dress.

In each of these stanzas, the sixth syllable of a hendecasyllabic line serves as the beginning of a new class: 'et' (and, 8), 'nec' (nor, 22), and 'ne' (in case, 25). The connective words lay bare the progress of Horace's argument as he seeks to attract Tyndaris to his country seat. 'et': you can escape not only the heat, as anyone might expect, but *also*, as you may not have supposed, enjoy the lyre; 'nec': nor need you fear drunken brawls – a concern whose significance deepens and is made specific with 'ne': lest wanton Cyrus lay his incontinent hands upon you. The rhetorical tacking of the poem, the accumulated emotional force of the argument, is structured within blocks of sense determined by the Horatian alcaic caesura.

Arranging units of sense in this way, instead of simply relying on lines or even stanzas as organizing units, makes Horace's alcaics beguilingly flexible, in that it allows him to craft sentences of elegant metrical structure, but without sacrificing naturalness. So the bolded phrase in this passage, where Horace famously urges serenity on his over-anxious patron Maecenas (3.29.29–34):

> prudens futuri temporis exitum
> caliginosa nocte premit deus,
> ridetque si mortalis ultra
> fas trepidat. | **quod adest memento**
>
> **componere aequus;** | cetera fluminis
> ritu feruntur

God in his providence hides future events in murky darkness, and laughs if a mere mortal frets about what is beyond his control. **Make sure to settle immediate problems calmly.** Everything else flows away like a river

From an observation on the strictness of limits, with admonitory stress on 'ultra' (beyond) at the limit of line 31, the passage moves to a description of a flowing river. Between those points comes a gnomic phrase: 'quod adest memento //

componere aequus', 'Make sure to settle immediate problems calmly'. That maxim gains points for being neatly framed between the caesura-markers. But not too neatly: at the same time it overflows not only the line-endings, but also a stanza-break. It thus enacts the fluidity of the river, while obeying its own injunction to keep within limits. Here is one of the hiding-places of the Horatian alcaic's power: its way of shifting the beginnings and endings of sense-units to the middle of lines, with the result that control never tyrannizes fluidity (as with regularly end-stopped lines) or vice-versa (as with mere enjambment). In English it took Milton's metrical art to achieve a similar tension between enjambment and medial caesuras. Critics who would dismiss the passage as the reiteration of a tired moral commonplace ('Always behave moderately') may as well read Horace in translation: the art resides in the metre. The way the poet propels his words through the alcaic strophe is a dynamic metrical event.

Only through attention to such minute metrical details can the claims of critics such as Murray and Wilkinson and Warren be justified: that the alcaic strophe, especially in the hands of its great master, Horace, is a marvel of expressiveness. It's one thing to read 'Dulce Et Decorum Est' knowing that Owen, in quoting Horace, undid his alcaics. But to have some sense of the metrical intricacies of Horace's metrical voice increases the sense of violence involved in Owen's erasure of the alcaic.

The persistence of Latin alcaics

In this chapter I have been trying to give some idea of the dynamism, intricacy, and expressive power of the alcaic strophe. Those qualities are so strong that they can even be detected *in potentia*, in the abstract metrical scheme, before a poet embodies them in actual words. They are evident even in the meagrely surviving fragments of Alcaeus. I have dwelt, though, on Horace's alcaics, not just because they have survived intact – 37 poems, 317 stanzas – but also because he brought specially adapted alcaics to such refinement as to have become, for most later readers and writers, the alcaic poet *par excellence*. For the modern poets I have so far discussed – Auden, Owen, Hollander – and for most of those I will yet discuss, when the alcaic impinges on their imagination, it is mostly Horace's alcaics they have in mind.

It needs noting, though, that the great majority of Latin alcaics are not only post-Horatian, but modern. Only one other important Roman writer, the first-century poet Statius, wrote in alcaics, and even then in only one poem of fifteen stanzas (*Silvae* 4.5), addressed to the poet's friend Septimus Severus, an orator and sometime writer who had come to Rome from his native Libya. The poet praises his friend's ready assimilation to life in the imperial capital. It is a competent and otherwise unremarkable poem, whose alcaics broadly 'avoid any metrical feature which is uncommon in Horace's alcaics'.[30]

Why did Statius choose to write in alcaics? Perhaps because Septimus himself seems to have written lyric verses ('barbiton ingenia', 60), and in any case to imitate Horace seems to have been a pastime of educated men in the first century. Pliny the Younger, for instance, mentions a friend who 'has lately turned to lyric poetry, and here he recalls Horace as successfully as he does [Propertius] elsewhere' (*Epistles* 9.22. 2 'nuper ad lyrica deflexit, in quibus ita Horatium ut in illis alterum effingit'). Yet for all this might suggest about poets imitating Horace's odes, Statius' poem remains the only surviving example of alcaics in all of post-Horatian Roman poetry. The implication is that Horace's mastery of so daunting a form discouraged later poets from risking the comparison, in something like the way that Beethoven's example seems for some time after his death to have inhibited his successors from composing symphonies. Whatever the reason, the relative paucity of alcaic stanzas is not just a modern, but an ancient, phenomenon.

Medieval writers did compose alcaics, but rarely.[31] Before the ninth century Horace was known in Europe chiefly for his satires, not the *Odes*, but even in periods when interest in the lyric Horace increased (as during the Carolingian period), poets tended to prefer trying their hand at sapphics rather than the more involved compound metre. Medieval alcaics were too few, and remain too obscure, to have themselves influenced modern writers: though they testify to the survival of the ancient metre into the middle ages, they constitute a blind alley so far as concerns the study of alcaics in the English tradition.

After Horace and Alcaeus themselves, it is the early modern neo-Latin poets whose example most matters. Aided by the increasing availability of new editions of Horace, and spurred by a revival of interest in the *Odes* themselves (as opposed to the satires and epistles), Renaissance humanist poets set out to imitate and rival Horace. They took up Horatian lyric metres far more often than their medieval counterparts, and alcaics in greater numbers than their ancient models.[32] Their study has been neglected, largely as the result of the logistics of modern academic departments. Classics faculties have ordinarily restricted their studies to classical antiquity, and often treated even late antiquity scantily, to say nothing of modern writers in Greek or Latin. English departments, for their part, have tended to ignore the fact that, in England as throughout Europe, 'Latin language and literature was the single most significant constituent of secondary education for *all* Renaissance and early modern writers and thinkers'.[33] Neo-Latin texts of all kinds were more widely read than vernacular literature, and the interrelations between neo-Latin and English literature are far more intimate and complex than modern English courses ordinarily acknowledge. Good editions of neo-Latin authors are scarce, and vernacular translations even rarer. The situation, though, has begun to improve: interest in neo-Latin is growing, and the outlines of a systematic academic discipline of Neo-Latin studies are beginning to take shape.[34] The Latin writings of most early modern English writers (the chief exceptions are Thomas More's *Utopia* and the Latin poems of John Milton) remain largely unexplored, 'as if they wrote only in the vernacular'.[35]

This means that students of the classical tradition in English should be wary. It is a mistake to assume alcaics written by an English poet of the sixteenth or seventeenth centuries must necessarily have been modelled directly on Alcaeus or Horace. Early moderns knew Latin alcaics as a living tradition. Neo-Latin lyric poetry is a vast topic far beyond the scope of this study, but it is worth acknowledging in passing some of the more conspicuous exponents of the Renaissance alcaic. Take for instance the late-fifteenth century Conrad Celtis. Like most neo-Latin poets during the Renaissance, his poems are composed mainly in elegiacs, hexameters, and hendecasyllabics; but among his four books of odes are a handful of alcaics. That he also wrote a volume of *Epodes* and a 'Carmen Saeculare' implies a particularly self-conscious cultivation of Horatian credentials. One could also point to the Pole Maciej Kazimierz Sarbiewski (Mathias Casimirus Sarbievius, 1595–1640), who achieved tremendous fame throughout seventeenth-century Europe as 'the Christian Horace'. In the four books of his *Lyricorum libri* he offers various examples of lively alcaic verses. The early sixteenth century Dutchman Johannes Secundus, in his celebrated polymetric sequence *Basia* (*Kisses*), includes an alcaic poem – the only one he ever wrote. It creates an incongruous fusion: allusion to Horatian injunctions to moderation on the one hand, and Catullan erotic urgency on the other. And there are the expert alcaic poems of Scotsman George Buchanan, a literary superstar throughout Europe in the sixteenth century, whose Latin verse paraphrases of the Hebrew psalms directly influenced Mary Sidney. Her version of Psalm 120, as we shall find in the following chapter, is the first poem in English alcaics.

English poets now known almost exclusively for their vernacular verse also composed Latin alcaics. George Herbert's alcaics form a part of an impressive and as yet underappreciated body of Latin verse.[36] The decline of Latin as a medium of imaginative literature has obscured similar achievements of other

English poets. John Milton's sole alcaic poem, 'In Obitum Procancelarii Medici', is a cardinal instance: a serious effort by a great artist who was nevertheless about to abandon his ambitions as a Latin poet and instead commit himself to English. Milton wrote it as a seventeen-year-old Cambridge undergraduate; its subject, Dr. John Gostlin, master of Caius, had also been a professor of medicine, and the poem elaborates on the truism even medical doctors themselves must eventually die. To produce verse tributes to deceased figures was a conventional exercise for university students and faculty, and many of Milton's Latin poems fall squarely in this tradition. 'As long as bishops and beadles were subject to mortality', quips one of the poet's great commentators, 'the young craftsman did not lack a subject.'[37] True enough, but Milton was no ordinary versifier, and his treatment of the alcaic shows a remarkable capacity for expressive, as opposed to a mechanical, handling of so complicated a strophe.

Most Latin alcaic verses written in the English-speaking world during the eighteenth and nineteenth centuries, however, are exercises or curiosities. Latin verse composition was 'gradually relegated to the place of an elegant private amusement, a sign of one's education at one of the great private schools'.[38] There are some exceptions – most notably the two exquisite alcaic odes of Samuel Johnson, unmistakably Horatian in style, but curiously romantic in tone.[39] Otherwise, we have alcaics as the virtuoso performances of academics, such as a certain Dr. Edward Hannes, who contributed his alcaic poems to a seventeenth-century anthology of Latin poetry; and, three hundred years later, the Sophoclean scholar Sir Richard Jebb, who composed strictly Horatian alcaic verses celebrating the appearance of a comet.[40] Or the light verse, often occasional, of well-educated amateurs the likes of the eighteenth-century Benjamin Loveling, 'a gentleman of Trinity College, Oxford', whose alcaic verses include those urging the virtues of wine and tobacco as social lubricants.[41] The tone is jocund, and the choice of metre ostensibly justified by its association with Horace's sympotic poetry, though Loveling, fortunately, doesn't for a moment imply that the relation is anything but superficial and even gently parodic. Latin verse composition was the afternoon pastime of many a Victorian clergyman, such as Charles Wordsworth, the Bishop of St Andrews, Dunkeld, and Dunblane. He rewarded a Norwegian official, whose hospitality he had enjoyed during a tour abroad, with a poem of five grateful alcaic stanzas.[42] There were all-rounders, such as William Herbert (1778–1847): twice Member of Parliament; later Dean of Manchester; translator of Icelandic, Danish, German, and Dutch poetry; writer of epic poems in English; and botanist (after whom a genus of crocus is named). Amid such various activities, he found time to compose and publish Latin verses, including some marmoreal alcaic verses on the death of Napoleon, which reflect a keen assimilation of Horatian norms.[43]

English poets, then, from the Tudors onward, were the heirs of an astonishingly long tradition of Greek and Latin alcaics, ancient and modern. It is one thing for English-speaking poets to extend the tradition by writing alcaics in Latin. It is another to receive the alcaic inheritance by introducing it into English, as Horace had introduced it into Latin. Having set out, then, the remarkable qualities of the alcaic in its various forms, Greek and Latin, it is time to consider its precarious fortunes as an English metrical form.

3

'Blossom Again on a Colder Isle'

Mary Sidney, Alfred Tennyson

There was an erasure at the heart of the first chapter of this book: Wilfred Owen's undoing of Horace's alcaic metre in 'Dulce Et Decorum Est', and its partial restoration in the ebulliently overt English alcaics of John Hollander. At the heart of this chapter there is a long silence. In the last years of the sixteenth century, Mary Sidney composed what is probably the first alcaic poem in the English language. Historical significance aside, it is a superb poem in itself, opening up opportunities for later poets to pick up and enrich the acoustic dimension of English poetry – had they chosen to do so. But this did not happen: for two and a half centuries, no significant poet followed Sidney in composing English alcaics. We hear formal echoes and allusions in the seventeenth and eighteenth centuries, but get no actual alcaics, even as English sapphics continued to be written in their scores. Not until the mid-nineteenth century was the silence broken, as Alfred Tennyson dusted off the English alcaic lyre and began to fiddle with it, producing, in his very different way, a variety of alcaic-based stanzas. As such Mary Sidney and Alfred Tennyson are the book-ends of this chapter: an unlikely pairing that illustrates the way study of the alcaic reveals unexpected connections in literary history.

'Again I call, again I calling'

It matters that the first English alcaic, Mary Sidney's paraphrase of Psalm 120, occurs as no mere metrical exercise by some obscure versifier, or on the margins of a career focused on other projects. Instead it arrives as an important component of a larger masterpiece of English literature, that compendium of verse paraphrases of the Psalms now known as the Sidney psalter, begun by Philip Sidney and, after his death, completed and revised by his sister. It is hard to overstate the importance of the Sidney psalter in the history of English prosody. The metrical variety of the settings is dazzling: of the 127 psalms that Mary Sidney rendered into English, there are 126 different verse forms (including, as we shall see, not just alcaics, but seven other classical metres). The Sidney psalter is a vast anthology of verse-forms for later poets to plunder, 'a School of English versification,'[1] and a great influence on the metrical imagination of later poets. George Herbert's *The Temple* is only the most conspicuously successful mirror of the psalter's metrical variety. Mary Sidney's English alcaic verse, then, is not just a metrical innovation in isolation, but part of an even larger landmark in the history of English metrics.

The fecundity of the Elizabethan metrical imagination can be situated not just within an English, but a much broader Latin, context. Victoria Moul has recently demonstrated that the extraordinary metrical inventiveness of early modern English poets 'sits within, and emerges from, a geographically wider and precedent Latin phenomenon.'[2] Moul describes a period of intense metrical experiment among late-sixteenth-century neo-Latin poets who were shaking up a hitherto relatively staid metrical tradition of Latin poetry in England. Departing from classical models, these poets composed Latin verse-forms that 'transformed the "soundscape" of Latin lyric verse.'[3] Poets writing in English responded to these Latin experiments by innovating English verse forms. Elizabethan metrical theorists struggling to find a way of adapting classical metres into English 'were thinking about these matters because the contemporary use of *Latin* metre underwent very rapid change in the second half of the sixteenth century.'[4] In short: metrical innovators in English verse were reflecting the metrical innovations of contemporary Latin, and this creativity is 'nowhere more evident than in the collections of psalm paraphrases' composed in Latin verse.[5] Moul singles out in particular the Sidneys' extensive reliance on two contemporary Latin psalter paraphrases, those of George Buchanan and Theodore de Bèze (also known by his Latin name Beza). 'These works,' she writes, 'seek to deploy the full range of classical verse forms to create a version of the psalter which unites the Biblical and classical lyric traditions.'[6]

Among the many implications of Moul's analysis, I propose three points that bear directly on Mary Sidney's alcaic version of Psalm 120. First, the fact of its being composed in a classical metre links it to a European tradition of neo-Latin psalm paraphrase that attempts to harmonize the Judeo-Christian and Greco-Roman traditions at the level of poetic metre. (This notion is evident already in St. Jerome, who compared the stylistic variety of Hebrew psalmody to the poetry of Pindar and Horace: it 'now rings with Alcaics, now swells to a Sapphic measure'.)[7] Mary Sidney advances that tradition by actually bringing alcaics into the English language for the first time. Second, her English alcaics form part of a collection, the Sidney psalter, which descends from neo-Latin psalters whose authors were not only writing in classical metres, but innovating new verse forms. Mary Sidney's alcaics, then, represent not just metrical innovation in themselves, but form part of the broader context of late-sixteenth-century neo-Latin metrical experimentation. And third, they belong to a tradition in which neo-Latin poets strive for striking metrical variety within a single book. In that sense the Sidney psalter descends from Horace's *Odes* (the *locus classicus* of lyric metrical variety) through the neo-Latin poets and especially Buchanan and Beza. The tradition then carries on from the Sidney psalter to George Herbert's *Temple* and Henry Vaughan and beyond. Smack in the middle of this tradition is Sidney's Psalm 120. The very first alcaics in English would have been significant enough for that reason alone, whoever the author and whatever the context. As it happens, the first English alcaics arrive already charged with significance, as part of a venerable tradition, and in a period of fervid metrical experimentation in *both* Latin and English.

One further context before turning to the poem itself. Mary Sidney's alcaic translation of Psalm 120 stands at the head of a sequence of fifteen psalms, the 'Songs of Ascents' or 'Songs of Degrees', celebrating the return of the Israelites from captivity in Babylon.[8] Of these, the first eight (120–7) are composed in unrhymed classical metres. As such they constitute an important instance of the larger Elizabethan effort at introducing quantitative metres into English.[9] More strikingly, the eight quantitative poems mix lyric and non-lyric metres as neither Horace nor any other ancient collection had done. The insight of Victoria Moul deserves quotation in full:

> No existing discussion of the sequence explains what would have been obvious to contemporary readers, but is now obscure: namely, that the choice of metres is not primarily, or indeed much at all, classical. No ancient verse collection contains such disparate metrical forms – including hexameter, alcaics, iambic metres and lyric metres. Such a sequence is, rather, distinctly contemporary: an imitation in English verse of the extraordinary metrical versatility and experiment of sixteenth-century Latin poetry.[10]

In sum: Mary Sidney's alcaic psalm initiates an eight-poem sequence that is itself the most metrically innovative passage in the most metrically innovative work of Elizabethan English literature, a phase of literature nurtured by the most metrically innovative phase of neo-Latin literature.

After such a build-up, a reader may wonder whether the poem itself disappoints. It does not. Psalm 120 is a poem of exile, whose mournful speaker sojourns ('too long, alas, too long') among hostile foreigners. Whether or not Sidney had Alcaeus in mind, it happens that the metre of the erstwhile political exile Alcaeus is a fitting way of joining classical prosody to the Hebrew lament.[11] The shifting metrical registers of the alcaic, moreover, suit the rhetorical tacking of the speaker, who alternates between confidence in God, disgust for the wicked, and pleading to the former for release from the latter:

> As to th'Eternal often in anguishes
> Erst have I called, never unanswered,
>   Again I call, again I calling,
>   Doubt not again to receive an answer.
>
> Lord, rid my soul from treasonous eloquence
> Of filthy forgers craftily fraudulent:
>   And from the tongue where lodged resideth
>   Poisoned abuse, ruin of believers.
>
> Thou that reposest vainly thy confidence
> In wily wronging, say by thy forgery
>   What good to thee? What gain redoundeth?
>   What benefit from a tongue deceitful?
>
> Though like an arrow strongly delivered
> It deeply pierce, though like to a juniper
>   It coals do cast which quickly fired,
>   Flame very hot, very hardly quenching?
>
> Ah God! Too long here wander I banished,
> Too long abiding barbarous injury:
>   With Kedar and with Mesech harboured.
>   How? In a tent, in a houseless harbour.
>
> Too long, alas, too long have I dwelled here
> With friendly peace's furious enemies:
>   Who when to peace I seek to call them,
>   Faster I find to the war they arm them.

All other considerations aside, the poem is a technical tour de force. There is a nice interplay between quantity and accent. On the one hand, there is sensitivity to the quantity of the English syllables. In many cases syllables that fall where the quantitative metre calls for *longae* are either obviously or plausibly 'naturally' long in English. In other instances it seems we are to understand a syllable to be long 'by position' (e.g., line 8, 'ruin **of** believers', or line 12, 'What bene**fit** from'). On the other hand, those quantities are balanced by Sidney's handling of the stress-accents, which more often than not coincide with the long positions, making the alcaic rhythm mostly legible to the ear. Sidney's fourth lines in particular achieve the stress-accent equivalent of the quantitative decasyllabic (/ u u / u u / u / u) without straining the English in the least: 'Doubt not again to receive an answer' (4); 'How? In a tent, in a houseless harbour' (20, where the metre cooperates with the alliteration and with Sidney's marvellous touch of assonance in 'How' and 'houseless'); and 'Faster I find to the war they arm them' (24). Among the challenges of writing classical lyric verse in English is to override the English reader's expectation of the iambic's alternation of unstressed and stressed syllables, and delivering instead the swing of the choriamb (– u u –). Sidney pulls off persuasively audible choriambs again and again: '**Doubt** not **again**' (4), '**trea**sonous **el** oquence' (5), '**Poi**soned ab**use**' (8), '**How**? In a **tent**' (20, where the choriamb is very effectively suspended for a moment with an anguished question), and '**furious en**emies' (22). This choriambic element, the hallmark of classical lyric verse, is made to ring clearly in the English ear.

Mary Sidney will have known her Horace, but there is no reason for expecting her to model her alcaics after Horace's alone. Overall they resemble the more flexible Greek alcaic. Very strikingly, the final syllable in every line is unstressed, a beautiful but relentless cadence that in this context suggests the speaker's deflation and exhaustion. Similarly she is quite happy to allow an unstressed syllable in the fifth position of the first three lines, where Horace's more rigid scheme stipulates a long: 'As to th'Eter<u>nal</u>, often in anguishes' (1); 'Lord, rid my soul <u>from</u> treasonous eloquence' (5); 'With Kedar and <u>with</u> Mesach harboured' (19). All the more striking, then, when she does land a stressed syllable in the fifth position, thus creating a sequence of three consecutive stressed syllables. It augments the urgency in the hendecasyllabic line 17: 'Ah, God! Too **long here wan**der I banished'.[12] The stakes are even higher in the enneasyllabic lines, whose three successive long syllables create the climactic 'Alcaic effect' that Wilkinson, West, and Morgan all relish. Here Sidney scores impressive hits such as this, in the poem's last stanza: 'Who when to **peace I seek** to call them' (23). But even where she avoids stressing the fifth position, she can do so expressively. In the third line of the first stanza, we read the fifth syllable as unstressed: 'Again I call, <u>a</u>gain I calling'. The iteration of 'again' occurs just at the position where, in a Horatian alcaic, the enneasyllabic line crests in the second of three successive long syllables. No Horatian stability for Mary Sidney: the unstressed syllable in the fifth position keeps up the alternation of longs and shorts, a metrical reiteration appropriate to the speaker's anxious petitioning, which resolves into the rapidity and regularity of the fourth line, where doubt momentarily gives way to assurance.

One aspect of Sidney's alcaics, though, does have a Horatian feel. Her hendecasyllabic lines invariably observe the Horatian caesura, breaking the line after the fifth syllable. The results are expressive. Much of the emphatic power in this poem emerges from the force of its accumulation of canny adverbs, which time and again assert themselves at the emphatic position – not, as typically in English verse, at the beginnings or endings of lines, but at the caesura: 'As to th'Eternall, | *often* in anguishes (1); 'Erst I have called, | *never* unanswered' (2); 'Of filthy forgers | *craftily* fraudulent' (6); 'Thou that reposest | *vainly* thy confidence' (9); 'Though like an arrow | *strongly* delivered' (13). Note especially the antithetical pairing of 'often' and 'never' in the same metrical position in lines 1 and 2, by which the speaker's urgent need to contact God is intensified by expressing itself both in positive and negative terms. Sidney is alive to other distinctively Horatian arrangements based on the caesura, as when she coordinates antithetical terms at corresponding positions within the half-line created by the caesura: 'Erst I have *called,* | never *unanswered* (2), or 'With friendly *peace's* | furious *enemies*' (22). Elsewhere patterning supports a plaintive anaphora: '*Though* like an arrow | strongly delivered / It deeply pierce, *though* | like to a Juniper (13–14). And, in a similar vein: '*Too* long alas, *too* | long have I dwelled here' (21), where the pathetic iteration 'too' comes framed, with an elegance very reminiscent of Horace, between the beginning of the line and the caesura. As a result, the word 'long' seems to break through the metrical boundary with the force of exasperation. The line makes full use of the resistance, the drag, that the Horatian caesura offers it. Fine effects: the product of the poet's attentiveness to the quiet violence characteristic of Horace's kind of alcaics. In Mary Sidney's poem, we have a snapshot of one moment in the development of English prosody, just when pressure of the classical form and its modern Latin tradition is shaping the contours of English verse, gracing it with new ways of moving.

The wilderness years

Under Mary Sidney's hand, the first English alcaics are so expertly realized, and made their appearance in so distinguished a context, that the stage was set for later poets to take up the form and establish it, as the sapphic was to be established, as a familiar English form. But this did not happen. Instead proper English alcaics disappeared from view. For the next two centuries and more, poets preferred instead to write in forms that suggested or evoked the alcaic, rather than attempting to replicate its metrical pattern. The foremost example is Andrew Marvell's 'Horatian Ode upon Cromwell's Return from Ireland'. The poem is 'Horatian' in part because of its theme: Marvell writes in a panegyric tradition that descends from those odes of Horace, very many of them in alcaics, that ostensibly praise Augustus and the leading figures of his regime,[13] but also includes modern panegyric verse in both Latin and English.[14] Marvell's ode invites readers also to see, in the indentation of the last two lines of the stanza, a visual allusion to the shape of the alcaic strophe. (He appears to have imitated a stanza-form that Richard Fanshawe hit upon in his translations of Horace's odes.)[15] Beyond that orthographic clue, little about his stanza behaves like an alcaic. Complex compound rhythms are replaced by simple, sturdy English iambic lines (a pair of tetrameters, followed by a pair of trimeters), and the sense-units tend to coincide with rhymed couplets:

> So restless Cromwell could not cease
> In the inglorious arts of peace,
>   But through advent'rous war
>   Urgèd his active star.

(9–12)[16]

The stanza splits itself in half, not by the rhymes alone, but also by the neat antithesis that confines 'peace' to the first couplet and 'war' to the second. Bipartite division does not comport with the three-stage progression of an alcaic. Neatly balancing antitheses, on the other hand, pervade Marvell's poem. The stanza-form emphasizes the contrast between royal and common (53–6):

> That thence the Royal actor borne
> The tragic scaffold might adorn:
>   While round the armed bands
>   Did clap their bloody hands

Or, in a famous stanza (61–4), resistance versus resignation:

> Nor called the Gods with vulgar spite,
> To vindicate his helpless right;
>   But lay his comely head
>   Down, as upon a bed.

Marvell's metre, whose metrical association with the alcaic is as much a matter of what the eye takes in as what the ear can hear, may owe something to the example of John Milton's translation of Horace's so-called Pyrhha ode (*Odes* 1.5).[17] That poem of Horace's is not composed in alcaics, but the 'fourth asclepiad' – a stanza composed of two twelve-syllable lines, a seven-syllable line, and a final line of eight syllables. In other words, its third line enacts a contraction from the expansive opening two lines, and the fourth line is longer than the third but shorter than the first two. It echoes, though in different proportions, the relative line-lengths of the alcaic, and in that sense may be seen as an analogue to the alcaic. (The fourth asclepiad will resurface in Chapter 5, where we will find W. H. Auden and others trying to wield it in English verse.)

Because of this association, Milton's rendering of Horace's asclepiads bears comparison with Marvell's 'Horatian Ode' measure. Milton's stanza form is more nearly 'Horatian' because it eschews end-stopped lines, preferring instead the frequent and expressive enjambment characteristic of Horace's lyrics, and avoids the seduction of rhyme in favour of less overt poetic features such as internal patterning and variation of rhythm:

> What slender youth bedewed with liquid odours
> Courts thee on roses in some pleasant cave,
>   Pyrrha? For whom bind'st thou
>   In wreaths thy golden hair,
> Plain in thy neatness? O how oft shall he
> On faith and changèd gods complain: and seas
>   Rough with black winds and storms
>   Unwonted shall admire:
> Who now enjoys thee credulous, all gold,
> Who always vacant always amiable
>   Hopes thee; of flattering gales
>   Unmindful? Hapless they
> To whom thou untried seem'st fair. Me in my vowed
> Picture the sacred wall declares t' have hung
>   My dank and dropping weeds
>   To the stern god of sea.[18]

Milton himself insisted he had translated 'according to the Latin Measure, as near as the language will permit', though this means not attempting to replicate the classic metre, but rather handling English iambic-based lines flexibly, and with a high tolerance of metrical substitutions. The visual effect – two longer lines followed by two indented shorter lines – is a crucial dimension. It helps, too, that the handling of the form does justice to principles famously set forth in his note 'The Verse' prefixed to *Paradise Lost*. Its sense is 'drawn out variously from one verse to another', and it is an example of (at least a partial) recovery of the 'ancient liberty ... from the troublesome and modern bondage of rhyming'. For all these reasons, it feels closer to the movement of Horatian lyric than Marvell's. Three major poets, then – Mary Sidney, Marvell, and Milton – offered to any successors three differing ways of suggesting alcaics in English.

One of Horace's twentieth-century editors, H. W. Garrod, found such a successor in William Collins, whose 'Ode to Evening', he thought, picked up on Marvell's metric and so linked the ode to the Horatian lyric tradition.[19] There is some justice in this. Collins's stanzas diverge from Marvell's in alternating two pentameter and two trimeter lines, as Milton's does, and it is freer with enjambment than Marvell's:

> For when thy folding-star arising shows
> His paley circuit, at his warming lamp
> The fragrant hours, and elves
> Who slept in buds the day

> (21–4)[20]

But such fluidity from line to line is in fact untypical of this poem, whose lines more often run like these (13–16):

> As of the rises, 'midst the twilight path
> Against the pilgrim bourne in heedless hum:
> Now teach me, maid composed,
> To breathe some softened strain.

Collins's measure does not resist the trend of eighteenth-century verse to express itself in couplets, a movement inconsistent with the tripartite character of the alcaic strophe. But because of its shape, metrical and orthographical, it has remained an effective way of signalling some sort of relation to Horatian lyric. The examples of Marvell and Collins have proven durable. Their influence can be seen, for instance, in the lovely verses from 2002 by the American poet Rachel Hadas, translating Horace *Odes* 1. 24.[21] Her stanza-form echoes that of Collins (alternating couplets of pentameter and trimeter) and Marvell (rhyming couplets), as Collins and Marvell themselves approximate Horace in the general shape of their stanzas. 'General' is the operative word: for Hadas was translating a poem Horace composed in sapphics, not alcaics. The stanza-forms of Marvell and Collins do resemble alcaics and can be made to stand for them, but can just as well be made to stand for 'Horatian lyric' generally.

English had to wait until the nineteenth century for a poet of major stature to attempt, as Mary Sidney had done, a stricter English replication of the alcaic strophe. In 1849, not quite six years before Tennyson was to publish his first experiment in that metre, an alcaic poem appeared among the verses of Arthur Hugh Clough. It reflected an emerging interest among literary people in the possibility of vernacular versions of classical metres. Just two years earlier Clough had published an article on classical lyric metres in the vivid but short-lived journal *Classical Museum*, and in 1848 had published a mock-epic poem in English dactylic hexameters. These last two points are crucial, as pointing to a broader context into which his own alcaics, and later those of Tennyson, came to be. The last half of the nineteenth century saw an extraordinary flourishing of debates about poetic metre. They involved not only technical matters (e.g., challenges to traditional notions of scansion), but extended to, and indeed were prompted by, questions surrounding the reform of universities, the curriculum of schools, the rise of the English as an academic subject, the role of the British Empire, and the relationship of the study of classics to all of these.[22] Clough's participation in those controversies began with his dissatisfaction with the stagnant Latin curriculum he endured at Oxford in the 1830s. His complaints echoed those of Sir William Hamilton who, in an influential 1831 article in the *Edinburgh Review*, had criticized the universities, 'but Oxford in particular', for the 'obscurantism and backwardness of its curriculum' that made no connection between the classics and the modern world, and failed to acknowledge the advances of contemporary German classical scholarship.[23] Clough entered into these controversies by becoming first a subscriber, and later a contributor, to the new journal *Classical Museum*, whose liberalizing attitudes towards classical studies included a frequent discussion of the possibilities of rendering classical metres into English verse. The example of German poets, who had been producing hexameter verses in that language, was catching on in England. 'After a lull of two centuries', notes Joseph Patrick Phelan, 'the possibility of producing an English metre analogous to the classical hexameter was once again being seriously considered, and even encouraged.[24] The hexameter debates are a familiar subject, but what is striking about Clough is his decision to attempt, after a lull of *more* than two hundred years, an alcaic poem in English:

ALCAICS
So spake the Voice; and, as with a single life

Instinct, the whole mass, fierce, irretainable,
    Down on that unsuspecting host swept
    Down, with the fury of winds that all night

Up-brimming, sapping slowly the dyke, at dawn
Full through the breach, o'er homestead, and harvest, and
    Heard roll a deluge; while the milkmaid
    Trips i' the dew, and remissly guiding

Morn's first uneven furrow, the farmer's boy
Dreams out his dream: so over the multitude
    Safe-tented, uncontrolled and uncon-
    trollably sped the avenger's fury.[25]

The title encourages readers to understand the poem as a mere exercise. If it is less than a fully-realized poem, its prosodic craftsmanship is nevertheless of a very high order. No other English alcaic more nearly conforms to the metrical template. More consistently even than in Mary Sidney's psalm, the disposition of stressed and unstressed syllables in the words as they would be spoken coincides with the alcaic's pattern of longs and shorts. Here and there the metre may encourage readers to gently promote or suppress an accent, but no word demands a noticeably unnatural pronunciation to align it with the underlying metrical scheme. The only systematic exception to the alcaic pattern is this: in his first and second lines, Clough alternates a masculine with a feminine ending. He meets with remarkable success, too, in contriving a persuasive succession of three stressed syllables in the first three lines of each stanza; and even where this doesn't occur (e.g., 9: 'Morn's first unevĕn furrow, the farmer's boy'), the result, if not Horatian, is at least a perfectly acceptable alcaic line by Greek standards. There is anyway the possibility that the unexpected short syllable in 'uneven' is mimetic, enacting a moment's metrical unevenness.

Sticking so close to the classical model entails losses and gains. It minimizes, maybe even cancels, the effect of metrical counterpoint. In Clough there is little of the suggestive friction that characterizes Mary Sidney's 'Ah God! too long here wander I banished', where English usage insists on reading the anguished adverb 'too' as stressed, even though a short syllable is expected in the third position. Without such metrical tension, Clough's verse is all melody and no undersong. A second limitation is the lack of freedom in diction and syntax. To get his rhythm right, Clough must resort to padding, multiplying repetitions (such as the *ands* in line 6), piling on adjectives, and coining inversions such as 'up-brimming' (5).

A further restriction involves length. It is hard to imagine a poet continuing with such strict fidelity to the metre without falling back on still more and graver wrenchings of English idiom.

As for the gains, the first is the metrical propriety. The alcaic is superbly suited to register such variations of containment, brimming, breach, and headlong rushing of the deluge as Clough conjures. One could point to a Horatian parallel in *Odes* 4.2.5–24, which compares Pindar's eloquence to a river rushing down a mountain side, and itself propels a deluge of words through the pattern of five whole sapphic strophes in a single, heavily enjambed sentence. Clough's breathlessness – his entire poem too corresponds to a single slinking sentence – springs not just from the enjambment from line to line but stanza to stanza. Such features could of course occur in any stanza-form, but note that the enjambment of lines 11–12 indicates the poet's awareness of the tradition that regards the third and fourth lines of the alcaic strophe as belonging to a single colon. More tellingly, the breathlessness is accentuated by Clough's way with Horatian caesura. Throughout the poem he effects a sort of tipsy arrangement whereby the break in the sense only just fails to correspond with the caesura, stranding little connective words on the left-hand side of the divide: 'So spake the Voice; **and,** | as with a single life' (1); 'Full through the breach, **o'er** | homestand, and' (6); 'Dreams out his dream: **so** | over the multitude' (10). The effect is to resist the pauses that the caesura might have produced. 'And', 'o'er', and 'so' are made into little cliff-hangers; to pursue the sense they anticipate is to spill over the internal metrical boundary. Where Mary Sidney made the caesura an occasion for balancing antithetical phrases, Clough makes it the ground on which to stress imbalances and enact overflowing. From first word to last, tumbling as it does through stanzas that expand and contract, the poem is a tour-de-force of headlong momentum. With it the alcaic had its second birth in English, and, if not exactly a poem in the deepest sense, it is at least an illuminating demonstration of what qualities the English alcaic might achieve.

Alfred Tennyson was to prove the poet who would do most to discover what those qualities could be. Tennyson may well have known Clough's ' Alcaics': Hallam Tennyson in his biography records his father's general appreciation of Clough's verse.[26] Before Tennyson came to them, English alcaics had ranged from Clough's more rigid replication on the one hand, to fluid approximations like Marvell's on the other, to Mary Sidney's somewhere in between. As it happens, a similar variety would emerge within Tennyson's own alcaics.

'A metre which I have invented'

'The grandest of all measures', Tennyson called the classical alcaic strophe.[27] But could he bring the alcaic over into English? Tennyson not only attempted it, but also applied himself, as no previous poet, to making the alcaic a vehicle of serious poetic expression in English. On and off, over the course of forty years, he explored the possibilities of the English alcaic in a series of remarkable poems running the gamut from strict accentual-syllabic replications to freer, more innovative adaptations. The freest of these deserves to be seen as a new English stanza-form in its own right. Tennyson's alcaic poems reveal, for the first time, a great English poet returning again and again to the alcaic, and allowing it to shape his aural imagination.

The very beginning of Tennyson's career as a poet involves an encounter with Horace's alcaics. In the first volume of his 1822 schoolboy edition of Horace, on an interleaf between pages 126 and 127, the young Tennyson inscribed his own translation of Horace *Odes* 3.3,[28] one of the six poems, the so-called Roman odes (3.1–6), that together constitute the longest sequence of alcaic stanzas in Horace. From a metrical point of view, Tennyson's translation is notable for beginning like this:

> The people's fury cannot move
> The man of just and steadfast soul
> > For he can brook
> > The tyrant's look
> And red right-arm of mighty Jove:
> What! though the echoing billows roll
> And on the lonely sea-beach dash

(1–7)

The translation extends to 97 iambic lines of various length, fluctuating from the dimeters in 2–3 to hexameters and everywhere in between. The arrangement of the first four lines, however, is unique. It cannot quite be taken as an integral quatrain, since 'soul' in line 2 comes to be rhymed with 'roll' in line 6. Nevertheless the metrical figure of lines 1–4 resembles the metre of Marvell's Horatian ode, in alternating two longer with two shorter lines, and indenting the shorter two, though in Tennyson's case the shorter lines are dimeters rather than trimeters. This raises at least the possibility that the young Tennyson may have begun translating Horace's ode by echoing the shape of the alcaic strophe, possibly following the example of Marvell or Collins, but thereafter abandoning the attempt, as though requiring a more spacious line. If there is any truth to that, it means that the schoolboy Tennyson – for four lines at least – participated in a seventeenth- and eighteenth-century tradition of representing Horatian lyric in a very approximate form.

Tennyson's mature involvement with the alcaic begins in 1833, with the composition of the verses that would eventually appear as section 9 of *In Memoriam*.[29] Or so I propose: my notion is that the stanza-form of *In Memoriam* deserves to be understood in light of the alcaic strophe. But that claim requires demonstration at length, which I will reserve for Chapter 4. Here instead I concentrate on a series of poems which, though they all appeared after *In Memoriam*, nevertheless are clearer and more overt instances of alcaic reception, and as such lend themselves to being discussed first. They represent a decades-long quest to develop a metrical form in English that would echo the metrical motion of the alcaic.

The quest begins in 1855 with the appearance of 'The Daisy', a recollection of a tour of Italy Tennyson had made in 1851 with his wife, Emily. Four years later, the poet finds himself lonely and missing her in an Edinburgh hotel during a tour of Scotland. He discovers, pressed within the leaves of a book, a flower they had plucked in an Italian alpine meadow, and this triggers a reverie (lines 101–8):

> And I forgot the clouded Forth,
> The gloom that saddens Heaven and Earth,
>   The bitter east, the misty summer
> And the grey metropolis of the North.
>
> Perchance, to lull the throbs of pain,
> Perchance, to charm a vacant brain,
>   Perchance, to dream you still beside me,
> My fancy fled to the South again.

Packed with images of 'cypress avenues' (64) and 'sun-smitten Alps' (78), and ringing with a beguiling echolalia of chimes and internal rhymes, the poem is among the sunniest and most musical examples of epistolary verse in English. Metre aside, the poem's matter already links it in various ways with Latin poetry. Tennyson's description of Como (70–84) leads him to recall Virgil's praise of that lake in *Georgics* 2.159–60.[30] More generally, there is the roving description of the Italian countryside typical of Catullus, Horace, and others.[31] There is an image, a commonplace in Latin literature, of a cold, dreary Britain remote from the bright centres of classical culture.[32] And there is the intimate epistolary approach found in so many of Horace's odes and satires. These classical dimensions constitute a literary and cultural context that help to justify Tennyson's choice of strophic form: 'a metre which I invented, representing in some measure the grandest of all metres, the Horatian Alcaic'.[33] A look at the first stanza of 'The Daisy' reveals the freshness of Tennyson's reception of this 'grandest of all metres':

> O love, what hours were thine and mine,
> In lands of palm and southern pine;
> > In lands of palm, of orange blossom,
> Of olive, aloe, and maize and vine.

The stanza, allowing for occasional resolutions, can be scanned like this:

```
u / u / u / u /
u / u / u / u /
  u / u / u / u / u
u / u / u u / u /
```

Here's a new twist in the story of English alcaics. Tennyson makes no attempt to reproduce, in the manner of Mary Sidney and Clough, the alcaic's accentual-syllabic count. Instead he gives us a poem of familiar 'English' rhythms, essentially iambic for most of the stanza. The regularity of the iambic tetrameter of the first two lines serves well enough to 'represent' (Tennyson's own term correctly delimits the extent of his ambition) the parallel hendecasyllabic lines of the ancient metre. Yet neither is Tennyson's metre quite like Marvell's adaptation, because shrewd touches in the third and fourth lines give the stanza something more of the feel of an alcaic.

Tennyson varies the third line into iambic pentameter catalectic: the extra half-foot not only gives the line nine syllables (as in the ancient alcaic), but also leaves it with a feminine ending, thus setting it off metrically from the others, just as the indented left-hand margin sets it off visually. By this trope Tennyson signals his understanding of the distinct nature of the alcaic third line. Just as Horace had so often arranged that the climax of the poem should occur in the third line, so too in 'The Daisy' the sense of the stanza often peaks (sometimes, in this alpine poem, literally peaks) in the third line:

> How young Columbus seemed to rove
> Yet present in his natal grove,
> > **Now watching high on mountain cornice**
> And steering, now, from a purple cove

> (17–20)

O Milan, O the chanting quires,
The giant windows' blazoned fires,
   The height, the space, the gloom, the glory!
A mount of marble, a hundred spires!

(57–60)

What more? we took our last adieu,
And up the snowy Splugen drew,
   But ere we reached the highest summit
I plucked a daisy, I gave it you.

(85–8)

The fourth line Tennyson treats with even greater skill. Its deployment on the page – flush with the left-hand margin – would lead us to expect a return to the tonic iambic tetrameter of lines 1 and 2. But instead we are dealt, again, nine syllables. That is technically unlike the alcaic, since it makes lines three and four of equal length. It resembles the alcaic, though, in this sense: the expected iambic pattern is broken up in the middle of the line by that sparkling classical foot, a choriamb (/ u u /), bringing into Tennyson's poem the most characteristic rhythmic element in the alcaic strophe, conveying the tongue-tripping rapidity of the alcaic fourth line without the jackhammer doubling of dactyls that strict metrical equivalence would require. By means of the minutest alteration of the fourth line, Tennyson acknowledges a hallmark of the ancient verse form and reproduces the headlong descending motion of the fourth line, all without the least obtrusiveness. He turns out to be the first poet to introduce the choriamb in an English alcaic based mainly on iambic metrical patterns (as opposed to English stress-accents patterned after longs and shorts). 'The Daisy' is a breakthrough for the English alcaic. It takes a middle path between stricter attempts at replicating the alcaic syllable-count and accents on the one hand (such as Sidney's and Clough's), and the approach of Marvell and Collins on the other hand, whose iambic stanzas are made to resemble, by their shape, a lyric metre. In 'The Daisy', the dominant English metrical foot, the iamb, is made to give way to the graceful Greek choriamb in the fourth line: so equal debts are paid to the English and classical models.

Horace's voice, Horace's accent

No more than four months passed before Tennyson embarked, in January 1854, on his second alcaic experiment, 'To the Rev. F. D. Maurice'. This Reverend

Maurice, who in 1852 had served as godfather at the christening of Tennyson's son, had run into trouble the next year for his liberal views on the nature of eternal punishment. 'Mr Maurice,' wrote Hallam Tennyson, 'had been ejected from his professorship at King's College [London] for non-orthodoxy. He had especially alarmed some of the "weaker brethren" by pointing out that the word "eternal" in "eternal punishment" (*aionios*), strictly translated, referred to the quality not the duration of punishment.' Hallam Tennyson records his father's approval of Maurice's notion that 'real Hell was the absence of God from the human soul'.[34] The ousted theologian's plight led Tennyson, who 'abhorred the belief in eternal punishment',[35] to write this invitation to stay at the poet's house at Farringford on the Isle of Wight (1–20):

> Come, when no graver cares employ,
> Godfather, come and see your boy:
>   Your presence will be sun in winter,
> Making the little one leap for joy.
>
> For, being of that honest few,
> Who give the fiend himself his due,
>   Should eighty-thousand college councils
> Thunder 'Anathema', friend, at you;
>
> Should all our churchmen foam in spite
> At you, so careful of the right,
>   Yet one lay-hearth would give you welcome
> (Take it and come) to the Isle of Wight;
>
> Where, far from the noise and smoke of town
> I watch the twilight falling brown
>   All round a careless-ordered garden
> Close to the ridge of a noble down.
>
> You'll have no scandal when you dine,
> But honest talk and wholesome wine,
>   And only hear the magpie gossip
> Garrulous under a roof of pine.

Here metre plays a more important role than in 'The Daisy'. The Italian atmosphere of the earlier poem, with its nods in the general direction of Roman poets, had made the alcaic a reasonable, though hardly inevitable, metrical model. 'To the Rev. F. D. Maurice', on the other hand, is so explicitly Horatian in tone, subject, and allusiveness that the alcaic metre becomes indivisible from its meaning.

The poem is 'Horatian' in being a verse epistle to a friend, in its expression of tolerance, and in its invitation to dine under the poet's humble roof, far from metropolitan cares. The parallels include direct allusions. Most pointedly: 'Far from the noise and smoke of town' (13) connects Tennyson's poem with a passage of one of Horace's masterpieces, *Odes* 3.29.9–12, in which he urges Maecenas, one of the leading figures in the Augustan regime, to set aside the weighty affairs of state and the bustle of the capital to join the poet in his rural retreat in the Sabine hills:

> fastidiosam desere copiam et
> molem propinquam nubibus arduis:
>   omitte mirari beatae
>   fumum et opes strepitumque Romae.

> Leave behind your blasé surfeit, and the pile that almost touches the clouds overhead. Stop looking with admiration at prosperous Rome with its smoke, wealth, and noise.[36]

Tennyson's allusion is feelingly apt: Horace's ode is particularly relevant to Maurice's situation. Maecenas, too, had suffered a kind of humiliation and demotion. Once among Augustus' two or three most intimate confidantes, he is supposed to have fallen from imperial favour around 23 BCE, roughly the same time that Horace published his first three books of odes.[37] Such a parallel could not have been lost on Maurice. But the allusion is uncommonly comprehensive, as including not only a very specific recollection of Horatian matter ('far from the noise and smoke of town' is nearly a quotation of 'fumum et opes strepitumque Romae'), but at the same time quoting the alcaic metre (in the sense of re-creating it, transposing it, into an English strophic form). Expert in classical languages, Maurice would have recognized not only the semantic quotation, but also the metrical allusion. Tennyson's poem produces the opposite effect of the dissociation of metre from matter that makes Wilfred Owen's metrical misquotation of Horace so discordant. Unlike Owen, Tennyson quotes a line of Horace by creating an English metre whose analogy with the alcaic strophe accommodates, rather than alienates, the quotation. Receiving this verse-epistle from his friend, Maurice would not only have perceived the overall allusion ('you, Maurice, are like Maecenas, recently disappointed and diminished, and I, like Horace, bid you to escape the capital's intrigues and congestion by staying with me in my wholesome country retreat'). He would also have felt the warmth and authority of Horace's familiar voice – specifically, the accent of his voice, as expressed metrically – speaking to him through Tennyson's invitation.

When, in line 18, Tennyson offers Maurice the promise of 'wholesome wine,' he is reaching back again to Horace's *Odes*, and once again to a poem addressing Maecenas. In it, Horace explains that he can offer his distinguished guest only cheap local Sabine wine in modest cups, nothing like the fine wines (Falernian, Caecuban, and Formian) to which Maecenas would be accustomed:[38]

> vile potabis modicis Sabinum
> cantharis, Graeca quod ego ipse testa
> conditum levi
>
>   . . . . .
>
> Caecubum et prelo domitam Caleno
> tu bibes uvam: mea nec Falernae
> temperant vites neque Formiani
>   pocula colles.

(Odes 1.20.1–3; 9–12)

> You will drink from modest cups a cheap Sabine wine that I stored away in a Greek jar . . . . At home you can drink Caecuban and the grape that is crushed in the presses of Cales; my cups are not mellowed by the vines of Falernum or Formian hillsides.

There are moral undertones to be felt in the way Horace protests the modesty of his refreshments:'come and enjoy a respite not just from the weighty responsibilities of a statesman's life, but also its oppressive and potentially corrupting luxuries'. Tennyson can similarly offer his friend Maurice, recently stung by public rebuke and displaced from his position of prestige, the remedy of 'wholesome wine.'

We could debate, Tennyson tells Maurice, the propriety of Britain's involvement in the Russo-Turkish War (three months later, in March 1854, England will have entered the war in Crimea). Or a happier alternative: we could leave such topics behind in favour of 'dearer matters' (29–40):

> We might discuss the Northern sin
> Which made a selfish war begin;
>   Dispute the claims, arrange the chances;
> Emperor, Ottoman, which shall win:
>
> Or whether war's avenging rod
> Shall lash all Europe into blood;

> How gain in life, as life advances,
> Valour and charity more and more.

Tennyson, in these lines, is reaching back to the following passage from a celebrated satire of Horace (*Sermones* 2.6.65–76), in which the city-bound poet pines for the simple pleasures of country life:

> O nights and feasts divine! When before my own Lar we dine, my friends and I, and feed the saucy slaves from the barely tasted dishes. Each guest, as is his fancy, drains cups big or small, not bound by crazy laws, whether one can stand strong bumpers in gallant style, or with mild cups mellows more to his liking. And so begins a chat, not about other men's homes and estates, nor whether Lepos dances well or ill; but we discuss matters which concern us more, and of which it is harmful to be in ignorance – whether wealth or virtue makes men happy, whether self-interest or uprightness leads us to friendship, what is the nature of the good and what is its highest form.[39]

The rustic surroundings, the simple fare, the freedom from arbitrary regulations of table etiquette, all create an atmosphere of warmth and honesty that forbids gossip (about whose country house is biggest) or trendy chit-chat (the merits of the latest celebrity dancer). Instead, the talk turns to practical ethics. So, too, Tennyson's Farringford will offer Maurice a respite from feverish London ambitions, the theological squabbles of Maurice's former colleagues, and the bloody disputes between nations. Instead their conversation will take refuge in the weightier matters of the law.

And Tennyson's penultimate stanza (41–4) –

> Come, Maurice, come: the lawn as yet
> Is hoar with rime, or spongy-wet;
>   But when the wreath of March has blossomed,
> Crocus, anemone, violet,

– brings in Horace not only by recalling his description of the onset of spring, but also by using language similar to Milton's very Horatian invitation to his own friend in Sonnet 17.2–8:

> Now that the fields are dank, and ways are mire,
> Where we shall sometimes meet, and by the fire
> Help waste a sullen day, what may be won
> From the hard season gaining? Time will run
> On smoother, till Favonius re-inspire
> The frozen earth; and clothe in fresh attire
> The lily and the rose.[40]

'The voice is Milton's,' observed D. S. Carne-Ross, 'but the sonnet is studded with Horatian allusions.'[41] By alluding to Milton, Tennyson effortlessly brings in a train of Englished Horatian associations, which harmonize with his own distinctly English version of Horace's alcaics. In short: in 'To the Rev. F. D. Maurice', Tennyson creates a dense nexus of thematic, verbal, and metrical reminiscences of Horace and the Horatian tradition that run even deeper than in his first alcaic experiment, 'The Daisy'.

Could it be that Tennyson felt, in this closer thematic involvement with Horace, the need for a closer approximation of the alcaic metre? For he saw fit, in 'To Maurice', to alter the elegant metre he had invented for 'The Daisy'. The change comes in the fourth line, the one which, in the earlier poem, features the adroit echo of a choriamb: u / u / u u / u /. In 'To Maurice', that line begins instead with a pair of dactyls: / u u / u u / u /. Though small, the alteration is significant: it brings the metre more directly into conformity with the pattern of the classical alcaic fourth line, which also begins with two dactyls: / u u / u u / u / u. It may be that in more nearly approaching a strictly Horatian line, Tennyson has allowed a slight diminution of the metrical subtlety he had achieved in 'The Daisy'. There is not only the loss of the fine effect of the Greek choriamb interrupting the pattern of English iambs, but also the slightly risky introduction of the double dactyls, which in English now smacks of limericks and other kinds of light verse. As ever with translation (as conventionally understood), so too with metrical translation a greater degree of literal fidelity usually produces estrangement from the texture of the original. But the metrical alteration, towards strict syllabic imitation, signals the direction in which Tennyson would move in his next experiment with English alcaics.

'A much freer and lighter movement' – or not

Nine years passed before Tennyson would take up the metre again in 'Milton: Alcaics'. Here Tennyson drastically changes his approach: rather than continuing to 'represent' the alcaic by creating analogous English strophes, he abandons conventional English measure altogether, attempting instead to replicate the strict syllabic template of the classical alcaic, as Sidney and Clough had done.

> O mighty-mouthed inventor of harmonies,
> O skilled to sing of Time or Eternity,
> 　God-gifted organ-voice of England,
> 　　Milton, a name to resound for ages;

Whose titan angels, Gabriel, Abdiel,
Starred from Jehovah's gorgeous armouries,
　　Tower, as the deep-domed empyrean
　　　　Rings to the roar of an angel onset –

Me rather all that bowery loneliness,
The brooks of Eden mazily murmuring,
　　And bloom profuse and cedar arches
　　　　Charm, as a wanderer out in ocean.

Where some refulgent sunset of India
Streams o'er a rich ambrosial ocean isle,
　　And crimson-hued the stately palm-woods
　　　　Whisper in odorous heights of even.

The poem's metrical structure looks, at first glance, nearly identical to Sidney's 'Psalm 120' and Clough's 'Alcaics', even in featuring feminine line endings throughout the stanza, which creates the effect of a double dactyl in the second half of lines 1 and 2, just as in Sidney's psalm. The syllable-count perfectly reproduces that of the ancient metre in all four lines (11-11-9-10). A closer look, though, discovers little alterations that make 'Milton: Alcaics' move with a very different gait. Clough had observed the Horatian caesura, and Sidney not only observed it but played upon it with particular expressiveness. But Tennyson shows no inclination to make poetic sense of the caesura: twice he overruns it, and often it is the site of distinctly unemphatic words ('of', 2, 'that', 9). Both Sidney and Clough between them lay significant stress on the 'pivot syllable', the fifth position of line 3 surprisingly often, given the difficulties of achieving three successive stressed syllables in English. Not so Tennyson. Once, among four possible lines, he lands a stressed syllable in that key position: 'Tower, as the deep dómed empyrean' (7). That is expressive, since what could convey the lofty apex of the heavens better than the *o* of 'domed', unambiguously long in quantity and stressed in accent, placed in the climactic position of the stanza's climactic line? In the other three lines, though, the pivot syllable is occupied by the most inconspicuous unstressed words possible: 'of' (2), 'and' (11), 'the' (15). The result is that his third lines become effectively iambic, since they are less likely than Sidney's to involve a stressed syllable in the fifth position, or than Clough's a stressed syllable in the first position. At least one contemporary, C. S. Calverley (who enters my account again in Chapter 4) noticed this aspect of Tennyson's enneasyllabic lines and felt it a defect. 'I should admit that the second syllable of words like "disallowed," "warranted," or "organ-voiced" is short, and I think

Mr Tennyson made a false quantity when he placed "organ-voiced" where he did in the *Milton* alcaics.' And then, with respect to 'organ-voiced', Calverley points to the difficulty of achieving a convincing pivot-syllable in the English enneasyllabic: 'He might plead that without the aid of some actual Latin adjective such as "atlantean," or some exceptional English compound, such as "un-swan-like," for a central word, it seems impossible to imitate the most frequently recurring form of the Horatian third line'.[42]

There are evidences of Tennyson's own diffidence about the quality of this poem. First: it originally appeared in the magazine *Cornhill* in 1863, together with three other poems under the heading 'Attempts at Classic Metre in Quantity', and again the next year in a volume of poems as one of four 'Experiments in Quantity'. Not that either the word 'attempt' or 'experiment' must imply failure: Tennyson after all authorized the poem's reprinting within the covers of a book, where 'experiment' replaced the earlier and perhaps less confident 'attempt'. Both words, though, imply a kind of special pleading on this poem's behalf. All poems are 'attempts' and many are 'experiments', but authors confident of their success will call them simply 'poems'. Specifically: 'The Daisy' and 'To the Rev. F. D. Maurice' are both attempts and experiments with respect to an ancient metre and its relation to English, but both are also fully-realized and thoroughly successful poems. 'Milton: Alcaics' is an interesting attempt and a valuable experiment, and no more. Second: Tennyson made a further disclaimer for the poem. 'Milton: Alcaics', he protested, was 'not intended for Horatian Alcaics .... The Greek Alcaic, if we may judge from the two or three specimens left, had a much freer and lighter movement.'[43] This statement was a rejoinder to Calverley's criticism, which had stung him.[44] But it is not clear that Greek liberties produced verses that move with freedom and lightness. They rather weakened the metrical pulse. English metrics are already more lax and ambiguous than Greek or Latin quantitative metres, and compound metres are already difficult to hear in English. The greater strictness of the Horatian alcaic (its fixed caesuras, its mandatory long syllables in the fifth position of lines 1–3, the way that the pivot syllable serves as a dependable point of reference) helps English alcaics achieve shape and definition. To attempt a Greek alcaic in English risks producing lines that seem to resolve into iambs, which the English ear is all too habituated to listen for. The distinction between Greek and Horatian alcaics is more meaningful in the classical languages; an English alcaic that aims for Greek freedom is likely to end up not freer but merely formless.

And as for 'lighter', there are non-metrical elements of Tennyson's poem that work against that effect. The diction is grandiloquent. Even in the second half of the poem, in which Tennyson declares his preference for the bucolic side of Milton, as opposed to 'the loud, resounding topics of angelic struggle',[45] veins of deep back-vowels bleed purple: 'all that bowery lonelieness / The brooks of Eden mazily murmuring, / And bloom profuse'; 'some refulgent sunset'. Extreme syntactic inversion and dislocation (Me rather…charm) is very specifically Horatian, but it retards the onward flow. There may be some justification for the omission of a definite article in line 12 ('out in ocean' – is it meant to be a Hellenism?) but it feels suspiciously like an instance of *metri gratia*. Tonally, sonically, syntactically, metrically, 'Milton: Alcaics' is rather more ponderous than light and fleet-footed. 'Attempt' suits it better than 'experiment' – Tennyson was right the first time. Tennyson's exercise is valuable at least as a test case about the limits of replicating the Greek metrical template in an English prosodic context.

'Blossom again on a colder isle'

Among the further grounds for diffidence about 'Milton: Alcaics', and a further bit of evidence of the poet's own misgivings, is that though Tennyson continued to experiment with alcaic forms, he abandoned strict imitation of classical syllabics. Instead, with 'To Professor Jebb, with the Following Poem', he returned to his earlier method of feeling his way towards an English stanza-form somehow answerable to, without strictly replicating, the metrical template. This next poem appeared in 1889 as an introduction to his long blank-verse 'Demeter and Persephone'. Sir Richard Jebb (1841–1905), eminent classicist and editor of Sophocles, here enters our account for the second time: he was mentioned near the end of Chapter 2 as among those learned Englishmen still composing Latin alcaics late in Victoria's reign. Jebb had 'directed H[allam] T[ennyson] to the *Homeric Hymn to Demeter*', and Hallam liked the poem well enough to request from his father an English adaptation.[46] Jebb was therefore the indirect instigator of 'Demeter and Persephone', and he went on to help Tennyson with the classical sources for the poem.[47] The subject of the dedicatory verses is the capacity of classical things to be transplanted (literally and figuratively) to the distant reaches (geographical and temporal) of northern Europe:

> Fair things are slow to fade away,
> Bear witness you, that yesterday
>   From out the Ghost of Pindar in you
> Rolled an Olympian; and they say

That here the torpid mummy wheat
Of Egypt bore a grain as sweet
   As that which gilds the glebe of England,
Sunned with a summer of milder heat.

So may this legend for awhile,
If greeted by your classic smile,
   Though dead in its Trinacrian Enna,
Blossom again on a colder isle.

Two transplantings feature explicitly in this poem. The first is of ancient Egyptian wheat into modern English soil ('Martin Tupper claimed to have "resuscitated mummy-wheat", and he exhibited it in the library of the Royal Institution', reported the *Literary Gazette* of 18 June, 1842).[48] The second transplanting, charmingly, is Tennyson's notion of the Demeter legend being 'transplanted' from ancient Greece to a modern British context: the very English poem he is presenting to Jebb.

Less obvious, though, is a third kind of transplanting: metrical. For all its classical references (to Pindar, Homer, the Demeter myth, and the classicist Jebb himself), 'To Jebb' lacks the variety of specifically Horatian allusions that pack 'To Maurice'. One hitherto unnoticed Horatian connection, though, should be pointed out. In the first stanza, Tennyson refers to a poem Jebb composed in ancient Greek to commemorate the 800th anniversary of the University of Bologna. Tennyson, who had received a copy, commends this act of Pindaric inspiration: 'yesterday / From out the Ghost of Pindar in you / Rolled an Olympian [ode]', (2–4). That word 'rolled' is not, in English, an ordinary synonym for poetic composition. The *OED* gives only one earlier example of that usage, lines 12–13 from Abraham Cowley's 'Praise of Pindar': 'So Pindar does new Words and Figures roul / Down his impetous Dithyrambic Tide'. (Ricks notes that Tennyson had a copy of Cowley at Somersby.)[49] In using 'roll' to describe the headlong momentum of Pindar's odes, both Cowley and Tennyson are surely translating a phrase of Horace, who praises the art of the Greek poet Pindar for the way he '*rolls* fresh words through daring dithyrambs' ('per audicis nova dithyrambos / verba *devolvit*', *Odes* 4.2.10–11). In English, then, to use the verb 'roll' in the sense of 'produce poetry' is to allude to that particular ode of Horace.[50] This is the same ode, indeed the same passage, which I suggested above as a model for Clough's 'Alcaics'.

It merits a brief look, then, at the opening lines of Horace *Odes* 4.2, where the poet, in a characteristic *recusatio*, declines a request from Iullus Antoninus, Augustus' step-nephew, to write a poem in the elaborately grandiose, and metrically exuberant, style of Pindar:

Pindarum quisquis studet aemulari,
Iulle, ceratis ope Daedalea
nititur pennis vitreo daturus
  nomina ponto.

monte decurrens velut amnis, imbres
quem super notas aluere ripas,
fervet immensusque ruit profundo
  Pindarus ore,

laurea donandus Apollinari,
seu per audaces nova dithyrambos
verba devolvit numerisque fertur
  lege solutis,

(1–12)

Anyone, Iullus, who strives to compete with Pindar relies on wings that have been waxed with Daedalus' skill, and is destined to give his name to a glassy sea. Like a river rushing down a mountainside, swollen by rains above its normal banks, Pindar boils and surges immeasurably on with his deep booming voice, deserving the award of Apollo's bay, whether he rolls down new words in his daring dithyrambs and is carried along in free unregulated rhythms . . .

'Not for me that kind of high-flying verse', Horace goes on to say; 'I am no swan, like Pindar, but a miniaturist who, like a painstaking bee fashioning the cells of a honeycomb, confines himself to poems of modest scale.' There's irony in Horace's refusal, which no commentator fails to note: Horace's own verses, in their sonority and precipitous enjambments, enact the very Pindaric grandiosity they pretend to disavow. What does tend to pass unremarked, though, is the way that this poem concerns itself with the transplanting of poetic metres from one language and culture to another. No, Horace does attempt to reproduce Pindar's famously complex choral metres (Horace calls them 'free unregulated rhythms' because Romans of his day, unaware of the intricate prosodic correspondences of Greek choral lyric, felt Pindar's poetry to be a kind of metrical chaos). But on the other hand, the poem *does* find Horace in the act of transplanting something else, a different Greek metrical form into Latin: the sapphic stanza. That's to say: among the subtexts of the poem is the question of the propriety of adapting metres from one language to another, and its method is to disavow the adaptation of one kind of Greek metre (Pindar's) by announcing that disavowal through the adaptation of another kind of Greek metre (Sappho's).

The terms of Tennyson's praise of Professor Jebb (that in his poem commemorating the founding of the University of Bologna, Jebb was like the ghost of Pindar *rolling* an ode) links 'To Jebb', both verbally and thematically, to Horace *Odes* 4.2. That is perfectly fitting, because the metre of 'To Jebb' is exactly the same as that of 'To the Rev. F. D. Maurice', and represents Tennyson's abandonment of a strict metrical imitation of the alcaic in the Milton ode, and a return to the familiar ground of English adaptation. It is doubly Horatian, in that, as in Horace's poem, it represents both a refusal to strictly imitate an earlier poet's metre, and at the same time a stealthy approximation of the earlier poet's stylistic effects. Tennyson's retreat from the more rigid conception of the alcaic is itself the new development, and its implication is that we ought to be a little less sanguine about the transplantability of foreign metres than about Egyptian wheat. The alcaic can indeed be transplanted from its ancient Mediterranean homelands and even 'blossom again on a colder isle', but it will thrive better if allowed also to evolve (as 'Milton: Alcaics' was not allowed to evolve) into a kind of prosodic flora better suited to the metrical climate of the English language.

'Cast in later Grecian mould'

'To Jebb' involves no metrical innovation. For that, Tennyson waited until 1891, when he would produce his final and freest alcaic experiment, 'To the Master of Balliol'. Like the poems to Maurice and Jebb, it is an occasional piece addressed to an eminent classicist: this time, none other than the great translator of Plato, Benjamin Jowett (1817–93). And once again, the alcaic poem serves as a preface to another, longer poem on classical themes: in this case, 'The Death of Oenone', adapted from an episode (10.259–489) of the fourth-century epic poem *Posthomerica* by Quintus Smyrnaeus. At the time of its composition, Jowett had been preparing a third edition of his translation of Plato,[51] a fact that allows Tennyson here again, as in 'To Maurice', to sound that familiar Horatian note: 'Illustrious friend, can you lay aside your weighty responsibilities long enough to savour the simpler pleasures of life?'

I

Dear master in our classic town,
You, loved by all the younger gown,
   There at Balliol,
Lay your Plato for one minute down,

II

And read a Grecian tale re-told,
Which, cast in later Grecian mould,
    Quintus Calaber
Somewhat lazily handled of old;

III

And on this white midwinter day –
For have the far-off hymns of May,
    All her melodies,
All her harmonies echoed away? –

IV

Today, before you turn again
To thoughts that lift the souls of men,
    Hear my cataract's
Downward thunder in hollow and glen,

V

Till, led by dream and vague desire,
The woman, gliding toward the pyre,
    Find her warrior
Stark and dark in his funeral fire.

There is nothing remarkable in the iambic tetrameter of the first two lines of the stanza: all of Tennyson's alcaic stanzas begin the same way. But a surprise both to ears and eyes greets us in the third line, where the Horatian enneasyllabic is cut down to just five syllables: a trochee and a dactyl (/ u / u u). And there is a further surprise in the fourth line, whose rhythm (/ u / u u / u u /) is unlike any other fourth line in the earlier poems. Or rather *almost* unlike: for it is exactly the reverse of the fourth line of 'To Maurice' and 'To Jebb' (/ u u / u u / u /). The final line of 'Balliol' is a metrical palindrome.

The result of these prosodic innovations is a stanza which, without renouncing its kinship to the alcaic, nevertheless deserves to be seen as a new English strophic form. It shares with the alcaic proper the parallel first two lines, the short third, and the dactylic fourth. But the differences amount to more. Not only is the third line curtailed to five syllables, but its rhythm (/ u / u u), in which unstressed syllables predominated, contrasts drastically with the predominating long syllables of the Horatian enneasyllabic (u – u – – – u – u). And the fourth line, which in the Greek and Horatian varieties plunges forward with the rapidity of a double dactyl, is here made to slow down. Not that it lacks for dactyls, but they have been moved to the end of the line to make way for an initial trochee.

These changes are not without critical point. When, for instance, Tennyson opines, justly, that Oenone's story is a tale which 'Quintus Calaber / Somewhat lazily handled of old,' we feel the initial trochee of the fourth line (Sómewhat) slowing down the movement of the line by preventing a succession of dactyls that would not have suited 'lazily'. Later in the poem, the correspondence of the rhythm of line three with that of the first five syllables of line four is at one with the rhetorical correspondence of the anaphora: 'All her melodies, / All her harmonies ...'. With 'To the Master of Balliol', then, Tennyson's alcaics led him farther than ever from the strict pattern of the ancient strophe. More than in any of his other alcaic poems, it can be seen as a new English stanza in its own right.

But its roots are in the alcaic, and to set it beside its four companion poems is to witness the evolution of that form in English. It is not often that a new metrical scheme is born; still less so when, as in this case, instead of springing fully-formed from a poet's head, it grows out of repeated experiments in adapting an established form from a foreign language. Tennyson's alcaics move from a fairly loose Horatian reminiscence ('The Daisy') to a closer approximation of the classical form with more specific Horatian references ('To Maurice'), to an even stricter exercise in replicating the Greek, not the Horatian, alcaic ('Milton'). They then move away from strict imitation, reprising a previous metre ('To Jebb'), followed by a final elaboration, derived from the alcaic but now so loosely as to constitute an invention in its own right. It would be hard to imagine how the trajectory of any five related poems could better illustrate the range of options available to an English poet receptive enough to allow a classical metre to shape and enrich the poetry of his native tongue.

So far as I can tell, Tennyson never referred to the English alcaics of Mary Sidney. He may not have heard of them: not till the mid-nineteenth century were critics beginning to talk very frequently about the long-neglected Sidney psalter. An anonymous writer in *Notes and Queries* in 1851, four years before the publication of 'The Daisy', calls attention, rather cautiously, to the fact that Mary Sidney's rendering of Psalm 120 'is in Alcaics and, I think, very successful, considering the difficulty of the metre'.[52] That reviewer could not have known that the poet was already at work who would at last begin to fulfil the promise of English alcaics. And yet these poems discussed in this chapter do not, for me, represent Tennyson's deepest engagement with the alcaics, which antedates all of them, and is the subject of the next chapter.

'The Same, But Not the Same'

Tennyson's In Memoriam Stanza

'In outline and no more'

Ancient metres may work on the English imagination in ways that are far from straightforward.

> I sometimes hold it half a sin
>> To put in words the grief I feel;
>> For words, like nature, half reveal
> And half conceal the soul within.

Tennyson, *In Memoriam* 5.1–4[1]

I sometimes think this stanza half reveals and half conceals the character of the alcaic strophe. What's at issue in this chapter is the English quatrain known as the In Memoriam stanza: four lines of iambic tetrameter, rhymed *a b b a*. Or rather not that stanza-form in the abstract, or as used by just anyone, but as uniquely handled by Tennyson in *In Memoriam* itself. My claim: that the In Memoriam stanza is an instance of the alcaic presence in English verse, and possibly, as a matter of artistic excellence, the greatest instance. In this case, though, the relationship is not straightforward, but diffuse and oblique. Fruitfully oblique: an unacknowledged source of the power of Tennyson's verse lies in its being like, but not too much like, the alcaic strophe. Tennyson has reasons for wanting Horace to be a presence, but not an entirely welcome presence, in his poem. Distance is as important as proximity. Horace's presence in *In Memoriam* includes his presence as a metrical effect: the alcaic metre is transposed, but ambiguously, into the form of the In Memoriam stanza.

In Memoriam comes with no such acknowledgement of metrical indebtedness as in the very title of 'Milton: Alcaics', or the note accompanying 'The Daisy' ('a metre which I invented, representing in some measure the greatest of all metres, the Horatian Alcaic), or the tell-tale fourth-line double-dactyl of 'To the Rev. F. D. Maurice'. If anything, it's the other way round. *In Memoriam* is much concerned with half-presences and approximations, and Tennyson is explicit about the power of poetic form ('measured language') as itself a measure for fending off unwelcome explicitness:

> But, for the unquiet heart and brain,
>   A use in measured language lies:
>   The sad, mechanic exercise,
> Like dull narcotics, numbing pain.
>
> In words, like weeds, I'll wrap me o'er,
>   Like coarsest clothes against the cold;
>   But that large grief which these enfold
> Is given in outline and no more.

(5.5–12)

It's not just that Tennyson's words express his grief while obscuring a direct view of it. 'Measured language' implies a link between his reticence and his chosen metre: a stanza-form sufficiently like the alcaic that it can be made, in the right context, to allude to it, without ever being made completely to identify with it. In the In Memoriam stanza, Tennyson gives us a subtle and elegant manifestation of the alcaic presence in English, but that presence is a matter of context, implication, and partial evasion. Tennyson's stanzas are alcaic 'in outline and no more', and all the more interesting for remaining oblique. So Tennyson, much later in *In Memoriam* (75.1–8), addresses his dear departed Arthur Hallam:

> I leave thy praises unexpress'd
>   In verse that brings myself relief,
>   And by the measure of my grief
> I leave thy greatness to be guessed;
>
> What practice howsoe'er expert
>   In fitting aptest words to things
>   Or voice the richest-toned that sings
> Hath power to give these as thou wert?

Here again there is textual, even specifically *metrical*, awareness. The bald statement of theme ('Since no words could ever give a just account of your character, Arthur, these poems, while they may ease my grief, must leave others only to guess at your greatness') is couched in terms that recall metrical form ('the *measure* of my grief', with the insinuation bolstered by its following so soon after the word 'verse'). Yes, the In Memoriam stanza is indeed the *measure*, in the formal sense, of Tennyson's grief, but another poetic measure is hinted at in the superlative construction 'Or voice *the richest-toned* that sings'. 'The *grandest of all metres*, the Horatian Alcaic': the standard Tennyson was later to claim he was aiming for 'in some measure' in the verse-form of 'The Daisy'.[2] We could read the undertone like this: 'Not even if I were to commemorate you in the richest of all metres, the Horatian alcaic, could I do justice to your memory, Arthur. So in the present poem I speak of you in a metre "in some measure" representing the alcaic, though an approximation: the exact relation of my English stanza and Horace's is unexpressed, given in outline and no more. The presence of the alcaic is to be felt, but obscurely.'

The In Memoriam stanza is not itself an adaptation of the alcaic. But given certain similarities with the ancient metre, and in the context of the poem, with its pervasive classical and often specifically Horatian allusive atmosphere, Tennyson handles the form in such a way as to invite reading it in light of the alcaic strophe.

FitzGerald's *Rubáiyát*: 'Somewhat as in the Alcaic'

The idea of reading one metrical form 'in light of' another ought to be uncontroversial. To take just one instance: another famous elegy, Geoffrey Hill's poem 'September Song', is now familiar enough to have become the frequent object of commentary not only in the academic press, but also on websites and blogs, where it is sometimes referred to as a sonnet. It is not a sonnet, strictly speaking. It is composed of fourteen lines, yes; but it is unrhymed, the metre and line-lengths are highly variable, and only three or four lines could be defended as meeting the standard of iambic pentameter. But it would be risking pedantry to object too strongly to invoking the term 'sonnet' in relation to the poem. 'September Song' may be said to invite comparison to stricter versions of the sonnet in general, both as to form (the fourteen lines, a plausible *volta*) and theme (as part of a tradition of sonnets which are also elegies, such as Milton's 'On the Late Massacre in Piedmont'). Then there's the context of Hill's own work, in which elegaic sonnets and sonnet-sequences are conspicuous.[3] Part of the meaning of 'September Song' derives from its evoking the sonnet, approximating it nearly enough to warrant the comparison, but without fully becoming one. On one reading, it can be construed as a devolution from the strict sonnet form; on another, an arrested or incomplete sonnet; on still another, neither devolved nor arrested, but a fully-formed alternative to a strict sonnet. In any case, the most fruitful critical account will come from reading Hill's poem *in light of* the tradition of strict sonnets, and weighing the critical implications of 'September Song' as an almost-but-not-quite-sonnet.

In just this way, reading the In Memoriam stanza under the aspect of the alcaic strophe is my method in this chapter. An obstacle looms, though: a historical one. Cultivated readers of the twenty-first century have little problem reading 'September Song' in light of the sonnet form it approximates, because the sonnet remains well-known. But the same readers are unlikely even to know about the alcaic at all, let alone to recognize, in the contours of the In Memoriam stanza, a similarity to that ancient form. Nineteenth-century readers, though, were not so unprepared. That educated Victorians could actually feel alcaic resonances in certain English verse forms can be illustrated by the works of two of Tennyson's contemporaries, Edward FitzGerald and Charles Stuart Calverley.

Nobody familiar with Latin poetry can read FitzGerald's *Rubáiyát of Omar Khayyám* without being reminded of Horace's *Odes*:

> The Moving Finger writes; and, having writ,
> Moves on: nor all your Piety nor Wit
> Shall lure it back to cancel half a Line,
> Nor all your Tears wash out a Word of it.

(LI)[4]

All this is of course very close not only to the themes, but also the phrasing, of (at least) two passages out of Horace:

> cum semel occideris et de te splendida Minos
>   fecerit arbitria,
> non, Torquate, genus, non te facundia, non te
>   restituet pietas;

Odes 4.7.21–4

> Once you have died and Minos has pronounced his solemn verdict, neither high birth, nor eloquence, Torquatus, nor piety will bring you back[5]

> Eheu fugaces, Postume, Postume,
> labuntur anni nec pietas moram
>   rugis et instanti senectae
>   adferet indomitaeque morti:

> non si trecenis quotquot eunt dies,
> amice, places illacrimabilem
>   Plutona tauris,

Odes 2.14.1–7

Ah Postumus, Postumus, the fleeting years slip by, nor will piety check the onset
of wrinkles, old age, and invincible death – no, not if on every day that passed
you killed three hundred oxen to appease Pluto, who has no tears

Beyond these thematic echoes are formal echoes too, and FitzGerald was anxious
they should be recognized. To his publisher, Bernard Quartich, on 10 August
1879, FitzGerald wrote to apologize for having overlooked an error in the proofs
of the fourth edition of his *Rubáiyát*. Though it was 'but a *word* wrong', it was
nevertheless 'a word that alters all the meaning and the fact', and justified,
FitzGerald urged, the inclusion of an unsightly erratum-slip. The mistake that so
concerned him, though, was not a misprint in the poems themselves, but in the
author's preface, where he was raising a recondite point about poetic metre. The
uncorrected version had read:

> With regard to the present translation. The original Rubáiyát (as, missing an
> Arabic guttural, these *tetrastychs* are more musically called), are independent
> stanzas, consisting of four lines of equal, though varied, prosody, sometimes *all*
> rhyming, but oftener (as here attempted) the third line suspending the cadence
> by which the last atones with the former two. Sometimes as in the Greek Alcaic,
> where the third line seems to lift and suspend the wave that falls over the last.

The mistaken word was 'sometimes' in the last sentence: FitzGerald had meant
'somewhat'. 'The blank line in the Stanza', he explained, 'does *not* "sometimes"
resemble that in the Alcaic, but does ALWAYS "somewhat" resemble it, which
makes all the difference, surely.'[6] Surely it does: rather than *occasionally* behaving
just like the third line in an alcaic, the corresponding line in a Rubáiyát quatrain
only approximates – but *always* approximates – that aspect of the Greek metre.

Is the distinction so important? The general sense (of a broad metrical
resemblance between the alcaic and the Rubáiyát stanzas) is clear enough in
either phrasing: who would care about the difference between 'sometimes as in'
and 'somewhat as in'? FitzGerald only noticed the error after the edition had
gone to press, but cared enough to intervene at that late stage, even offering, as he
proposed in a post-script, to correct the error by hand, in pen, in each copy of the
edition. His anxiety tells of his interest in seeing that his stanzas be understood
as pervasively (rather than occasionally) reminiscent of alcaics. Not equated

with them, or confused with them: approximation ('*somewhat* as in the Greek Alcaic') is the positive aim. They are to be read only *in light of* the strict alcaic model. FitzGerald wanted his readers to appreciate not only his poem's generic and thematic resonances with the classics (with the genre of eclogue, for example, and with Lucretius, both of which he mentions elsewhere in his preface),[7] but also wanted them to hear the metrical resonances with the alcaic.

One can see what he meant. Though the Rubáiyát stanza's metre may be perfectly standard English iambic pentameter, it is the A A B A rhyme-scheme that led FitzGerald to associate it with the alcaic. That orphaned third line has the effect of bracketing 1–2 as a unit, and setting up 4 as a return to the tonic key of 1–2. The result is a climactic third line that 'seems to lift and suspend the wave that falls over the last,' a characterization that remarkably anticipates Wilkinson's description of the alcaic as 'the gathering wave of the first two lines, the thundering of the third, and the rapid backwash of the fourth.' One can feel that motion in the following stanza, where the nub of a distinctly Horatian concern (compare for instance *Odes* 1.11) comes with the coincidence of the crucial word 'tomorrow' at the formal crux of the strophe:

> Ah, my Belovéd, fill the cup that clears
> TO-DAY of past Regrets and future Fears –
> 　　*To-morrow?* Why, To-morrow I may be
> Myself with Yesterday's Sev'n Thousand Years.

(XX)

So too in the following meditation on death's inevitability, and the awkwardness of having to leave to our successors what we ourselves inherited from our predecessors (cf. *Odes* 2.14). The crucial concession, that 'we' ourselves must die, fittingly comes with the cresting third line:

> And we, that now make merry in the Room
> They left, and Summer dresses in new Bloom,
> 　　Ourselves must we beneath the Couch of Earth
> Descend, ourselves to make a Couch – for whom?

(XXII)

Horatian themes mingle with quasi-alcaic form.

FitzGerald in his preface specified the Greek rather than the Horatian alcaic. Rightly so, since the more variable Greek version allows for more short syllables, including in the fifth foot of the hendecasyllabic lines, which often makes them move more nearly like English iambics. But this in no way diminishes the spectral presence of Horace in the *Rubáiyát*. The salience of the third line holds for both the Greek and Horatian versions of the stanza. And FitzGerald's mere mention of the word 'Alcaic' in the preface is enough to conjure the ghost of Horace, especially when we then meet Horatian themes – friendship, drinking, the acknowledgement of mortality – in stanza upon stanza of the *Rubáiyát*.

Nineteenth-century critics not only felt the overlap of the Rubáiyát stanza and the alcaic, with its attendant Horatian undertones; they also associated it with other of Tennyson's alcaic experiments. Of special interest is the now obscure late-Victorian critic Stephen Gwynn, and his notion about the origins of the stanza-form of Tennyson's 'The Daisy'. 'The suggestion for this curious quatrain,' he wrote in 1899, seven years after Tennyson's death, 'almost certainly came from FitzGerald's famous Persian measure.'[8] No, it certainly did not: FitzGerald did not begin writing his *Rubáiyát* until 1857, by which time 'The Daisy' had already been in print for two years. Yet Gwynn's anachronism is revealing. Apparently unaware of Tennyson's declaration that he had invented the stanza-form of 'The Daisy' specifically to represent 'in some measure the grandest of all metres, the Horatian Alcaic',[9] Gwynn, not unreasonably, assumed its derivation from the Rubáiyát quatrain, which FitzGerald himself had linked to the alcaic. Gwynn's misapprehension merely points up the readiness of Victorian critics and readers to associate these two English quatrain forms with alcaics.

FitzGerald's *Rubáiyát*, then, is a significant instance of alcaic reception in English. This fact is almost entirely ignored, and the neglect is especially lamentable, since the immense popularity of the poem on both sides of the Atlantic means that the alcaic has probably made its influence felt in English most widely through the *Rubáiyát* than through any other means. It deserves a chapter in itself, rather than this brief excursus, whose point is this: that nineteenth-century critics rightly felt, more keenly than we can today, the presence of the alcaic in English forms that approximated it.

A forgotten Victorian critical commonplace

In which light consider a remarkable Victorian poem, composed not in English but in Latin by the poet, translator, and wit Charles Stewart Calverley (1831–1884). After three vivid alcaic stanzas describing a fierce winter storm, we hear of a feast being prepared within (11–20):

> Tu Falernum
> Prome, dapes strue, dic coronent
>
> Crateras; ignis cor solidum, graves
> Repone ramos. Jamque doloribus
> Loquare securus fugatis
> Quae socio loquereris illo;
>
> Hunc dedicamus laetitiae diem
> Lyraeque musisque. Illius, illius
> Da, quicquid audit: nec silebunt
> Qui numeri placuere vivo.[10]

Bring out the wine, prepare the feast, order the cups to be filled to the brink; build a solid core of fire and stoke it with hefty logs. And, all grief having departed, confidently say the kinds of things you might say to that dear companion of ours. We dedicate this day to cheer, music and poetry. Raise a toast to him, whatever he may be called, and let not be silent the songs he liked to hear when he was alive.

One could be forgiven for thinking that Calverley's poem is a clever variation on Horace's Soracte ode (*Odes* 1.9), whose speaker, as we have seen in earlier chapters, similarly calls for feasting, wine, and a crackling fire against the wintery cold outside. And indeed those thematic parallels, together with his elegant alcaic stanzas, do make Calverley's poem undeniably Horatian. But there is a complication: Calverley's last two sentences have no warrant in the Soracte ode. Nothing there prepares us for the abrupt revelation that Calverley's speaker and interlocutor are remembering a departed friend (*socio . . . illo*, 16) and are resolving to carry on conversing and singing as would have pleased him were he still living.

The explanation of that unexpected development is that yes, Horace is behind this poem, but at one remove. The immediate source is not Horace but Tennyson. Calverley's poem is, as it turns out, a translation of all but the first stanza of *In Memoriam* 107, the section that marks the birthday of the bereaved poet's friend, Arthur Hallam:

> The time admits not flowers or leaves
> To deck the banquet. Fiercely flies
> The blast of North and East, and ice
> Makes daggers at the sharpen'd eaves,
>
> And bristles all the brakes and thorns
> To yon hard crescent, as she hangs

> Above the wood which grides and clangs
> Its leafless ribs and iron horns
>
> Together, in the drifts that pass,
>   To darken on the rolling brine
>   That breaks the coast. But fetch the wine,
> Arrange the board and brim the glass;
>
> Bring in great logs and let them lie,
>   To make a solid core of heat;
>   Be cheerful-minded, talk and treat
> Of all things ev'n as he were by:
>
> We keep the day with festal cheer,
>   With books and music. Surely we
>   Will drink to him whate'er he be,
> And sing the songs he loved to hear.

Nobody with Horatian ears can fail to hear, behind these lines, the Soracte ode with its determination to make merry within despite the cold weather without:

> But fetch the wine,
> Arrange the board and brim the glass;
>
> Bring in great logs and let them lie,
>   To make a solid core of heat;
>   Be cheerful-minded,

These lines come close to paraphrasing this alcaic stanza of Horace's:

> dissolve frigus ligna super foco
> large reponens atque benignius
>   deprome quadrimum Sabina,
>   O Thaliarche, merum diota:

(Odes 1.9.5–8)

> Thaw the cold by piling logs generously on the hearth, Thaliarchus, and serve the four-year-old wine more lavishly than usual from its Sabine jar.

The allusion to Horace deepens the urgency of Tennyson's poem, though the moral point differs, since Horace's poem is more concerned with the speaker's own mortality than somebody else's. *In Memoriam* 107, then, is a Horatian poem: not a re-writing of Horace, exactly, but best read in light of the Soracte ode. This means that when Calverley came to translate Tennyson's already deeply Horatian verses in to Latin, the choice to render them into Horatian alcaics constitutes an act of embedded literary criticism. He proposes, not through discursive statement but through the style of his translation, an analogy between the alcaic strophe and the In Memoriam strophe. Elsewhere he was explicit about the Horatian link. 'A stanza of *In Memoriam*', he wrote, 'is a thing compact, *teres atque rotundum* [polished and rounded – itself a Horatian phrase], as in a stanza of a Horatian Ode.'[11] That, by 'Horatian Ode', he meant mainly odes in alcaics is borne out in practice: every time he translated one of Horace's alcaic poems into English, regardless of theme, he rendered it into In Memoriam stanzas.[12] Including, significantly, the Soracte ode itself, whose opening Calverley translates into these Tennysonian lines:

> One dazzling mass of solid snow
>   Soracte stands; the bent woods fret
>   Beneath their load; and, sharpest-set
> With frost, the streams have ceased to flow.

(1–4)

This poem completes a marvellous triangulation. At one corner is Tennyson, whose *In Memoriam* 107 emulates and transforms (at the second corner) Horace's Soracte ode. Connecting the two at the third angle is Calverley, who translates Tennyson's poem into Horatian alcaics, and Horace's poem into the In Memoriam stanza of Tennyson.

Both Tennyson and Calverley had good reasons for associating the In Memoriam stanza with the alcaic. Among its likenesses are the general tightness of its four tetrameter lines (the Horatian compactness that Calverley noted) as against the longer lines typical in both English and Roman elegy. More specifically, there's the way the third line achieves a distinct peaking, and the fourth a distinct falling off. Wilkinson's sense (that line 3 of an alcaic involves a 'pivot' at which the stanza peaks and from which, in line 4, it falls away) is tellingly echoed in Christopher Ricks's characterization of the In Memoriam stanza: that it 'rises to a momentary chime' (the rhyme produced in line 3) 'and then fades'.[13] The triple movement of the stanza, for Ricks, issues from its 'continual receding from its affirmations, from what it momentarily clinches'.[14] The first two lines propose, the rhyme in line 3 clinches, and the fourth line recedes. Both the ancient and the English quatrains, then, can be thought of as sharing a tripartite character. An apprehension of this general quality led Calverley to demonstrate it *in practice* by Englishing Horace's alcaics à la *In Memoriam*, and vice-versa.

Nor was Calverley alone. He shared in a late-nineteenth-century critical sensibility that associated the In Memoriam stanza with the Horatian alcaic. We find it in critics, translators, and poets alike. The foremost Victorian translator of Horace, the Oxford classicist John Conington, thought it 'very probable' that the In Memoriam stanza would 'be found eventually to be the best representation of the Alcaic in English'.[15] That slight equivocation ('eventually') bespeaks misgiving not about the stanza's suitability itself, but the inadvisability of anyone but Tennyson attempting to use it, at least so long as the master was alive. 'With all its advantages' as an analogue for the alcaic, the In Memoriam stanza nevertheless

> has the patent disadvantage of having been brought to notice by a poet who is influencing the present generation as only a great living poet can. A great writer now, an inferior writer hereafter, may be able to handle it with some degree of independence; but the majority of those who use it at present are sure in adopting Mr Tennyson's metre to adopt his manner.[16]

By 'those who use it at present' Conington meant Calverley, whose translation of Horace *Odes* 3.2 'reminds us of Mr Tennyson', and this will not do, since 'Mr Tennyson's manner is not the manner of Horace'.[17] (One understands what he meant, but there are also continuities between Tennyson and Horace that make the Tennysonian echoes more resonant, less discordant, than Conington's judgment implies.) It is for this reason that Conington himself resisted the temptation, in his own translations, to turn Horace's alcaics into In Memoriam stanzas. But that eschewal, and his criticism of Calverley, were to be understood as mere contingencies: when, in the course of time, translators will have learnt to use the In Memoriam stanza without inviting obvious comparison with Tennyson, then it would 'very probably' prove the most apt analogue to the alcaic, even better than the metres Tennyson had devised for 'The Daisy' and 'To the Reverent F. D. Maurice'.[18]

Other critics agreed, and with fewer reservations. Typical of them is the anonymous writer who, surveying recent translations of Horace in the *Quarterly Review*, praised Calverley's choice of the In Memoriam stanza as the medium for 'transplanting' the alcaic, regretted that Conington had ruled it out for himself, and asserted that 'The "In Memoriam" stanza conveys the gravity at least and the dignity of the Alcaic'.[19] Another reviewer repudiated Conington's claim that the In Memoriam stanza 'associates itself too much with a modern poet and a modern poem', and went on to declare Calverley's alcaic translations an unmitigated success.[20] Yet another reviewer congratulated a (now forgotten) translator, Rutherford Clark, for extending what by then constituted a tradition of following 'Mr Calverley and the advice of Prof. Conington in rendering the weightier Alcaic Odes into the metre of "In Memoriam" –; and all these are powerfully and effectively done.'[21] This custom of associating the In Memoriam stanza with alcaics survived into the early twentieth century: Calverley's translations remained in print until 1913, and even as late as 1925, A. E. Housman, in a private letter, praised them as 'the most poetic versions of Horace' he knew.[22]

What's to be gained from excavating this strand of Victorian critical opinion? This insight: how great a gap has opened up between us and Tennyson's contemporaries in registering the contours of an ancient poetic form. Victorian critics (and the readership they imply) had no difficulty associating the metre of *In Memoriam* with the alcaic strophe. They understood the implications of Calverley's clever project of turning Horace's alcaic poems into In Memoriam stanzas and *In Memoriam* into alcaics. Even critics who, like Conington, worried about its Tennysonian overtones, nevertheless granted the propriety of the In Memoriam stanza as an English analogue to the ancient metre. Calverley's translations, and their critical reception, demonstrate how natural it was for the best Victorian readers to experience *In Memoriam*, in its formal aspect, as an extraordinarily prolonged engagement with the idea of the alcaic strophe.

I write this in anticipation of a critique that would suspect me finding in *In Memoriam* an echo of the alcaic where it does not exist. I turn for support to Calverley, Conington, Clark, Housman, et al. as witnesses from an era when the cadences of the alcaic were regularly absorbed by schoolchildren who grew into adults capable of instinctively recognizing rhythmical echoes which most of us now can recover only through study. I do feel the need for their corroboration, since my claim about the In Memoriam stanza is especially nuanced: that it is meant to encourage association with the alcaic while at once discouraging too conclusive an association, and that such allusive diffidence complements the themes of *In Memoriam* as a whole. However sound or feeble my argument, the Victorian consensus at least demonstrates that it is no folly to read *In Memoriam* again, for the first time in a century, in light of the Horatian alcaic.

The art of minute alterations

Tennyson had Horace's *Odes* in mind at the very inception of *In Memoriam* in 1833. This fact is obscured, though, by Tennyson's numbering of the book's sections, which does not correspond to the order of composition. The first section of *In Memoriam* was not the first to be written. The evidence instead points to section 9 as the first poem to have been composed, and it is distinctly Horatian:[23]

> Fair ship, that from the Italian shore
> Sailest the placid ocean-plains,
> With my lost Arthur's loved remains,
> Spread thy full wings, and waft him o'er.
>
> So draw him home to those that mourn
> In vain; a favourable speed
> Ruffle thy mirror'd mast, and lead
> Thro' prosperous floods his holy urn.
>
> All night no ruder air perplex
> Thy sliding keel, till Phosphor, bright
> As our pure love, thro' early light
> Shall glimmer on the dewy decks.
>
> Sphere all your lights around, above;
> Sleep, gentle heavens, before the prow;
> Sleep, gentle winds, as he sleeps now,
> My friend, the brother of my love;
>
> My Arthur, whom I shall not see
> Till all my widow'd race be run;
> Dear as the mother to the son,
> More than my brothers are to me.
>
> (9.1–20)

The speaker addresses the ship bearing the body of Arthur Hallam back to England, but at the same time alludes to another ship, the one Horace addresses in *Odes* 1.3, praying for the safe journey of his friend Virgil within. Both poems belong to the classical category *proemptika*, 'send-off poems', wishing the travelling friend a prosperous journey.[24] The allusion has been acknowledged by all Tennyson's major commentators.[25] The links to the classical world generally are reinforced by his mention of Italy in line 1, and by an apt Virgilian allusion ('placid ocean-plains', translating 'placida aequora', *Aeneid* 10.103). Horace's poem begins like this:

> Sic te diva potens Cypri,
> sic fratres Helenae, lucida sidera,

> ventorumque regat pater
> obstrictis aliis praeter Iapyga,
>   navis, quae tibi creditum
> debes Vergilium, finibus Atticis
>   reddas incolumen precor,
> et serves animae dimidium meae.

(Odes 1.3.1–8)

May the goddess who rules over Cyprus, and Helen's brothers, those bright stars, and the lord of the winds, tying up all the others except Iapyx, guide you, o ship, for you hold Vergil in trust and owe him to me. Be sure to discharge him intact on the shores of Attica, I pray you, and save one who is half my soul.

This connection to Horace matters. Throughout *In Memoriam*, Tennyson will allude to Horace dozens of times, as the Roman poet's themes (friendship, conviviality, and the contemplation of death) so often overlap with his own. Specific Horatian odes often seem to have precipitated various sections of *In Memoriam*, particularly those that have, for Christopher Ricks, 'a Horatian elegaic serenity'.[26] In the case of this poem, a familiar Horatian frame (concern for a troubled or imperilled friend) harmonizes with *In Memoriam* generally. In similar fashion, some years later, as I noted in the previous chapter, Horace's ode to Maecenas (3.29) would supply Tennyson with a frame, and indeed with some of the very words, for addressing his beleaguered friend, the Rev. Dr. Maurice. Just as in that poem, where the Horatian subtext permitted a deep but unobtrusive compliment (Maurice as comparable to Maecenas), so here it is a discreet compliment to Arthur Hallam to be compared, by implication, to Virgil. It is true that in Horace's ode Virgil is alive, not dead, and his ship is departing rather than arriving; but even those reversals are neatly pointed, as achieving pathetic irony. And the wholly apposite phrase in line 8, 'animae dimidium meae' (half my soul,) is picked up and used not once but twice in *In Memoriam*.[27]

In an atmosphere so dense with Horatian associations, is there also the allusive tug of Horace's signature metre? Yes, because in Tennyson's hands, any given In Memoriam stanza can be delicately adjusted, when needed, to resemble the alcaic. This is accomplished mainly through metrical substitutions, sometimes in combination with placement of caesuras, the timing of enjambments, and other kinds of phrasal and rhythmic punctuation. Consider again the first stanza of *In Memoriam* 9:

> Fair ship, that from the Italian shore
>   Sailest the placid ocean-plains

> With my lost Arthur's loved remains,
> Spread thy full wings, and waft him o'er.

A tiny metrical alteration in the second foot of line 3 changes the character of the line. We find not the expected iamb, but a spondee instead ('With my | **lost Ar** | thur's loved remains'). As such the line has something in common with the third line of a Horatian alcaic which, as we have seen, typically begins with a short syllable and builds to a climactic three successive long syllables. 'With **my** | **lost Ar** | thur's **loved** | re**mains**': the second through fourth syllables, making three successive stresses, strikingly gather into themselves the emotional energy of the stanza, and constitute its climactic moment. Tennyson throughout *In Memoriam* sedulously eschews the feminine line-endings typical of alcaic third lines; but the spondaic substitution in the second foot means that the resumption of the iambic pattern feels like a kind of falling-off. Given that in any In Memoriam stanza, the rhyme in line 3 rises to a kind of pinnacle ('rising to a momentary chime' – Ricks), the added presence of those three stressed syllables makes this particular line 3 feel, in its rising, peaking, and falling off, distinctly like an alcaic third line.[28]

To take a single parallel example, one of the best-known passages from all of Tennyson, section 54:

> Oh, yet we trust that somehow good
>   Will be the final end of ill,
>   To pangs of nature, sins of will,
> Defects of doubt, and taints of blood;
>
> That nothing walks with aimless feet;
>   That not one life shall be destroy'd,
>   Or cast as rubbish to the void,
> When God hath made the pile complete;
>
> That not a worm is cloven in vain;
>   That not a moth with vain desire
>   Is shrivell'd in a fruitless fire,
> Or but subserves another's gain.
>
> Behold, we know not anything;
>   I can but trust that good shall fall
>   At last – far off – at last, to all,
> And every winter change to spring.
>
> So runs my dream: but what am I?
>   An infant crying in the night:

> An infant crying for the light:
> And with no language but a cry.

Nobody could miss the pathos of the diction, but what's more likely to go unnoticed is a well-timed metrical subtlety. In stanza four, the iambic structure of the third line yields, you might say, to the pressure of the speaker's yearning, so that the second foot swells from an iamb to a spondee, producing three consecutive stressed syllables ('At **last** – | **far off** | – at last, to all'). The effect is especially strong as the spondaic substitution 'far off' is itself set off by dashes: the poet hopes that God's justice will come, but the point is that it will be deferred. The effect is climactic: Tennyson's three consecutive long syllables bring the stanza, and arguably the entire poem, to its emotional and metrical peak.

This, too, is the effect of 9.3: 'With **my loved Ar**thur's lost remains'. So it is doubly striking when, passing to the fourth line of that poem, we immediately find another metrical substitution. This time it is a trochee: '**Spread** thy | full wings, and waft him o'er.' That initial trochee imparts to the line a rhythm (/ u u / u / u /) that feels like a shorter form of the alcaic fourth line (/ u u / u u / u / u).[29] When such a line follows a third line featuring a medial spondaic substitution, with its effect of a mid-line peak or pivot, then the resulting effect is a distinct English echo of the last half of an alcaic strophe, with its mid-line peak running into a more rapid fourth line, followed by a tonic return:

> With **my loved Ar**thur's **loved** remains,
> **Spread** thy full **wings** and **waft** him **o'er**.

Tennyson can create such fourth lines simply by leaning on the first syllable.[30] The alcaic effect created in lines three and four is subtly supported by one more detail: that the first and second lines of the stanza both involve resolutions (a spondee, a trochee) that land the stress on their first syllable. Since Horace's alcaics regularly begin with long syllables, this makes Tennyson's stanza just that much more like an alcaic. All this is achieved with tiny metrical nudges.

None of the Victorian critics goes into such detail about the metrical minutiae, but Conington did put his finger on an apposite critical principle. Reflecting on Calverley's choice of the In Memoriam stanza as an analogue for Horatian alcaics, he acknowledged the wisdom of preferring a humble 'English' iambic measure:

> [...] it is evident that he chose the iambic movement as the ordinary movement
> of English poetry; and it is evident, I think, that in translating Horace we shall be

right in doing the same, as a general rule. Anapestic and other rhythms may be beautiful in themselves, but they cannot be manipulated so easily [...][31]

This judgment is counterintuitive: one might at first suppose that Horace's complex metrical patterns would best be suggested by triple metres such as anapests (or dactyls, or other non-iambic combinations such as choriambs). Such stanzas, though, would suffer this disadvantage: their metrical patterns must remain fixed. They cannot be varied ('manipulated' is the crucial word in Conington's remark) without risking devolving into the iambic patterns English ears are trained to hear, or lapsing into no clear form at all. Good old familiar iambs, on the other hand, lend themselves better to produce the suggestion of classical measures, because the iambic line is malleable: we expect it to be varied with metrical substitutions. If the underlying metrical grid is clear enough, an iambic poem can support frequent local substitutions, and longer passages can even modulate through changes of rhythm, without losing metrical integrity and deliquescing into formlessness. Since the basic form of the In Memoriam stanza already suggests the alcaic to Victorian sensibilities, all Tennyson needs to do in order to impart a distinctly Horatian sound is to bring in the occasional, well-judged, metrical alteration. With a spondaic substitution in the second foot of one line, and trochaic substitution at the beginning of the other, this stanza is altered – 'manipulated' – just enough to bring it notably closer to the rhythms of the alcaic, while keeping well within the limits of the English form. These alterations need not be frequent to achieve their effect: Tennyson need mould the stanza to resemble the alcaic only when he wants to, and he lays on the full alcaic effect sparingly.[32]

The alcaic feel is apt in 'Fair ship, that from the Italian shore', since that section's Horatian associations are particularly strong. In addition to the allusion to Horace's poem on Virgil's departing ship, and the reference to Italy, there are other Horatian elements. One of them occurs in the third line of this stanza:

> All night no ruder air perplex
>   Thy sliding keel, till Phosphor, bright
>   As our pure love, thro' early light
> Shall glimmer on the dewy decks.

(9.9–12)

Here, a spondaic substitution in the second foot produces another succession of three stressed syllables coinciding elegantly with the cresting emotion: 'As **our pure love**, thro' early light'. An even subtler Horatian effect: the matter of enjambment in the second stanza:

> So draw him home to those that mourn
> 　In vain; a favourable speed
> 　Ruffle thy mirror'd mast, and lead
> Thro' prosperous floods his holy urn.

The lineation of 'So draw him home to those that mourn / In vain', in this already Horatian context, recalls one of the most dramatic moments of yet another Horatian poem, *Odes* 3.13. There Horace contemplates the impending death of a young sacrificial goat who will, for that reason, never come to adulthood. The kid's forehead, Horace writes, is 'swollen with budding horns, marking him out for love and warfare – all **in vain**':

> cui frons turgida cornibus
> primis et venerem et proelia destinat:
> **frustra:**

> (4–6)

The sudden irruption of 'frustra' (in vain) at the beginning of the line is widely admired. The tone may be unclear (critics divide over whether the effect is of sympathetic pathos or chilly detachment), but the abrupt evocation of the animal's doom is trenchant. So when Tennyson writes of his own doomed friend in this way –

> So draw him home to those who mourn
> 　In vain:

– his timing of the line-break, where 'in vain' leaps out at the beginning of the line, is perfectly Horatian. No need to press the link too hard: the verbal echo does not mean Arthur Hallam is a sacrificial victim, rather than the accidental victim of an unforeseen stroke. It does, however, show how readily Tennyson can mirror the very movements of Horace's verse, once a Horatian atmosphere is established.

One last Horatian filiation. Horace designed his first book of odes to begin with an ostentatious display of his metrical versatility. Each of the first nine poems of *Odes 1* is written in a different metre: first asclepiad, sapphic, second asclepiad, fourth archilochean, fourth asclepiad, and so on until the ninth poem. This polymetric sequence is an unprecedented feat which classicists refer to as the Parade of Metres. As it happens, the final poem in the sequence, *Odes* 1.9, is the Soracte ode, and as such it constitutes the first appearance of the alcaic strophe in Horace's oeuvre, and indeed in all of Latin literature. After the Soracte ode, all of the other metres hitherto used are repeated elsewhere throughout the work. Horace signals, then, the special importance of the alcaic strophe by saving it to be the last of the nine poems in his Parade of Metres. It makes a striking parallel that Tennyson should have placed the first poem he composed for *In Memoriam*, the first poem whose movements resemble those of the alcaic, in the *ninth* position of the sequence.

Horace half-embraced: *In Memoriam* 89 and 90

A rejoinder to my analysis of the first stanza of *IM* 1.9 might run like this: 'Granted, it suited Victorian critics and writers to associate the In Memoriam stanza with the alcaic. And granted that, if adjusted here and there in just the right way, Tennyson's stanza can be made to catch something like the climactic movement of an alcaic third line, or the dactylic ripple of the fourth. In poems like the one you cite, with an evident Horatian context, then yes, it might make sense to hear a bit of a metrical echo of the alcaic. But surely such stanzas are exceptional rather than typical'. Yes, in a way, since fending off Horace's influence is as important to *In Memoriam* as inviting it.

Against the first stanza of *IM* 9, set the following lines (130.13–16), which find the speaker suffering the paradox of sensing, all at once, proximity to and distance from his dead friend's spirit:

> Far off thou art, but ever nigh;
>   I have thee still, and I rejoice;
>   I prosper, circled with thy voice;
> I shall not lose thee tho' I die.

Tennyson here minimizes his metre's relation to the alcaic. Every line is firmly end-stopped, resisting imitation of Horace's frequent enjambments. The iambic beat predominates (a spondee in the first foot of the first line is the only pronounced departure). We do not find here the combination of metrical resolutions that, in section 9, brought the third and fourth lines so notably closer to the cadences of the alcaic. But at the same time neither is the *sense* of the stanza very Horatian. Tennyson's intimation in this stanza (that his friendship with Hallam will survive mortality) is far from Horace's, that friendship's very value derives in part from the irredeemable finality of death.

This point of difference means that Horace poses a bit of a problem for Tennyson. On the one hand, *In Memoriam*'s pervasive allusions to Horace are appropriate. Many of Horace's odes are celebrations of friendship,[33] or meditations on mortality,[34] often simultaneously, and what is *In Memoriam* if not a contemplation of friendship in light of a friend's early and unforeseen death? It would have been odd for Tennyson not to have used Horace as a reference-point. On the other hand, though, Horace is in many ways not a fitting model. For *In Memoriam* is also an exploration of certain kinds of Christian belief, and in the end professes an – equivocal, very complicated – faith in immortality and the ultimate permanence of human relationships that Horace, resolutely this-worldly and convinced of the finality of death, cannot be called on to endorse.

This gap between Horatian and Christian morality might have undermined the poem, but Tennyson knows how to generate from it a productive tension. Throughout *In Memoriam*, though Horace is regularly invoked, thematically and formally, he is only ever half-embraced: the poem alludes to Horace in part to resist, and make a point of resisting, too close an identification with him. Horace has too much to say about friendship and death for Tennyson to ignore him, and the particular shapeliness of Horace's tight stanzas suits Tennyson's lyrical and meditative cast of mind. Much of his poem's drama, though, springs from Tennyson's struggle to resist the intellectual persuasiveness of materialism, especially as expressed in terms of contemporary scientific theories that anticipated Darwin. For all the beauty of Horace's odes, for all their worldly wisdom and consolatory powers, their force depends in part on the confidence with which they insist on acknowledging death as annihilation. A certain kind of unbeliever finds that frankness salutary. But even a deeply admiring Christian such as Tennyson, who, as we have seen in the previous chapter, identifies with Horace in many ways, must draw the line at Horace's philosophy.

Two adjacent sections of *In Memoriam*, 89 and 90, bring out the point. In them we find, expressively juxtaposed, two distinctly Horatian poems. Section 89 in particular reads like one of Horace's odes transposed into an English frame. It is set in the Tennyson family home at Somersby in the Lincolnshire countryside. Here, the speaker reminisces, his beloved Arthur used to come to escape London, exult in the glories of nature, drink and dine *all'aperto*, and philosophize. All the elements of classical symposium are there, except those obnoxious to Christian sensibilities (such as *hetairai*, the women trained to wait on and entertain the men at such gatherings). It is a sort of version of a Horatian sympotic poem, the kind that reaches its apogee in the great ode to Maecenas (*Odes* 3.29) which, as we saw in the previous chapter, finds the poet enticing his illustrious friend to abandon his business in Rome for Horace's villa in the countryside. Tennyson makes the link to Horace's poem explicit: arriving at Somersby, he says, Hallam used to shake off 'the dust and din and steam of town' (8), words that allude to, and half-translate, Horace's appeal to Maecenas to abandon 'the smoke and wealth and noise of Rome' ('fumum et opes strepitumque Romae', 12). As if to make allusion double-sure, there's this happy memory: that it was bliss, back when Hallam was alive,

> Beyond the bounding hill to stray,
>   And break the livelong summer day
> With banquet in the distant woods;
>
> (30–2)

That phrase 'break the day' (the sense is 'to while away the hours') is not English idiom, but Latin. In this context it recalls a line from yet another alcaic Horatian ode (2.7), addressed to Horace's friend Pompeius. The two men had served together under Brutus at the battle of Philippi in 42 BCE, but thereafter taken different paths: Horace back to Rome and civilian life, while Pompeius had remained abroad and a soldier until a complicated political settlement (around 30 BCE) permitted his return to Italy. The two men had been parted for perhaps more than a decade, and Horace rejoices at the reunion with his friend (1–8):

> O saepe mecum tempus in ultimum
> deducte Bruto militiae duce,
>   quis te redonavit Quiritem
>   dis patriis Italoque caelo,
>
> Pompei, meorum prime sodalium?
> cum quo morantem saepe diem mero
>   fregi coronatus nitentis
>   malobathro Syrio capillos.

My friend, so often carried with me into moments of the utmost peril when Brutus was in charge of operations, who has restored you to your father's gods and the sky of Italy, to be a citizen once again? Pompeius, dearest of my comrades, many's the time that in your company I have broken the long day's tedium with neat wine, my garlanded hair glistening with Syrian perfume.

What's crucial is the Latin phrase *diem mero / fregi* (6–7) 'I have broken the day with wine', in the sense of breaking up the tedium of the day by drinking. This idiom Tennyson picks up in *In Memoriam* 89 as 'break the livelong summer day / With banquet'. Is 'break the day' (as opposed to 'break up the day') quite idiomatic English? No, but it is pitch-perfect: a quiet but distinct Latinism, a momentary slip into a Roman accent, effortlessly linking the English poem to Horace's ode, paying Tennyson and Hallam the compliment of association with Horace and Pompeius. Two specific verbal echoes, then, to two specific odes (both written in alcaics) make clear that section 89 ought to be read in light of Horace's sympotic poetry celebrating friendship. The Roman predecessor's feelings are neatly mirrored in the English poet's lyric. So far the resonance between ancient and modern is harmonious, and the allusion appears straightforward.

There is a touch of discord in Tennyson's movement between Roman and English planes. The point of the Horatian allusions lies more in the disjunction than in the obvious similarities. Horace's friends, Maecenas and Pompeius, are not dead but alive: Horace can expect the company of one of them soon enough, and enjoys his reunion with the other right now. The pronouns and verbs in both of Horace's poems are in the second person. Tennyson's friend, on the other hand, is dead; he can only address his poem to the trees Hallam used to love, and all the pronouns associated with Hallam himself are in the third person – a disturbing discontinuity from the Horatian models. Contrast this kind of allusiveness with Tennyson's later poem 'To the Reverend F. D. Maurice', which also alludes to, and virtually translates, line 12 of the Latin, 'fumum et opes stepitumque Romae', this time as 'far from the smoke and noise of town.' In 'Maurice', the allusion signals a happy harmony between an ancient and a modern friendship. But the very same allusion in *In Memoriam* 89 produces dissonance, not harmony: Horace's relation to Maecenas is not snugly apposite to Tennyson and Hallam, since Tennyson has lost his friend to death. Horatian allusion suits 'Maurice' with a neatness that does not obtain in the elegy to Hallam. It's natural for *In Memoriam* to evoke the friendship-poetry of Horace, but the evocations reveal Horace's inadequacy to Tennyson's predicament: they do not quite fit. Horace can console, but only up to a point.

If section 89 reads like a Horatian sympotic ode, its neighbour, section 90, is like a Horatian meditation on death, and very much like one in particular, the so-called Postumus ode (*Odes* 2.14). 'Ah, Postumus, Postumus,' the poem begins, 'the fleeting years slip by, nor will piety check the onset of wrinkles, old age, and invincible death'. This unflinching acknowledgement of death's inevitability is wholly characteristic of Horace. The implication is that facing the brutal facts is better than repairing to euphemism or consolatory bromides. The ode impressed itself on Tennyson's imagination, especially the final two stanzas of the poem (21–8), which are memorably unsparing:

liquenda tellus et domus et placens
uxor, neque harum quas colis arborum
    te praeter invisas cupressos
      ulla brevem dominum sequetur:

absumet heres Caecuba dignior
servata centum clavibus et mero
    tinget pavimentum superbo,
      pontificum potiore cenis.

Earth must be left behind, and home, and beloved wife; and of all the trees that you cultivate none except the abhorrent cypress will follow you, their short-lived master. Your heir, who deserves it better, will use up the Caecuban [wine] that you have locked away with a hundred keys, and he will stain your expensive floor with that proud wine, which is choicer than the pontiff's banquets.

Here we have not just an insistence on death's inevitability (which Christianity affirms), but also of death's irredeemability (which Christianity denies). Moreover, even if you could be redeemed from death, it would not be well with you: you would return to find everything changed in your absence, and that all you held dear had fallen into the hands of your indifferent heirs. All the better, Horace avers, that you *can't* come back from the dead.

So it is a little surprising to find that precisely this poem underlies *In Memoriam* 90, in which Tennyson considers the distress that might result if the dead, including his own Arthur Hallam, really could return to the world, hoping to re-inhabit the beloved scenes and resume the society of their earlier lives.[35] Would they really be welcome? Oh, everyone in bereavement *claims* to long for reunion with their loved ones:

'Twas well, indeed, when warm with wine,
   To pledge them with a kindly tear,
   To talk them o'er, to wish them here,
To count their memories half divine;

(9–12)

But such a resumption would be impossible: they would no longer belong in a world that had moved on from them:

But if they came who past away,
   Behold their brides in other hands;
   The hard heir strides about their lands,
And will not yield them for a day.

Yea, tho' their sons were none of these,
    Not less the yet-loved sire would make
    Confusion worse than death, and shake
The pillars of domestic peace.

(13–20)

This is exactly the alarming premiss of the last two stanzas of Horace's Postumus ode. When Horace warns his friend that he must resign himself to losing not only earth and home, but also his 'beloved wife', he throws strong emphasis on this final loss by separating, through enjambment, the word 'uxor' (wife) from its modifier and isolating it starkly at the beginning of the next line (21–2):

liquenda tellus et domus et placens
uxor

Tennyson seizes on that detail and develops its implications with 'behold their brides in other hands'. That elaboration (that the dead must not only relinquish their brides, but see them pass into the hands of other men) is warranted in two ways. One is a matter of biography: Arthur Hallam was to have married Tennyson's sister Emily who, less than a decade after his death, and eight years before the publication of *In Memoriam*, did indeed become someone else's wife, a navy man called Richard Jesse. (Their firstborn son was called Arthur Henry Hallam.) There is also a textual warrant: 'behold their brides in other hands' draws on the stanza of Horace's ode that imagines an indifferent heir depleting Postumus' cherished wine collection and carelessly staining his expensive floor with it. In Horace the dead man's wine, in Tennyson the dead man's wife, falls into other hands.

This points to a second, more precise, allusion: with 'the hard heir strides about their lands', Tennyson distinctly echoes 'absumet heres Caecuba dignior' (your heir, who deserves it better, will use up the Caecuban wine). As such, when Tennyson writes this couplet – 'Behold their brides in other hands; / The hard heir strides about their lands', the marvellous tightness of the rhyme, the proximity of the interior B-rhyme, makes the Horatian allusion more intense. It fuses into a single rhyme two specific points of reference to the Latin ode. It is worth noting, too, another Horatian echo. Horace tells Postumus he must leave behind 'all of the trees that you cultivate', which calls to mind not section 90 but 89, whose speaker dolefully addresses not his dead friend, but the elms and sycamores that Hallam had once loved and must now forsake.

Tennyson is in that sense Horace's heir, his literary heir, though he is anything but indifferent and anything but 'hard'. And yet here again there is something uneasy in his inheritance of Horace's poem. Part of the problem is clear enough: Horace's ode insists on the finality of death, and however much Tennyson may admire and wish to emulate him, too complete an assimilation of Horace on this point would not suit a poem that affirms, however equivocally, the Christian promise of resurrection. (The very equivocation is un-Horatian.) A trickier problem is Horace's claim that the dead not only return no more, but that were it possible, reunion with living loved ones would prove disastrous. The anachronism of your reappearance, Horace indicates, would cause either resentment (among those who thought their inheritances secure) or unbearable confusion (among loved ones unable to reconcile this figure from the past with their present, altered, affections). Tennyson will have none of this. He raises the Horatian notion in order to reject it. He protests that he would not at all resent Arthur Hallam's return to the world. On the contrary, he craves it:

> Ah dear, but come thou back to me:
>   Whatever change the years have wrought,
>   I find not yet one lonely thought
> That cries against my wish for thee.
>
> (21–4)

This amounts to a repudiation of Horace's position. It makes definitive a misgiving Tennyson had raised in the first two stanzas:

> He tasted love with half his mind
>   Nor ever drank the inviolate spring
>   Where nighest heaven, who first could fling
> This bitter seed among mankind,
>
> That could the dead, whose dying eyes
>   Were closed with wail, resume their life,
>   They would but find in child and wife
> An iron welcome when they rise:
>
> (1–8)

That is: 'He who first suggested that the dead would not be welcome if they came to life again knew not the highest love.'[36] So who is that 'he' who first proposed so odious a notion? Tennyson names no names; from a purely rhetorical view it's effective to leave obscured in the mists of time the author of so obnoxious a doctrine. But anybody who catches the references to the Postumus ode will be tempted to propose, as I think I am the first to do, that it is Horace he's quarrelling with. If Horace was not strictly the 'first to fling / This bitter seed among mankind', nevertheless he certainly repeated it, and gave it devastatingly articulate expression in the elegant alcaic stanzas of his ode. That's to say: Tennyson repudiates Horace in all but name, as the perpetuator, if not the originator, of the malign notion that reunion of the departed and the bereaved would be an evil rather than a good. Such an idea could not come from someone who had fully loved: 'He tasted love with half his mind'.

We can draw a line from Tennyson to Wilfred Owen and his 'Dulce Et Decorum Est', as discussed in the first chapter of this book. Both poets invoke Horace in part because their themes (patriotism and war, friendship, mortality) readily call to mind passages from the *Odes* which are *loci classici* of those commonplace subjects. In both cases the allusion to Horace involves some kind of repudiation. This brings in the matter of prosody, since the relationship of both poets to Horace involves their way of inheriting the alcaic metre. If Owen knew the alcaic and meant to distort its metrical pattern, then he is a 'hard heir'. When Horace appears, as it were from the dead, to visit the twentieth century and inhabit a modern poem, Owen gives his predecessor an 'iron welcome', partly by doing violence to the Horatian metrical inheritance as he disfigures the alcaic metre. 'Behold your *words* in other hands, Horace'. Like the cold-blooded heir who inherits Postumus' wine only to stain the dead man's expensive floor with it, Wilfred Owen inherits Horace's words – 'dulce et decorum est pro patria mori' – only to defile them. If Owen did not understand the alcaic metre and was not trying to defile it, the fact remains that he did unmake it, and the metrical misquotation is a fact of the poem. In either case the poetic heir has had his own way with the metrical inheritance.

Tennyson's own repudiation of Horace is subtler, and its tonal effects are far more delicate. His is generally in sympathy with Horace: the In Memoriam stanza's approximation to the alcaic suits the broad overlapping of Tennysonian and Horatian themes throughout the work as a whole. But in specific poems such as 89 and 90, the effect of Horatian allusion is to demonstrate that a complete embrace of Horace is impossible: Horace's ultimate disbelief forbids it. 'I sometimes think it half a sin / To put in words the grief I feel', and it would have amounted, not to a sin, but a lapse of discretion, had Tennyson, in *In Memoriam*, embraced the alcaic as clearly and explicitly as he did in later poems. Here, tactfully, he gives us Horace's metre 'in outline and no more'. The half-embrace has its formal manifestation in an English stanza-form sufficiently like the alcaic to call it to mind and sometimes to imitate it closely, but still sufficiently different to resist a more complete metrical identification, such as in the five alcaic-style poems Tennyson would later write.

Could Horace 'resume his life' and revisit the world to see what Tennyson, his heir, had done with the alcaic strophe, he would find his signature metre altered, but not despoiled in the manner of the hard and heedless heir that he had imagined. It is a feat of keen textual consciousness that these ideas are conveyed in the very metrical form in which Tennyson writes.

'Who would keep the ancient form?'

In Memoriam is not 'about' poetic form. But one of the poem's characteristic words, 'form', and others like it, such as 'measure', encourage readers to keep questions of poetic form in mind. At times this amounts very nearly to allegorizing the In Memoriam stanza as an emblem of the larger concerns of the poem.

Nothing could seem further from the inner world of *In Memoriam* – its unremitting rumination, its fluctuations of hope and despair, its interiority only occasionally broken by lashings of equally volatile English weather – than a brilliant military triumph in the sun-smitten eastern Mediterranean in the first century BCE. Yet Horace's Cleopatra ode (*Odes* 1.37), which celebrates Octavian's defeat of Antony and Cleopatra, nevertheless played a part in the making of *In Memoriam*. The stanzas in question (*IM* 105.17–24) find Tennyson, on the third Christmas since Hallam's death, in no mood for festive gaiety in the absence of his friend:

> But let no footstep beat the floor,
>   Nor bowl of wassail mantle warm;
>   For who would keep the ancient form
> Thro' which the spirit breathes no more?
>
> Be neither song, nor game, nor feast;
>   Nor harp be touch'd, nor flute be blown;
>   No dance, no motion, save alone
> What lightens in the lucid east.

'But let no footstep beat the floor' picks up the opening words of the Cleopatra ode: 'Nunc est bibendum, nunc pede libero / pulsanda tellus' (Now let the drinking begin! Now let us thump the ground with unfettered feet'). Octavian's victory, Horace declares, means that war-time austerity can at last give way to celebration. Aside from that single word 'no', Tennyson's 'Let no footstep beat the floor' neatly translates the distinctly un-English idiom 'pede libero / pulsanda tellus'. Why would Tennyson go out of his way to allude to Horace's Cleopatra ode, when there are any number of English ways of saying, 'Now's not the time for dancing'?

One plausible answer: with that allusion, Tennyson once again simultaneously invites and fends off Horatian associations. The fending off is clear enough: Tennyson's 'no' takes a Horatian moment of celebration and abruptly cancels it. As in sections 89 and 90, what suited Horace (enjoyment of living friends, but insisting on the permanence of death) does not quite suit Tennyson's poem. In this case Horace's call for joyous abandon ('Now let the drinking begin! Now let us thump the ground with unfettered feet') is the more pointedly rejected because expressed in Horatian terms. The question of embracing or rejecting the Horatian inheritance is complicated by a point of diction: the use of the word 'form':

> But let no footstep beat the floor,
>> Nor bowl of wassail mantle warm;
>> For who would keep the ancient form
> Thro' which the spirit breathes no more?

'Who would keep the ancient form?' The use of 'form' here touches the plane of textuality in the same way that 'measure' had done in 'the measure of my grief.' On the denotative level, the last two lines of this stanza ask: 'What is the point, what is the propriety, of keeping up our customary Christmas celebrations ("the ancient form") now that the friend whose presence animated them is dead?' Read as evidence of the poet's formal consciousness, though, the lines can be parsed like this: 'Why would I, an English poet of the nineteenth century, express my bereavement in a metre that approximates, and in some sense preserves, a verse form used by poets of remote pagan antiquity, the fossil remnant of outworn creeds?' What's at issue is not only the propriety of the proposed Christmas celebrations (whether such traditional observances should be preserved or jettisoned) but the propriety of the metre (whether a Greco-Roman verse form, or a version of it, suits or disgraces the modern Christian poem). The question of continuity is especially vivid in this instance, since the line 'Nunc est bibendum, nunc pede libero' is itself an inheritance, indeed also a near-translation, from a surviving fragment of Alcaeus (Campbell 332.1–2), in which the death of one of the poet's political rivals prompts a call for celebration:

> νῦν χρῆ μεθύσθην καί τινα πὲρ βίαν
> πώνην, ἐπειδὴ κάτθανε Μύρσιλος.

nun chrē methusthēn kai tina per bian
pōnēn, epeidē katthane Myrsilos.

Now must men get drunk and drink with all their strength, since Myrsilus has
died.[37]

Though these are the only two extant lines, they show the poem was composed
in alcaics. Horace effectively quotes these lines in his Cleopatra ode ('Now let the
drinking begin! Now let us thump the ground with unfettered feet'), to which
Tennyson himself clearly alludes with 'But let no footstep beat the floor'. This
literary pedigree makes Tennyson's question ('But who would keep the ancient
form?') trebly pointed. Tennyson's own poem does indeed keep the ancient form,
in the sense of preserving the themes, and approximating the metre, of two
ancient poems, one Greek, one Latin. But this act of literary reception is
only partial, as it rejects the celebration enjoined by the ancient poems, and
uses an English metre whose relationship to the 'ancient form' is ambiguous.
The use of the word 'form' joins the metrical technique to the larger
moral problem: Tennyson's reluctance to identify with, fully to embrace, his
Horatian and Alcaic antecedents. 'Do we indeed desire the dead / Should still be
near us at our side?' (*IM* 51.1–2) The philosophical question has a formal
dimension: do I want Horace's metre to be insistently and unambiguously
present in this poem?

Swinburne's 'Sapphics' and re-membering a metrical body

A celebrated poem by another, slightly younger, Victorian poet offers at once a
parallel and a useful counter-example. The poet is Charles Algernon Swinburne,
whose speaker, in 'Sapphics' (1866), experiences, in vision, among much else, a
visitation from Aphrodite:

Saw the white implacable Aphrodite,
Saw the hair unbound and the feet unsandalled
Shine as fire of sunset on western waters;
    Saw the reluctant

Feet, the straining plumes of the doves that drew her,
Looking always, looking with necks reverted,
Back to Lesbos, back to the hills whereunder
    Shone Mitylene;

Heard the flying feet of the Loves behind her
Make a sudden thunder upon the waters,
As the thunder flung from the strong unclosing
    Wings of a great wind.

(9–20)[38]

Striking as Aphrodite's epiphany is, it is preceded, and possibly upstaged, by a visitation in different form: Sappho's *metrical* form. For Swinburne is writing English sapphics of unrivalled fluency, metrical dexterity, and quantitative richness. 'Here for once,' says Carne-Ross (having tested his ear on dozens of examples of English attempts at classical metres from the sixteenth century onwards), 'here for once is a line that moves and feels like Sappho's.'[39]

In her own venturesome reading of the poem, though, Yopie Prins collapses the distinction between Sappho the poet and her sapphic strophe. Her argument turns on the frequent coincidence of Greek terms for poetry and parts of the body. 'Melē' in Greek means both bodily limbs and lyric poetry; 'podes', 'dactyloi', 'kōla' are feet, fingers, and limbs, but also units of poetic metre. An accident of history – that most of Sappho's poetic *corpus* (to keep up the figure) survives only in mutilated fragments – allows for conceiving of Sappho as dismembered. To re-member her would be to reconstruct her metre. In Swinburne's poems, the sapphic metre (melē, 'lyrics') compels the presence of Sappho herself, reconstituted as her metrical body (melē, 'limbs'). In this way of thinking, Sappho is her metre. The real miracle of Swinburne's poem is not the conjuring of Aphrodite but the reconstitution of Sappho on English soil, in the modern age, through the sheer force of the sapphic metre.[40]

Prins notices that a certain fragment of Sappho survives only as a quotation in the Alexandrian scholar Hephaistion's treatise on metres as an example of the Aeolic dactylic tetrameter. Ingeniously, she observes that it 'has been preserved precisely because of its metrical appeal'. Hephaistion's scholarly treatment submits Sappho to metrical *analysis* (whose literal meaning is 'undoing'), but quoting and so preserving her verses is a reconstitution of part of an undone metrical body: 'Hephaistion repeats the rhythmic disarticulation and rearticulation of the Sapphic body, and turns Sappho herself into a metrical body that is manifested *through* and *as* metre.'[41] Maybe so, and in that sense the last lines of Owen's 'Dulce Et Decorum Est', with its metrical misquotation of the alcaic metre, would constitute an un-doing of Horace himself, a dis-membering instead of remembering.

Yet whereas Carne-Ross finds in 'Sapphics' a metrical triumph, Prins detects signs of a kind of failure, of which the poem itself is aware. She reads the dramatic enjambment from lines 12–13 ('Saw the reluctant // Feet') as punningly dramatizing the difficulty of hauling an ancient Greek quantitative metre ('feet') across the gap of time and space that separates it from the modern world: 'Swinburne is straining to recreate the melody of Sappho in sapphic stanzas, a vehicle of transport not quite as automatic as Aphrodite's chariot.'[42] What's more, the metre and its music come into English not only reluctantly, but merely partially. Swinburne's poem is aware of its own partial success. The music of Sappho does not quite come through in English. Swinburne's Sappho strangely *sees*, rather than hears, her music: 'only beheld among them / Soar, as a bird soars / / Newly-fledged, her visible song, a marvel / Made of perfect sound and exceeding passion, / Sweetly shapen' (55–9). For Prins, Sappho's song is 'visible' because here, in Swinburne, it is reconstituted as writing, and in a language, English, which cannot replicate the quantitative character of the ancient Greek prosody.

It is probably true that even the great majority of English readers, even were they familiar with the pattern of the sapphic stanza, would have a hard time recognizing it by ear alone. She adduces a principle of John Hollander that the English ear needs help from the eye (that is, to see the shape of a stanza on the page) to persuade itself that it can hear the complicated metrical patterns of classical verse replicated in English. Pressing that point, she concludes that despite Swinburne's metrical adroitness, 'the meter of the sapphic stanza' remains, in the end, not a sonic but 'a graphic phenomenon . . . . a written form that appeals to the eye rather than the ear, an inscription rather than an utterance.'[43] However superb Swinburne's approximation of the sapphic stanza (and it is a 'marvel'), it must fall back on patterns of stressed and unstressed syllables, mere analogies of the true Greek quantities. The result is 'a mark of their absence', a visual notation that plots the pattern of sounds we can no longer hear.[44]

I take Prins's 'reading Sappho as if she were a metrical body'[45] as illuminating of Tennyson's metre in *In Memoriam*. I would put it more cautiously, but Horace, too, can be read as a metrical body, especially with respect to the alcaic strophe. The alcaic is his signature lyric metre: it is, in Prins's terms, Horace's body. To reconstitute his strophe in English is in that sense to try to reconstitute Horace in the modern world. It is one thing for *In Memoriam* to invoke Horace semantically, as it often does, by quoting his words or taking up the themes and situations of his odes. It is another thing to imitate his metre, for this is to bring Horace *bodily* into the modern poem. That conjured presence, like Sappho's in 'Sapphics', is reluctant and partial: any English analogue of the alcaic is in part 'visible song', its audible utterance requiring, to be perceived, the assistance of graphic inscription. The In Memoriam stanza is in that way also a marker of an absence, a song that cannot quite be clearly heard, and of a presence that cannot quite be completely recovered.

I wrote above, though, that 'Sapphics' offers not only a parallel, but a counter-example, to *In Memoriam*. For all that 'Sapphics' involves demonstrating the limitations of re-embodying sapphic song, for all that it remains 'less a reincarnation of that form than its spectral emanation',[46] it nevertheless differs from *In Memoriam* in both intent and effect. Swinburne pointedly sets out to re-create the sapphic metre as nearly as the English language and his own talents permit. His intent, whether he succeeds or not, is to try to compel the presence of Sappho by embodying her as rhythm. He wants to conjure Sappho. Despite her haughtiness, she does appear in the poem. Imperfect as it is – merely in English, merely stressed-based, relying heavily on its graphic element – the metre of 'Sapphics' really is the sapphic metre in English.

Not so in Tennyson, whose task is trickier: he has as much reason for wanting to fend off Horace's spectral presence as to invite it. To faithfully reproduce Horace's metre in *In Memoriam*, to come as close to alcaics as Swinburne comes to sapphics, would give Horace's voice too great a place. In 'Sapphics', the speaker is as it were possessed by the sapphic rhythms: 'eros is allegorized as rhythmic effect',[47] and the speaker is in its power. Tennyson could not allow such a thing in *In Memoriam*. Horace's insistence that friendships must end with death, and can never be redeemed, is as uncompromising as Sappho's voice is overpoweringly erotic. It cannot be reconciled with Tennyson's faith. Part of the pathos of the metre in 'Sapphics' is that Swinburne wants to fully voice sapphic song but must concede the impossibility. Whereas part of the prosodic feeling of *In Memoriam* is of holding back, lest it come too close to the alcaic, so close that the power of a re-membered, re-collected Horace should compromise the emphasis on Christian redemption. It comes close enough as it is.

'Changes wrought on form and face'

English approximations of classical metres always carry a strain of pathos, simply because they can only ever be mere approximations. That fact is profoundly relevant to another network of themes in *In Memoriam*. If Tennyson's predicament were simply to deal with the grief of bereavement, and having to choose whether to side with Horace or Christianity on the question of immortality, then *In Memoriam* would be a much simpler poem than it is. But Tennyson also frets over a murkier problem: the question of the persistence, mutability, and transplantability of 'forms'. In most instances the 'form' in question is the personhood of his dead friend. If Arthur Hallam now partakes of immortality, what *form* does he now take? Has he retained his individual character, or has he now blent, indistinguishable, into the cosmos? Has he progressed so far beyond mere mortals as to make any putative association with Tennyson pointless? Is his form far off or near? Has he a body? Is he embraceable?[48] At some points in the poem, this concern for the state of his friend's form is generalized: what if recent scientific notions are right, that no species, including humans, has a fixed form? What continuity may hold between ancient forms of species and their evolved modern versions? If spirits were transplanted from this world to the next, could they meaningfully retain their old forms in that new context?

Each of these questions about human and other natural forms implies questions about the persistence and mutability of the alcaic form: whether it can and ought to survive into modern English; whether its form should be fixed or mutable; whether embracing it compromises individual identity. Among the many passages where the question of changes in poetic form can be felt behind broader themes is section 82:

> I wage not any feud with Death
>> For changes wrought on form and face;
>> No lower life that earth's embrace
> May breed with him, can fright my faith.
>
> Eternal process moving on,
>> From state to state the spirit stalks,
>> And these are but the shatter'd stalks,
> Or ruin'd chrysalis of one.

(1–8)

I accept, says Tennyson, that 'eternal process ... from state to state' – from this world to the next – means that Arthur must change his form, that his body (at least) is a mere discarded casing, as of a chrysalis, or support, as of the stalk of a plant. But the seed of a dead plant may be transplanted and take root elsewhere:

> Nor blame I death, because he bare
>> The use of virtue out of earth:

> I know transplanted human worth
> Will bloom to profit, otherwhere.

'Transplanted' here is the operative word. On the textual level, it implies a hopeful response to the question 'who would keep the ancient form?' Though the proper Horatian alcaic may have died, it is possible to bear 'the use of virtue out of death'. The old stanza-form can be transplanted into another language in a remote time and place, and 'bloom to profit' there. My interpretation wins some warrant from the fact that 'transplanting' is the very term that Tennyson himself would later use, in 'To Jebb', as a figure for the reception of classical themes and metrical forms in English literature. There, as we saw in Chapter 3, he uses the image of transplanting to describe the survival of an episode of Greek literature: his adaptation of the *Homeric Hymn to Demeter*:

> So may this legend for awhile,
> If greeted by your classic smile,
>   Though dead in its Trinacrian Enna,
> Blossom again on a colder isle.

Which transplanting included, in these very verses, the transplanting into English soil of a metrical form, a version of the alcaic strophe, which, 'though dead' with respect to Latin, might, in this and other English versions that Tennyson would write, 'blossom again on a colder isle'. So it makes sense to find, in *IM* 82, the terms 'transplanting' and 'form' in close proximity, where the primary sense of 'form' in this poem is the physical constitution of a human body. 'Blossom again on a colder isle' chimes with 'I know transplanted human worth / Will bloom to profit, otherwhere' as a way of accepting 'changes wrought on form and face'. Confidence in Arthur Hallam's survival (in some form) has a formal analogue: that Horace's stanza, transplanted, can survive too.

And yet in the very next stanza, a recursive Tennyson undermines that bit of hopefulness:

> For this alone on Death I wreak
>   The wrath that garners in my heart;
>   He put our lives so far apart
> We cannot hear each other speak.

(13–16)

Tennyson's anxiousness about the transience, mutability, or permanence of human form returns. And, as here, it is usually expressed in terms linked to similar concerns about poetic form. 'We cannot hear each other speak': this sense of being unable to quite communicate emerges often in the poem. In an earlier section, the speaker, dreaming, receives the visit of a consoling 'angel':

> He reached the glory of a hand,
>   That seemed to touch it into leaf:
>   The voice was not the voice of grief,
> The words were hard to understand.

(69.17–20)

'We cannot hear each other speak', 'the words were hard to understand' – again and again throughout *In Memoriam* Hallam's presence can be sensed, but full communication is just out of reach.

So too with Horace: the In Memoriam stanza conjures the great poet of friendship and mortality, summons him across time and space to enrich Tennyson's poem with his thematic associations and historical perspective and poetic authority. But Horace cannot fully enter into the (precariously, but in the end distinctly) Christian frame of *In Memoriam*. The effect of being *precariously* Christian is a vital quality of the poem, and the poet's willingness to entertain, and to at least risk succumbing to, Horatian notions of the finality of death is reflected in the way that the In Memoriam strophe intermittently approaches, and then recedes from, correspondence with the alcaic. Horace's metrical presence in the poem is like Arthur Hallam's: spectral, suspended between two worlds; invoked, sensed, as if at any moment about to fully materialize but never actually doing so, and so always remaining separate. So too the alcaic hovers within hailing of the In Memoriam strophe, but the communication remains indistinct. It's the genius of the In Memoriam stanza to strike that balance, so apposite to the relationship of the bereaved poet to his friend: it evokes the constant presence of a ghost – the alcaic – though all the while keeping separate.

The problem posed by Horace's Postumus ode, and Tennyson's remonstrance in *IM* 90, is this: if the deceased should manage to return, would he be recognizable or welcome in his new form? That question is framed at the level of metre in *In Memoriam*. If Horace's metre reappeared in England nineteen centuries later, would it be recognizable in its new form? Would it be welcome? The answers, in the case of Horace's alcaic strophe, are yes and no: yes, recognizable, sometimes clearly glimpsed; but no, not completely welcome. In Tennyson's own words (87.14): 'The same, but not the same.'

'The Ear Grows Dissatisfied'

Robert Bridges, W. H. Auden

'Far-sought effects'

Robert Bridges, Poet Laureate, died at 85 in April of 1930. That same year Faber and Faber brought out the debut volume of a twenty-three-year-old poet called W. H. Auden. The historical coincidence links two of the century's leading connoisseurs of 'learned rhythms', as Bridges called the compound metres of classical lyric. (Auden, for his part, in his inaugural lecture as Professor of Poetry at Oxford, championed 'complicated verse-forms of great technical difficulty'.)[1] Both loved the alcaic strophe and wanted to bring it over into English. Bridges was thwarted, but in his pursuit of something else – his experiments with syllabic verse – lay the seeds of the younger poet's success. Auden was to pioneer a flourishing of alcaics in English that continues to this day. His victory, though, would be a sort of pyrrhic one, partly for technical reasons (it was achieved by sacrificing the audible dimension of the alcaic strophe), and partly because of cultural changes that diminished readers' capacity to appreciate his success. As such, this chapter returns again and again to two related questions: the extent to which complex metrical forms such as the alcaic in English can really be heard, as opposed to merely scanned; and what place alcaics can have in a late-twentieth century culture increasingly losing touch with the classical inheritance.

The case of Bridges and Auden brings to the fore an uncomfortable proposition, implied throughout this book, most strongly in the previous chapter. That is: it is a matter of some doubt whether the complex patterns of classical lyric metres, when adapted to English verse, can actually be heard. Yopie Prins's analysis of Swinburne's 'Sapphics' strongly implies that even in that masterful English adaptation, Sappho's metrical voice is largely unheard, at least until our apprehension is conditioned by visual clues, such as the graphic figure of the stanza on the page, and contextual clues (in Swinburne's case, the very title

'Sapphics'). On this line of reasoning, the pleasure we take in the stricter versions of English alcaics, such as those of Mary Sidney or Arthur Hugh Clough, is rather more abstract than auditory. Equipped with visual and contextual clues, we agree to listen for metrical pattern. But do we hear it, or are we constructing in the imagination an alcaic rhythm that English stress-based verse cannot convincingly bring home to the ear alone?

Most people who can pick up on the beat of English poetry at all tend to be perfectly satisfied with the familiar iamb. Some listeners may be able to hear and appreciate other metres, such as the trochees of Blake's 'Tyger' or Poe's 'Raven', or the gangly dactyls of limericks. To ask more of the average English reader is to require overcoming centuries of literary acculturation. The problem arises even with the familiar forms. 'There are only a few skilful and happy readers of Milton', Samuel Johnson thought, 'who enable their audience to perceive where the lines end and begin', and he admitted that 'blank verse seems blank verse only to the eye'.[2] The lyrics of Alcaeus and Sappho were designed for vocal performance, but what about English alcaics on the page? 'Did the printing press', asks Christopher Ricks, 'minister to a situation in which literature itself could not but tyrannize through the eye?'[3] If the audible dimension of even English iambic pentameter is already vexed, how can English classical metres be expected to be available to the ear?

This problem caught up to the metrical connoisseur Robert Bridges, in the course of a famous tract on the minutiae of poetic metre. 'While everyone', he wrote in the 1894 version of *Milton's Prosody*, 'has a liking for the fundamental common rhythms',

> it is only after long familiarity that the ear grows dissatisfied, and wishes them to be broken; and there are few persons indeed who can take such natural delight in rhythm for its own sake, that they can follow with pleasure a learned rhythm which is very rich in its variety.[4]

The salient words, brought into uncomfortable proximity, are 'pleasure' and 'learned'. Many readers take those terms as roughly antithetical. It does not make sense to expect readers of English verse to crave a 'learned' classical metre such as the alcaic. It may produce pleasure of an arid intellectual kind. How many of us, though, even those of us trained to recognize the complexities of compound classical metres, are really taking 'natural delight in rhythm for its own sake?'

On the same page, Bridges conceded it was 'easy to see how the far-sought effects of the greatest master in any art may lie beyond the general taste'.[5] He was referring specifically to the eccentric prosody of *Samson Agonistes*, but could just as well have been pointing to classical lyric metres. Certainly the metrical subtleties of the Horatian alcaic I describe in the second chapter of this book qualify precisely as the 'far-sought effects of a great master'. Milton may have been content to address his verse to a 'fit audience and few', but Bridges implies that, by the dawn of the twentieth century, those fit to detect the master-strokes of Milton's prosody had become a very few indeed. Some of Bridges's contemporaries positively discouraged complex metres. A 1904 essay on 'The Future of English Verse', by Bridges's influential friend Henry Newbolt, championed a simple understanding of English prosody that emphasized the beat and dispensed with fussing about metrical feet and other prosodic niceties: 'To everyone but a few makers of authoritative books,' he wrote 'the stresses in English are more important than syllables.'[6] Just count the beats, and leave the complexities to the pedants. Later in his essay the very terminology of classical versification comes in for crude satirizing:

> Look at the simplicity of it: You set out to write a poem, say in short couplets; you put the words of your story in their natural order, with their natural pronunciation and stresses; you do not need to trouble yourself about iambs and trochees; anapests or dactyls are no more to you than anacondas or pterodactyls; when you have got four beats or stresses you have got a line, and you go on to the next.[7]

What could be less metrically demanding than this, either for writers or readers? On the other hand, *Milton's Prosody* emerges incidentally (in its parenthetical asides, such as the ones I have been tracking here) as an expression of dismay at the metrical timidity of English poets and their readers. 'The fundamental common metres' could only delight Bridges for so long before his ear grew dissatisfied and longed for more, and he wished others shared his appetite for the richer and more various 'learned rhythms'. (He will have had very personal reasons for lamenting the limited appeal of 'learned rhythms': he had himself lately been composing English poems in classical measures, including alcaics – about which more below.)

In June 1927 Bridges furnished his friend, R. C. Trevelyan, with a copy of the recently completed draft of *The Testament of Beauty*, composed in a daringly experimental syllabic metre. The metrical form itself engaged Trevelyan's interest: 'As to the metre, there can be no doubt it is admirably suited in movement and emotional effect to the subject matter.'[8] He records, however, his wife's indifference to the metrical experiment:

> My wife, who does not pretend to understand the metre, enjoyed the poem immensely, without troubling herself about the scansion. Perhaps this is the

wisest thing to do; yet I do not myself get the fullest enjoyment out of a poem that is so distinguished for its metre, unless I fully understand the metre as I read it.[9]

These two readers may be taken to represent two very different types. The one does not trouble themselves about scansion. The other cannot fully enjoy a poem *without* grasping the metrical principle, and wants to train themselves to grasp it. That momentary diffidence about the whole notion of prosody's value, that led Trevelyan to float the possibility that to ignore it is 'perhaps ... the wisest thing to do', ought to give pause to somebody like me, writing a book like this. What kind of pleasure am I taking in extraordinarily complex forms, hoping readers will share it? I doubt it is a spontaneous and untutored pleasure. T. S. Eliot wrote of Ezra Pound's poetry that its metrical subtleties required of readers 'a trained ear, or at least a willingness to be trained'.[10] Among Pound's chief virtues is his way with versification. A good ear will carry you some way towards appreciating it, but proper relish requires a feel not only for modern English prosody, but also some grounding, however elementary, in the prosody of those other literatures (Greek, Latin, Anglo-Saxon, Provençal) that Pound sought to echo in his own verse. His critical writings imply that he could have wished every reader had, if not a trained ear, at least a willingness to be trained. Is this too much to ask?

And yet I feel a touch of unease. Though it would be odd for someone in my line of work to suggest that learning and pleasure are enemies, even for me the expression 'learned pleasure' may carry unpleasant undertones. It is not that aesthetic pleasure must be spontaneous in order to be genuine. 'Acquired tastes' are often the best. My wariness has rather to do with false notions of worthiness. Those of us who teach at universities have sometimes encountered students whose willingness to be trained, even when it did not entail notions of snobbery or social climbing, seemed to involve pretending to acquire a taste for kinds of literature they did not really enjoy, but felt obliged to. Some of them persist in dutiful self-deception and become professors of literature themselves, communicating to their own students a similar obligation to feign relish for what they do not enjoy. I do not count myself among them: I really do thrill to the unexpected choriambic riff in a line of Pindar or Pound or Basil Bunting. I do, however, respect the candour of the occasional student who wonders whether what I call appreciative attention to metrical details may really be just a taste for splitting impossibly fine hairs. The implication is that 'no ordinary person' (as Bridges puts it), approaching a stanza as complex as the alcaic, can really pick up its intricacies without erecting a wildly disproportionate scholarly apparatus – prolegomena, painstaking scansion, elaborate and possibly eisegetical interpretation. The metre exists not in itself but only in the preposterous academic superstructure surrounding it. As for Eliot's calling for 'a trained ear, or at least a willingness to be trained', Ben Glaser has astutely noted that 'in wondering about the "willingness to be trained" without explicitly naming the trainer (school, poet, critic, or perhaps ideally the poem?), Eliot reveals a career-long ambivalence about the role of criticism in modern prosody'. Metrical innovation brings along with it the 'paradoxical necessity of criticism as a supplement to the supposedly autonomous' poem.[11]

A similar anxiety about the thin line between metrical sensitivity and mere pedantry surfaces and resurfaces in Bridges. Throughout the various permutations of *Milton's Prosody* (he produced five versions between 1887 and 1921) the gap between 'the general taste' and his own metrical connoisseurship is never far from his mind, and fosters a defensive posture:

> The fact that rhythm is so much more evident than prosody, and is felt to lie so much nearer poetic effects, inclines people to think that prosody is pedantic rubbish, which can only hamper the natural expression of free thought and so on.[12]

Note the exasperated 'and so on'. Of course I am on Bridges's side: one purpose of this book is to defend a certain kind of very complex prosody as a means, rather than a bar, to pleasure and the expression of free thought 'and so on'. It is worth considering, though, how far the charge of pedantry has a point. Close investigation of some particularly knotty aspects of Shelley's versification led even Bridges to this confession:

> A consistent prosody is, however, so insignificant a part in what makes good English poetry, that I find I do not much care myself whether some good poetry be consistent in its versification or not: indeed I find I like some verses better because they do not scan, and thus displease the pedants.[13]

'I like some verses better because they do not scan' is a refreshing provocation. But in acknowledging that there are limits to metrical fastidiousness, Bridges simultaneously makes clear that the pedants of prosody are other people, not himself. He does not think that prosodic niceties are 'mere pedantic rubbish'.

Bridges was not alone in worrying that readers were missing the pleasures of prosody. George Saintsbury, by far the most aesthetically sensitive contemporary critic of versification, in his landmark 1910 study of English metre, urged readers (with characteristic cheer and gusto) to attend not only to poetry's beats but to 'read scanningly', that is, to discern and relish the counterpoint between beats and the disposition of metrical feet. In other words, he enjoined a willingness to be trained:

> I hope it is not impertinent or pedantic once more to recommend strongly this joint eye- and ear- reading. It does not at all interfere with the understanding of the sense or enjoyment of poetry, and it puts the mind in a condition to understand the virtue and meaning of the prosody as nothing else can. One of the innumerable privileges of those who have received the older classical education is that they have been taught (at least in some cases) to read scanningly.[14]

Saintsbury might well have worried about 'impertinence': the growing class of readers educated only in English literature, and the rise of English studies in schools and universities, meant fewer readers as well-trained in prosody as those who had enjoyed a classical education. His championing of the study and appreciation of complex prosodies could have been interpreted as not just 'pedantic' but as classist. The 'virtue and meaning of prosody', as against mere rhythm, was becoming a harder sell in the literary economy of the early twentieth century.

'No art of English poetry at all'

Bridges's impatience with simple verse-forms was, however, not new. Three centuries earlier certain Elizabethan poets and critics had famously grown impatient with vernacular English metres and yearned for an English poetry capable of reproducing the complex prosody of classical verse. The story is familiar to anyone acquainted with English poetry, but its relevance to Bridges's metrical experiments means it bears reviewing briefly here. 'Let us imagine', writes Derek Attridge, 'an educated Englishman of the 1560s or 1570s who, as a result of his grammar-school training in Latin' holds the simple, 'English' forms of accentual verse in contempt. Why? Because for him,

> lines of English verse had no metre, as he understood it; there was no complex pattern of syllables of different types, and hence no intellectual pleasure to be gained from observing how the pattern was kept and the rules obeyed, and no resulting sense of admiration for the skilful poet who, following the extensive and detailed precepts established by tradition and authority, had made from the loose and disordered flux of words a carefully constructed artefact.[15]

'No *intellectual pleasure* to be gained'. For Attridge's putative Elizabethan, English poetry was defective: it lacked a venerable tradition, was based on accents and syllable-counts, preferred simple over compound metres, was indifferent to quantity, and concealed its blandness with the barbarous medieval cosmetic of rhyme. There was, on this view, 'no art of English poetry' at all. Those sharing this disappointment contributed to that remarkable but failed movement to establish English verse on a foundation of quantitative prosody, modelled on Latin quantitative verse (as then understood). For one of these critics, William Webbe, writing in simple English metres was just too easy, 'beeing within the compass of every base witt'. 'Now a dayes', complained George Gascoigne to an Italian friend in 1575, 'in English rimes (for I dare not cal them English verses) we use none other order but a foote of two sillables, whereof the first is depressed or made short, and the second is elevate or made long; and that sound or scanning continueth throughout the verse.'[16] Gascoigne means what we would call accentual-syllabic iambic pentameter, unworthy of the name of poetry: 'And surely I can lament that wee are fallen into such a playne and simple manner of wryting, that there is none other foote used but one; whereby our Poemes may justly be called Rithmes, and cannot by any right challenge the name of verse.'[17] Compare Bridges on the distinction between mere rhythms on the one hand, and complex prosody on the other.

'Wee are fallen': the current metrical blandness is a lapse from earlier, more complex prosodies. Even in English 'we have used in times past other kindes of Meeters,' Gascoigne laments, and among them cites what he takes to be Chaucer's more subtle engagement with quantity, which he approves because it made use of 'the same libertie in feete and measures that the Latins do use'.[18] A similar sense of declension from the standards of Latin quantitative poetry drove other humanist scholars to disparage accentual-syllabic verse as a barbarous usurpation of classical poetry by '*Gothes* and *Hunnes*' – this from no less a figure than Roger Ascham in his influential treatise *The Scholemaster*.[19] To perpetuate accentual-syllabic verse in English, such critics thought, was to fail to get with the humanistic programme.

Imposing Latin quantitative rules on English verse resulted in lines like these, which Attridge cites from Richard Stanyhurst's 1582 version of the *Aeneid*. The translator renders (rather freely) Virgil's description of the inlet on the North African shore where the beleaguered Aeneas and his surviving ships take refuge:

> Heere doe lye wide scattered and theare clives loftelye steaming
> And a brace of menacing ragd rocks skymounted abydeth.

These lines are meant to replicate Latin dactylic hexameters, and within the translator's system, they do indeed. But the lines jar. The natural vowel quantity of 'rocks' is short, but here it scans long 'by position', according to the Latin rule that makes a short syllable long when followed by two consonants. That strangeness is slightly mitigated by the fact that, were the line read as accentual verse, 'rocks' would anyway be stressed. Not so the first word in the same line, 'And', which must also scan long by position, and even more sensationally the final syllable of 'menacing'. Stanyhurst's strict principles have wrested 'menacing' into an unnatural 'menacíng'. Syllables that naturally sound long, such as *lye* and *brace*, in Stanyhurst's system must scan as short, because of an odd quirk of culture: most Elizabethan Englishmen did not pronounce Latin as Romans did. The Romans would have pronounced the first syllable of *licet* with a short 'i', and of *calor* with a short 'a'. But Elizabethans pronounced those syllables as if they were English, sounding 'the first syllable of *licet* in the same way as Stanyhurst pronounced *lye*, and the first syllable of *calor* with a vowel-sound like that in Stanyhurst's *brace*'.[20] Because those Latin syllables were short, the 'same' sounds in English, it was thought, must scan short too – in defiance of the phonetic evidence of our daily experience of the English language. If for us this seems a triumph of theory over practical experience, that is one way of characterizing an Elizabethan humanist aesthetic in which metrical order is apprehended chiefly intellectually rather than aurally.

Some advocates of the quantitative movement sought a kind of compromise: less rigid applications of the Latin rules, greater scope for the way English was actually pronounced. The critic George Puttenham proposed a sort of hybrid prosody, in which both quantitative and accentual principles should be taken into account. Such efforts at compromise did not catch on, and this may be one explanation for the failure of later poets to emulate Mary Sidney's alcaics, elegant as they are. Nor could poets or readers finally agree on clear rules for determining the quantity of an English syllable. Even great poets were led to commit offences to common sense. Carne-Ross complains of 'the absurd pedantry of imposing on English the classical rule of length by position that led even a poet with so good an ear as [Philip] Sidney's to scan a work like *violence* as a quantitative u u /'.[21] By the early seventeenth century the quantitative movement was moribund. Among the many reasons for its failure, one stands out for our purposes: though it had rigour, it had little discernible aurality, cut no figure in 'the sensual ear'. Instead it elevated the intellectual apprehension of an abstract pattern above the plainly audible element. Readers who favoured quantitative English verse derived their satisfaction from 'observing how the pattern was kept and the rules obeyed', but without *hearing* rhythms corresponding to actual spoken English. Attridge's imaginary Englishman persuaded himself that he was hearing English quantitative verse, but 'quantity was always described in terms of the sound of the syllables, though in fact it bore no relation to it'.[22]

English poetry went down a different path. By the mid-seventeenth century, it was more or less settled that modern English versification should be based on stress-accent rather than formal quantity. The result has been that in modern English verse, rhythm is indeed 'more evident than prosody'. Happily, this does not mean that we have mere rhythms and no poems, as Gascoigne feared. The abstract pleasure of prosody is available to any readers who notice discrepancies between metrical template and the natural stress of a syllable, as when a trochee takes the place of an expected iamb. Some few readers consciously relish the less systematic role of syllabic duration – when, for instance, a distinctly long vowel sometimes reinforces a stressed syllable, or, with contrapuntal force, tugs against an unstressed one. But for most readers metrical nuance is caviar to the general, and it is the audible thumping of familiar English rhythms that matters, not the abstract pleasures – the unheard melodies – of prosody.

'No accepted grammar of the method'

There was a touch of Attridge's 'educated Englishman of the 1560s or 1570s' about Robert Bridges. During the same time he was writing and re-writing *Milton's Prosody*, he was also experimenting with classical lyric metres, including alcaics, in English. And not any old kind, but English alcaics on quantitative principles, such as the Elizabethan theorists of the quantitative movement might have approved. He was perhaps the last poet of any considerable standing to hazard the sort of poetry that the sixteenth-century classicizing critics such as Gascoigne had called for: English versions of classical forms based on quantitative, rather than accentual, measures. What led Bridges to revisit that long-abandoned project?

In 1898 he had made the acquaintance of a certain William Johnson Stone, author of an obscure tract, *On the Use of Classical Metres in English*, self-published that same year. In it Stone took up, after three centuries, the lost cause of the English quantitative movement, and bluffly urged 'the introduction of classical metres' into English poetry'.[23] Stone was disappointed that English poets had 'thrown quantity to the winds and written lines which resemble their models only in the number of the syllables and the exaggerated beat of the verse'.[24] The whole field of quantitative verse had been 'persistently shunned by the mass of sensible Englishmen.'[25] The relentless thumping of English accentual metres, together with defective teaching of the classics, had deafened both poets and readers. 'Our English ears are so vitiated by the combined effect of reading English accentuated verse and reading Latin and Greek without the true pronunciation or accentuation, that we are in general unable to detect quantity.'[26] One might have thought the actual problem was that reasonable people could disagree about the quality and duration of English syllables. But no, Stone insisted: 'English words, if pronounced accurately, have a distinct quantity, which is easily perceived by any one who will attend to it.'[27] It was just that simple. Accordingly he laid out, in the compass of eight pages, a list of criteria for determining the quantity of English syllables. By observing Stone's categories, English poets might compose verses 'not merely distantly similar' to Latin and Greek, 'but really and actually the same, governed by rules equally strict and perfect, and producing on the ear the same pure delight.'[28]

Bridges thought enough of Stone's treatise to arrange to have it reprinted and published together with his own 1901 edition of *Milton's Prosody*. That high compliment was not altogether an endorsement. He first persuaded Stone to revise, chastening his strident rhetoric (the tone of the first version, Bridges wrote, was 'rather that of a plea').[29] Stone's unexpected death, just before his treatise was re-issued, afforded Bridges some freedom to voice his reservations. 'Upon the advisability or even the possibility' of quantitative classical metres in English, he demurred: 'I do not myself express an opinion.'[30] About several of Stone's tests for determining the quantity of a syllable, Bridges confessed himself 'not so hopeful.'[31] More trenchantly: ingenious metrical theorizing is all very well, but 'there can be no accepted grammar of the method until some poet has written such poetry as can be, with or without minor developments, improved and accepted', and it is unclear 'whether or no such poetry be ever written.'[32] And yet Bridges took up Stone's challenge, composing a number of 'experiments in quantitative verse', which 'were made in fulfilment of a promise to William Johnson Stone that I would some day test his theory.'[33] He was careful to hedge these ambitious poems with qualifications and tactful disavowals. Stone's 'premature death', he wrote, 'converted my consent into a serious obligation. This personal explanation is due to myself for two reasons: because I might otherwise appear firstly as an advocate of the system, secondly as responsible for Stone's determination of the lengths of English syllables.'[34] The slightly uncomfortable implication is that Bridges undertook his quantitative verses with some reluctance, duty-bound to honour a promise he made to a dying protégé. It is hard to shake the sense that Bridges, in the course of trying to put it into practice, had found that Stone's system simply didn't work: 'Except for a few minor details, which I had disputed with Mr Stone, I was bound to take his rules as he had elaborated them; and it was not until I had made some progress and could think fairly well in his prosody that I seriously criticized it.'[35] He follows with a catalogue of specific doubts, misgivings, and objections to Stone's programme, but determines to conclude on a hopeful note. 'Yet the experiments that I have made reveal a vast unexplored field of delicate and expressive rhythms hitherto unknown in poetry: and this amply rewarded me for my friendly undertaking.'[36] That may be taken as a generous expression of courtesy to a dead friend whom he had encouraged in a project that did not quite come true.

Yet there are reasons to think that the author of *Milton's Prosody* still held out hope for an alternative to the relative crudity of thumping familiar English metres. He was happy to see several of his own quantitative poems, composed according to Stone's principles, printed in leading journals such as *Monthly Review*, *New Quarterly*, and *English Review*. This last journal featured a poem in elegiac couplets published a decade after Stone's death – long after Bridges might have decently claimed to have discharged his obligation to his friend. Moreover he saw to their inclusion, under the heading 'Poems in Classical Prosody', in editions of his collected poems. Whatever his misgivings, then, about Stone's idiosyncratic system of codifying the quantities of English syllables, Bridges appears to have maintained some faith in the possibility of 'delicate and expressive rhythms hitherto unknown in poetry'.

One of these poems in particular seems intended as more than a mere experiment. Less than a year after the publication of the dual edition of *Milton's Prosody* and Stone's essay, the second Boer War came to an end, and the two events led Bridges to attempt a victory ode in a broadly Horatian mode, composed in alcaic strophes according to Stone's prosodic principles. It is called 'Peace Ode: On the Conclusion of the Boer War, June 1902'. Bridges was sufficiently pleased with it to have it privately printed in elegant red goat-skin with silk doublures, one exemplar of which found its way into to the hands of King George V. As such it was not, like so many metrical experiments in classical metres, a mere squib or trifle. It begins like this:

> Now joy in all hearts with happy auguries,
> And praise on all lips: for sunny June cometh
>   Chasing the thick warcloud, that outspread
>   Sulfurous and sullen over England.[37]

(1–4)

The eye, running ahead of the ear, readily picks up the alcaic cues: in this case not just the suggestive disposition of lines on the page, but also Bridges's fidelity to the Horatian caesura after the fifth foot, specially demarked by lining up parallel terms ('hearts' and 'lips') in exactly that position. Bridges keeps to the Horatian caesura in all his English alcaics, and often arranges emphatic, parallel, or antithetical terms around it.

But readers who sound out the lines, expecting them to resemble accentual alcaics, will quickly be frustrated. Consider the fourth line. Historically, the decasyllabic line has presented the least problem for writers of English accentual alcaics. The dactyl-led descending cadence (/ u u / u u / u / u) comes relatively easily to English: 'Doubt not again to receive an answer' (Sidney); 'Milton, a name to resound for ages' (Tennyson), 'nothing amounted to more than hearsay' (Hollander). But Sidney and Tennyson were writing alcaics that tended to preserve the accentual element, and Hollander's alcaics are chiefly accentual. By that standard, Bridges's line 'Sulfurous and sullen over England' feels distorted. The first word, 'sulfurous', presents no problem at all, corresponding in accent to the first three elements of the metrical template (/ u u). But the fourth syllable in the Horatian template is long, so we expect to find in the English a stressed syllable. Instead we get simply 'and', an unaccented syllable. A naturally short vowel followed by two consonants becomes, as in Latin, 'long by position', and so 'and', despite its naturally short vowel, and despite being unaccented, in Bridges's poem coincides with the long syllable that always occupies the fourth position of line.

Stone had admired exactly this effect when, occasionally, other poets of the nineteenth century had allowed it to happen, as in the following little alcaic caprice of Tennyson's. Because the accents mostly fall where, in a Horatian alcaic, the longs would occur, a casual reader might have taken this poem as purely accentual, not noticing that Tennyson was also trying to suggest the duration of the vowels:

Up sprang the dawn unspeakably radiant,
Sending from all that luminous orient
    Far splendour; and sweet larks ascending,
    Hailed with a glorious hymn to sunrise.

Fortune was all-kind, and through the lovely vale,
Forth flamed the sun o'er silvery foliage.
    Thine early rising well repaid thee
    Munificently rewarded artist.

The line that caught Stone's eye was the final one, where the fourth syllable is meant to be read as long in quantity ('munificēntly'), to fit the classical alcaic template, even though it is also unaccented. It is the only really conspicuous clash between ictus and accent in the little poem, and Stone relished the counterpoint. 'It is a relief', he wrote, 'to find one combative accent' in a poem that otherwise allows ictus and accent to coincide.[38]

The same principle explains the first syllable in 'warcloud' in line 3 of Bridges's ode, which is to be scanned long by position. But the second syllable in 'cometh' (line 2) remains short, because of Stone's ruling that 'th', like 'sh' and in most cases 'ng', counts as a single letter. The second syllable in 'chasing' (line 3) must be scanned as long, not because the 'i' is followed by 'ng' (which counts as one letter), but because the next word begins with 'th', which also counts as one letter, and together with 'ng' forms a double-syllable that lengthens the vowel. In line 4, the first syllable in 'sullen' scans short, despite being followed by a double consonant, because, according to an idiosyncratic stricture of Stone's, 'where the accent is on the vowel', its natural quality 'is never in doubt', meaning it cannot be lengthened even by position.[39] That explains why the first syllable of 'happy' in line 1 remains short.

Even readers familiar with the alcaic strophe, if they expected to find it replicated in the English accentual way, would find these lines metrically defective. They would be listening for rhythm rather than prosody, and the expected rhythm is already spoilt in every line. In the fourth line, instead of the expected / u u / u u / u / u, they would hear instead / u u u / u / u / u. Only if they knew that Bridges was trying to write quantitative verse, and, even then, only if they knew Stone's peculiar rules for determining quantity, would readers be able to perceive what Bridges calls 'the prosody'. To mark the stressed accents in bold, and to underscore the 'long' syllables, illustrates how in the fourth, fifth, seventh, and ninth syllables the accent and ictus diverge:

<u>Sul</u>furous <u>and</u> **sul**len <u>over</u> **Eng**land.

That divergence is supposed to create a sensation of counterpoint, an elegant interplay of impulses, the prosody that Bridges values as so much richer than mere rhythm, and wishes more readers could appreciate.

For many readers, though, the result will be a muddle. One thinks of Stanyhurst's *Aeneid*. If I cannot clearly hear the syllabic quantities as Stone and Bridges want me to hear them, I will not perceive the alcaic pattern they are supposed to produce, except by working it out painstakingly on paper, ex post facto.[40] The element I actually *hear* (the stress accents) marks out no regular pattern at all. If I cannot hear Stone's system of quantities, it may be that I have a bad ear, or it may simply be a matter of acculturation. Stone himself allows for this second possibility: he hoped his system would invite suggestions for refinement and improvement, leading to an eventual cultural consensus, 'a gradual crystallization of opinion on these various points'.[41] No such consensus has emerged, of course, not because of any clash of opinions, but because of indifference. Almost nobody since the seventeenth century had been seriously interested in introducing a fixed system for determining the length of English syllables and creating a tradition of quantitative poetry in English. Stone's whole project would have vanished without a trace, were it not for the obliging response of a future poet laureate.

It is for this reason that Bridges's alcaics are significant. They represent a sort of historical impasse. They are the last serious attempt by a major poet to render into English a learned metre with the complex contrapuntal pleasures of quantitative prosody. Three centuries separate the alcaics of Bridges's 1902 'Peace Ode' from Mary Sidney's alcaic rendition of Psalm 120. In all that span of time, the most successful manifestations of the alcaic in English are those whose relationship to the classical stanza is oblique rather than strict. Marvell's 'Horatian Ode', Tennyson's more complex innovations, and FitzGerald's Rubáiyát stanza are not alcaics, but are meant to be read in light of alcaics. Proper English alcaics – those more or less achieving metrical equivalence, whether accentually or quantitatively – have so far been very rare. The alcaic, in other words, for all its long presence in English literature, had not yet become naturalized as an English verse-form. Bridges's writings on metre make clear the character of the impasse: the average English reader is not acculturated to pick out the metrical pattern of an intricate compound metre, even an accentual one. Readers prefer the relatively straightforward accentual rhythm of simple metres. Had the sixteenth-century proponents of quantitative prosody prevailed, English readers might have developed an ear for the alcaic and other classical metres. But that movement decisively failed, and Bridges's own late attempt at reviving it according to Stone's principles represents a late, last-ditch failure. There are limits to what untrained English readers are prepared to hear, and even the accentual pattern of the alcaic (to say nothing of its contrapuntal relations with ictus and duration) tests those limits too sorely. The story of alcaics in English might have ended with Bridges's ardent failed efforts.

A new prosody

It was W. H. Auden who would find a way for the alcaic at last to enter the repertoire of poets writing in English. The breakthrough involved constructing an alcaic based precisely on some principle *other than* the audible. Paradoxically, it was Robert Bridges who opened the way to that discovery – not through his experiments with alcaics, but with another alternative verse-form: syllabic verse. Here we return to *Milton's Prosody*, since it was his study of Milton that precipitated his own syllabic experiments. Bridges proposed a novel definition of elision by which, if it were accepted, *Paradise Lost* could be shown to have (almost without exception) ten syllables, and *Samson Agonistes* twelve. On such a view Milton's versification could be said to be syllabic. This theorizing led him to compose the syllabic verses that he included in *New Poems* and described as 'Neo-Miltonic Syllabics', a metre that 'pretends to offer their true desideratum to the advocates of Free Verse'.[42] Free verse was in fact a point of contention: *New Poems* was published in 1925, just three years after the appearance of 'The Waste Land'. In accounts of twentieth-century literary history, it is the development of free verse that gets the lion's share of attention. Bridge's experiments with syllabics were relatively unheralded. Much as he cherished the idea of quantitative prosody in English as an alternative to the 'fundamental common metres', he came, in the end, to favour syllabics, choosing them as the medium of his final major work, the long philosophical meditation *The Testament of Love*, begun in 1926 and completed a few months before his death. Bridges found in syllabics a way of resolving two conflicting impulses: his longing for innovation and his respect for tradition.

Such a resolution is possible because 'unlike free verse', syllabic verse 'possesses a definite heuristic character', and this formal quality aligns it with the 'psychologically satisfying' quality of traditional verse.[43] It is shapely and orderly, but at the same time its freedom from any one strict rhythmical pattern accommodates almost any kind of phrasing and syntax, including incorporating passages of foreign languages. Moreover, 'unlike both free and accentual-syllabic verse, it is still unembarrassed by connotations of violent aesthetic partisanship'.[44] These are the observations of the poet and critic Robert Beum, whose analysis of syllabic verse should be seen in a historical light. He was writing in 1957, when critics were still taking stock of the relatively recent phenomenon of syllabic verse. He is right that with syllabics, a poet could break free of the constraints of English iamb without automatically being classed with Ezra Pound & Co. Beum noted another advantage: syllabic verse's 'relative newness saves it from belittling comparison with a great body of prior masterworks in the same medium – a body which now exists for free as well as for accentual verse'.[45] Here was a new mode that offered an alternative to traditional English metres, but could at the same time be highly formal, and liberated its practitioners from invidious comparison to earlier masters.

Bridges's syllabics intrigued Auden. Bridges was high on the younger poet's list, literally: his name appears in a list of 'those elder modern poets … from whom I have learned most'.[46] On the one hand, Auden was enthusiastic about Bridges's syllabics: Christopher Isherwood recalled receiving from Auden a gift of *The Testament of Beauty* at a time when his friend was 'in the throes of his Bridges craze'.[47] On the other, Auden noticed and cautiously admired Bridges's quantitative experiments. 'So far as I know, Bridges was the first to write quantitative verse in English which ignores stress altogether.' This is significant, because it links Auden's interest in syllabic verse (which ignores stress) with the idea of writing in classical metres. Referring to a passage from 'Epistle I', one of Bridges's quantitative experiments, Auden observed that it 'is written in hexameters, but no ear that listens for stresses will hear them as such.'[48] He was flirting with the idea that one could write classical metres in a new way: without regard to audible stresses or quantity. Auden had formed an association between syllabic verse and the possibilities of classical verse forms. He may not have been aware of Bridges's characterization of syllabic prosody as 'the freest of free verse, there being no speech-rhythm which it would not admit', adding in particular its capacity to accommodate 'various tongues'.[49] But Auden would surely have known the second poem in Bridges's *New Verse*, 'Poor Poll', whose eponymous parrot can mimic English phrases 'as schoolmasters in Greek will flaunt their hackney'd tags / φωνᾶντα συνετοῖσιν and κτῆμα εἰς ἀεὶ, / ἡ γλῶσσ' ὀμώμοχ', ἡ δὲ φρὴν ἀνώμοτος / tho' you with a better ear copy ús more perfectly'.[50] Here syllabic verse – lines of twelve syllables each – allows for the integration of various quotations from ancient Greek in a way that contrasts with Owen's quotation of Horace (where the Latin alcaic measure is at odds with the English iambic pentameter). It differs, too from the classical quotations in Ezra Pound's *Cantos*, where integration of ancient metres is not possible, because in Pound's free verse there is no regular English metre to be assimilated into. Bridges's syllabic verses promised a new avenue for bringing the qualities of 'various tongues', including Greek and Latin, into English.

Bridges's example remained latent, though, until Auden discovered the syllabic verse of Marianne Moore. Or rather, it was the *stanzas* of her syllabic verse, her demonstration that syllabics could take the form of elaborate and intricate stanza-shapes, as opposed to the mainly stichic syllabics Bridges favoured. 'Before I had encountered Miss Moore's verse', Auden wrote,

> I was well acquainted with Robert Bridges's syllabic experiments, but he confined his verses to a regular succession of either six-syllable or twelve-syllable lines. A typical poem by Miss Moore, on the other hand, is written in stanzas, containing anything from one up to twenty syllables, not infrequently a word is split up with one or more of its syllables at the end of a line and the rest of them at the beginning of the next, caesuras fall where they may and, as a rule, some of the lines rhyme and some are unrhymed. This, for a long time, I found very difficult.[51]

The difficulty with Moore's syllabic prosody involved the question of audibility, what the ear can hear, as against what is intelligible only to the eye. 'To begin with, I could not "hear" the verse', Auden admits.[52] Whether syllabic verse can have, or ought to have, an audible dimension was a common subject of debate in the mid-twentieth century, as English-speaking poets of stature increasingly turned to syllabics.[53] Initial bemusement, though, turned to admiration and then emulation: Auden was to take up syllabics and make them a major part of his middle and late career. It is only after he took up syllabics, and only in that mode, that he at last brought over into English the intricate classical forms that so fascinated him, most notably alcaics, the favourite metre of 'the only Roman poet I really like.' Auden detects Horatian qualities in Moore's syllabics: 'In most cases', he wrote, 'one can make a pretty good guess at the influences which have contributed to a poet's style, but Miss Moore leaves us guessing. Was it Mallarmé, was it Horace, was it Emerson?'[54] He means not simply that Moore resembles Horace in the matter of tone (unsentimental, precise, fastidious) but also in the matter of form, in the elaborateness of her stanzas. T. S. Eliot detected a similar resemblance when he referred to a 'sort of Latin stateliness' in Moore's verse.[55] It makes sense, then, for Auden to have taken the next step of creating syllabics that are *explicitly* Horatian, replicating the syllable count of the alcaic strophe.

Auden's alcaic experiments date to as early as 1939. 'Crisis' (later reprinted as 'They'), finds Auden exploring the possibilities of the form. The syllable count (11-11-9-10) makes the stanza unmistakably alcaic, though the movement of the strophes does not always feel very Horatian. More often than not the stanzas fall into halves, into bundles of unrhymed couplets (lines 21–4).

> Our money sang like streams on the aloof peaks
> of our thinking that beckoned them on like girls;
>   our culture like a West of wonder
>   shone a solemn promise in their face.[56]

Does this bipartite structure reflect an actual dichotomy? Auden himself thought so. 'Crisis', the poet explained to a friend, 'turns on the division between reason and the heart, the individual and the collective, the liberal ineffectual highbrow and the brutal practical demagogue like Hitler or Huey Long.[57] This helps to account for the extraordinarily explicit collaboration of metre and matter in the following stanza, where the first two lines, with masculine endings, pertain to a 'father's rage', and the feminine lines take up 'a mother's distortions' (33–6):

> They arrive, already adroit, having learned
> restraint at the table of a father's rage;
>   in a mother's distorting mirror
>   they discovered the Meaning of Knowing.

Auden's schematic cast of mind, his lifelong habit of framing his thoughts in terms of antitheses, shaped both his poems and his essays. In this case, though, we find it altering the three-step movement of the alcaic. Nevertheless, these verses find Auden discovering a way of bringing alcaics into English that dodged the difficulties of either accentual or quantitative approaches. Syllabic stanzas accommodate, as Bridges predicted, a theoretically unlimited range of rhythmical movements (including the rhythms of other languages) without, like free verse, abandoning all metrical heuristic. Furthermore, by avoiding the nonce-syllabics of Marianne Moore and instead using syllabics to reconstruct classical stanzas such as the alcaic, Auden effectively generated a new prosody. In this novel versification, there are two voices. The first voice, the 'heard melody', is the natural speech-rhythm of the words as they are propelled through the syllabic template. 'Speech-rhythm', because the point of syllabic verse is precisely to avoid regular accentual patterning, and set 'ordinary' speech in motion against the fixed pattern of the syllable-count. The second voice is an abstract one, an 'unheard melody': the ghostly residual pattern of the alcaic strophe.

Take the decasyllabic line from the stanza above: 'they discovered the Meaning of Knowing'. Those unfamiliar with the alcaic strophe's cadence (and this must have included the majority of Auden's contemporary readers, and an even greater majority now) will hear the line only as it would be spoken in prose, with the main accents falling on three syllables, according to spoken convention rather than any metrical system: 'They dis**cov**ered the **Mean**ing of **Know**ing'. On the other hand, those who know the alcaic will have a hard time suppressing their memory of the cadence of the alcaic fourth line (/ u u / u u / u / u). Such readers will hear the counterpoint of the colloquial accent and the ghostly presence of the metrical ictus, indicated here by underscoring: '<u>They</u> dis**cov**<u>ered</u> the **Mean**<u>ing</u> of **Know**<u>ing</u>'. The counterpoint is distinct: accent diverges from ictus in six of the ten positions. Of all the three metrical patterns in an alcaic strophe, the decasyllabic line is the easiest to recreate in English accentual verse, so its avoidance here draws particular attention to the way that Auden's alcaics are meant deliberately to refuse an ordinary appeal to the ear.

This is something new. Ordinarily in syllabic verse, metrical counterpoint, if felt at all, depends on the sense of a disjunction between (on the one hand) more or less conversational rhythms, which might otherwise be taken for prose, and (on the other) the mathematical heuristic of the syllable-count. In the syllabic lyrics of both Bridges and Moore, the syllable-count is mostly arbitrary: their poems are nonce-forms corresponding to no conventional received English template. As such, readers bring no metrical expectations to the poem beyond the syllable-count. Auden, however, by basing his own syllable-counts on alcaics, creates a very different kind of syllabic. The syllable-count is not arbitrary but historical, reproducing the metrical body of Horace – but only the visible body. The audible body exists only as a negative in the ear of classically trained readers. Auden's stanza positions itself midway between Moore's nonce stanzas (by which English verse achieves, through syllabics, something like the elaborate stanzaic complexity of Horace's odes), and the metrical experiments of Bridges (whose quantitative alcaics were inaudible to most readers, but whose syllabic verse accommodated unconventional rhythms, even those of ancient languages). Christopher Ricks in a masterful study of literary allusion has observed that the best allusions are not wholly exclusive: the basic sense remains intelligible to readers who may not catch the additional resonances of the allusion.[58] In that sense Auden's syllabic alcaics constitute the best sort of metrical allusion. For readers ignorant of the alcaic, the syllabic scheme is nevertheless accessible, interesting, and metrically intelligible on its own terms. For that vanishing company of readers in the know, it is precisely the *absence* of alcaic cadences that creates a striking ghostly counterpoint to the alcaic syllable-count.[59]

Naturalized at last

This new kind of alcaic was no mere exercise, but became a kind of hallmark of Auden's middle and late career. The early forties found him producing three new alcaic poems: 'In Memory of Sigmund Freud' and the 'Prologue' and 'Epilogue' to *New Year Letter*. This marks a significant development: until now, all previous English alcaics by first-rate poets that strictly reproduce the syllable-count had either been impressive one-offs (Mary Sidney's Psalm 120 or Clough's 'Alcaics') or experimental curiosities (Tennyson's ode to Milton, Bridges's 'Peace Ode').

With his eulogy to Freud and the 'Epilogue' to *New Year Letter* we find Auden, first among English poets, writing several poems in the strict alcaic syllable-count which are both successful as poems and also major works, central to his larger oeuvre.

The elegy to Freud in particular represents a kind of advance in the direction of specifically Horatian qualities, since its frequent enjambment creates a forward momentum much more characteristic of Horace's alcaics than the more heavily end-stopped lines his of previous alcaic forays.[60] Consider this stanza (45–8):

> No wonder the ancient cultures of conceit
> in his technique of unsettlement foresaw
>   the fall of princes, the collapse of
>   their lucrative patterns of frustration:

Despite the greater fluidity between lines, though, Auden continues to bundle the stanzas into couplets of masculine and feminine endings. In that he crucially diverges from syllabics on the model of Bridges and Moore. By attending not only to the syllable-count but to the line-endings, he creates expressive effects: 'collapse' and 'frustration' are conveyed not only semantically, but also metrically, since Auden's first two lines (masculine) break down into the liquid rhythms of the last two lines (feminine). Auden in this way hints at the victory of the feminine. One of Freud's accomplishments, after all, is to 'give back to / the son the mother's richness of feeling' (95–6). But though it is true that 'Freud', with its greater syntactic limberness, more nearly approaches the classical alcaic, nevertheless the masculine and feminine line endings, bound into couplets, enforce an un-Horatian dualism. This fact cannot be concealed by Auden's new strategy of indenting the third line to the right of the fourth, as if to suggest a greater correspondence to the tripartite classical model. Auden's alcaics of early forties still dance the two-step.

It is ironic, then, that Auden should have learnt to develop a tripartite strophe, much more akin to the alcaic's, by venturing a different lyric metre, the fourth asclepiad.[61] Auden's success with alcaics would lead him to expand his repertoire of classical strophes. Most conspicuous among these would be the sapphic, long naturalized into English verse. With Auden it took on a wholly new career in pure syllabics. By contrast, the fourth asclepiad had rarely been attempted in English. It is easy to see why. It was never as well-known as the alcaic. Horace himself used it only seven times. It happens that one of Horace's most famous poems, *Odes* 1.5, the so-called Pyrrha ode, is composed in this metre, which consists of two twelve-syllable asclepiads ($-\ -\ -\ u\ u\ -\ -\ u\ u\ -\ u\ x$), followed by a dramatic curtailment in the form of a seven-syllable pherecratean (– – – u u – x), and rounded off by the eight-syllable glyconic (– – – u u – u x). In combination these units form a strophe as complex as the alcaic, though less subtle. The shift from the twelve syllables of the second line to the mere seven of the third is very abrupt: the alcaic's lines modulate their lengths less precipitously. And there is nothing in the asclepiad quite like the Horatian alcaic's third-line pivot. The four lines of the fourth asclepiad are less various: all of them begin with exactly the same rhythm in the first six syllables. One might describe the fourth asclepiad as a strophe which plays on three slight variations of the same basic choriambic rhythm.

Attempting it, though, Auden paradoxically created a stanza that in one respect feels closer to the movement of the alcaic. The poem in question, 'Ischia' (1948), reproduces the strict 12-12-7-8 syllable-count of the fourth asclepiad, but with a significant innovation. He made the third line stand out as alone ending with a feminine syllable:

> nothing is free, whatever you charge shall be paid,
> that these days of exotic splendour may stand out
> > in each lifetime like marble
> > mileposts in an alluvial land.

(65–8)

That is a distinctly alcaic stroke, since the alteration sets off the third line not simply as shorter than the others, but as having a different metrical movement. In this case, as opposed to the Freud ode, the orthographic figure of the poem on the page, with its double-indentation of the third line, is not merely cosmetic. It reflects an actual metrical difference. 'Ischia' is a significant development, too, in that its Horatian form combines, for the first time, with more explicitly Horatian matter: in this case, an affectionate description of the Italian landscape. As Horace would praise the Sabine countryside surrounding his mountain villa, Auden now relishes his own Italian retreat on Ischia. One of Auden's major commentators senses the link, finding the 'Horatian metre' (though he does not specify it, manifesting a critical tendency to collapse alcaics, sapphics, and asclepiads into a general 'Horatian' category) 'particularly appropriate to the kind of local descriptive-meditative poem that it is'.[62] Another critic, oblivious to the metre, nevertheless notes the poem's 'relevance to that part of Italy [Ischia] to Horace'.[63] I would add the fact of the poem's (muted) celebration of the downfall of Mussolini, a theme not incongruous with the Horace's alcaic Cleopatra ode (1.37). With 'Ischia', then, Auden expresses distinctly Horatian sentiments in an

English form which, though it is not an alcaic, in some ways comes closer to its movements than his earlier, stricter alcaics.

A later asclepiad poem would at last link Auden explicitly with Horace. In 'The Horatians' (1968) Auden addresses Horace's mild-mannered modern heirs who, like himself, shun Pindaric extravagance (49–68):

> Some of you have written poems, usually
> short ones, and kept some diaries, seldom published
>   till after your deaths, but most
>   make no memorable impact
>
> except on your friends and dogs. Enthusiastic
> Youth writes you off as cold, who cannot be found on
>   barricades, and never shoot
>   either yourselves or your lovers.
>
> You thought well of your Odes, Flaccus, and believed they
> would live, but knew, and have taught your descendants to
>   say with you, 'As makers go,
>   compared with Pindar or any
>
> of the great foudroyant masters who don't ever
> amend, we are, for all our polish, of little
>   stature, and, as human lives,
>   compared with authentic martyrs
>
> like Regulus, of no account. We can only
> do what it seems we were made for, look at
>   this world with a happy eye
>   but from a sober perspective.'

Here we are treated to a metrical switch: Auden has exactly inverted the pattern he had used two decades earlier in 'Ischia', and contrived to make the third lines *masculine*, to set them apart from the other three lines, which are now all feminine. As in the earlier poem, that differentiation creates, in this asclepiad poem, an alcaic effect, and indeed the poem's reference to Regulus connects it explicitly with one of Horace's greatest alcaic poems, *Odes* 3.5, a celebration of the conspicuous heroism of that Roman general. That is: even when he is writing asclepiads, Auden lends the stanzas an alcaic inflection. (The same passage also includes a reference to one of Horace's *sapphic* poems, 4.2, an elaborate disavowal of Pindaric metrical pyrotechnics). The overall tone, by which the speaker, appearing to apologize for the modest scale of his poems, thereby draws attention to their perfection, superbly catches the tone of a half-dozen other Horatian odes in various metres. (Compare the last two stanzas in particular to Horace's *recusatio* in *Odes* 1.6, a poem composed in sapphics). The first reader of 'The Horatians' was the Greek scholar E. R. Dodds, to whom Auden had confided in a 1968 letter that he had 'lately been obsessed by Horace', and made good on the claim by enclosing his draft of this poem.[64] 'The Horatians' demonstrates how thoroughly Auden's experiments with Horatian metres fed his self-identification with the Roman poet, and vice-versa. A retrospective Auden, in one of his final poems, named Horace 'adroitest of makers', one of the tutelary spirits of his lifetime.[65] In 'The Horatians' Auden places himself among Horace's 'descendants', emulating him not just by assimilating his modest tone and drollery, and not just by effortless allusion, but also through the creation of flexible new English forms of several kinds of Horatian stanzas, all of which evolved from his earliest alcaic experiments.

Auden returned to alcaics proper the next year when, a month after Apollo Seven, he slightly altered the form again, this time as a vehicle with which to report feeling distinctly underwhelmed by the recent 'Moon Landing' (1–6):

> It's natural the Boys should whoop it up for
> so huge a phallic triumph, an adventure
>   it would not have occurred to women
>   to think worth while, made possible only
>
> because we like huddling in gangs and knowing
> the exact time:

Here again Auden deploys a strict alcaic syllable count, but (yet again) with a strategic adjustment. Now all the line endings, even the first two (which ought strictly to be stressed) are unstressed. All the masculine endings have been changed to feminine. Auden's way, perhaps, of rendering a phallic triumph detumescent? Just the previous year, he had given the same prosodic form to a very similar impulse ('Ode to Terminus', 1–4):

> The High Priests of telescopes and cyclatrons
> keep making pronouncements about happenings
>   on scales too gigantic or dwarfish
>   to be noticed by our native senses,

The first and second line-endings are not just feminine, but dactyls: 'cyclatrons', 'happenings'. This trailing-off cushions what ought to have been the emphatic thud of the masculine ending of the alcaic hendecasyllabic. A month earlier, in

'Epistle to a Godson', Auden, going out of his way to avoid the oracular tone, which he hated, burnished his Horatian credentials by coming down firmly on the side of not coming down firmly on any side. Not only, he protests, have *I* no authority for issuing pronouncements, but neither have the rulers of this world (48–56):

> Yet who can
>
> issue proper instructions? Not, certainly,
> our global Archons, whose top-lofty slogans
>   are as off the beam as their syntax
>   is vague: (they would be figures of fun, if
>
> very clever little boys had not found it
> amusing to build devices for them, more
>   apt at disassembly than any
>   old-fire-spewing theogonic monster.)

Here again, for Auden, there is a touch of hubris in science's contraptions and the clever *boys* who contrive them; once again the feminine line endings accuse and deflate. That little device of prosody, that touch of un-assertion where metrical assertion is expected, helps convey the folly of asserting too hard.

Metrical form and cultural disinheritance

There is a bittersweet quality to Auden's achievement with alcaics. On the happy side of the ledger is the plain fact that Auden not only revived and reinvented the alcaic strophe for the twentieth century and beyond, but used it more extensively than any English poet. One could summarize his achievement like this: in an age which, as Bridges anxiously observed, seemed to have no more place for complex classical metres, Auden found a way of reinventing them. Rejecting Bridges's attempt to resuscitate a system of English quantitative verse, he instead applied Bridges's syllabic experiments to the alcaic. He found in the intricate stanzaic syllabics of Marianne Moore a model for suggesting in English the metrical complexity of the alcaic strophe, but went beyond her by consciously marking the endings of his syllabic lines as masculine or feminine, and patterning those line-endings to suggest similar effects found in Horatian strophes. Arranging his stanzas to correspond strictly with the syllable-count of the classical alcaic, he created not just what Yopie Prins would recognize as 'visual song', but something more: his alcaics produce, for classically educated readers, a counterpoint between the prosy conversational rhythms of the syllabic verse and the latent prosody of the classical stanza. His success with the alcaic experiments led him later to evolve English versions of other Horatian lyric forms, most notably fourth asclepiads (whose kinship to alcaics he underscored by allusion to specific Horatian odes) and, later, sapphics. All of Auden's English alcaics and their cousins became central to his middle and late career, and include some of his greatest poems. What's even more, as we shall see in the next chapter, they inspired a renaissance of English alcaics in the late twentieth and early twenty-first century. And the alcaic can in this sense be thought of as playing an important part in the development of syllabic verse in the twentieth century. For all these reasons, Auden is the most important English heir of classical poetry's greatest lyric form.

Yet his success is implicated with one of his most melancholy preoccupations: his sense of a certain kind of cultural disinheritance, the emerging dominance of a narrow technocratic version of science that threatened to sever our connections to the past, in particular the classical past. That concern can be detected in the two alcaic poems quoted immediately above. In 'Ode to Terminus' Auden has a go at the new technocrats by using classical references that they probably would not understand, and that ironize their role as destroyers of cultural memory. He calls them 'our global *Archons*', more destructive than 'any /old fire-spewing *theogonic* monster' (my emphasis). In 'Epistle to a Godson', addressed to Philip Spender, the son of his lifelong friend Stephen Spender, Auden complains (this time rather more genially and self-mockingly) that the rate of technological change has at last destroyed the practice of intergenerational tradition, by which fathers pass on their wisdom to their children. 'In yester times it / was different', but now the world alters so quickly that an old man's accumulated wisdom is of no relevance to the young. It is significant that this acknowledgement of severed continuity should be expressed in alcaic verses, itself an inheritance from older poets (Horace himself is a kind of godfather to Auden), which neither Philip Spender, nor indeed most readers by 1969, could be expected even to recognize, let alone appreciate.

Even highly literate critics could not be counted on to recognize it. Reviewing the volume in which 'Epistle to a Godson' first appeared, Clive James mischievously altered the typography, setting three of its stanzas as prose, as if to illustrate how the garrulous old poet had become a prisoner of his 'strictly prosaic later manner'. Only later in his review did James reveal to his *TLS* readers that he had been deceiving them: 'Epistle to a Godson' was actually composed in verse, not prose, but the elaborate syllabic quatrains, lacking any rhythmic element, read *like* prose, and so might just as well have been set as prose. Auden 'long ago ran out of metrical rules needing more than a moment's effort to conform to', James asserted – as if the verse-form Auden had chosen were merely being conformed to, or were easy to achieve. Most tellingly, James shows no sign of having a clue what alcaics are: he mistakes the form of the poem as an 'arbitrary syllabic' stanza.[66] No form, though, could have been less arbitrary. The remonstration of Edward Callan, in a letter to *TLS* a few weeks after James's review appeared, is bracing: 'What your reviewer sets as prose is a passage in Alcaic stanzas (based on a syllable count of 11, 11, 9, 10) – a form Auden has adapted from the Aeolian Greek. Perhaps not every reader would agree that the passage *reads* as prose, even when *set* as prose. The music of its movement is irrepressible.'[67] There are many grounds for legitimate critique of Auden's later work, but they ought to stand on the capacity to recognize one of the most persistent forms of prosody in the Western tradition.

There is a larger irony in this episode. The failure of people like Clive James to identify the specific features of classical literature, or of others to recognize classical forms at all, is itself a preoccupation of Auden's work. One of the clearest instances of this anxiety emerges, as Juan Christian Pellicer has shown, in Auden's 'The Shield of Achilles'. In that poem, 'a ragged urchin' accepts as axiomatic the barbarism of 'a modernity stripped of traditional features of civilization, a condition in which the traces of civilization are no longer recognizable'. (I would add that classical lyric metres themselves are among the 'traces of civilization' in danger of becoming 'no longer recognizable'.) Hence Auden's interest in 'curious prosodic fauna', and his extensive effort to preserve and renew alcaics, asclepiads, sapphics and other recondite metres. His motives could be mistaken as pedantic. They are in fact moral concerns.[68]

Pellicer's further analysis deserves to be quoted at length:

The 'ragged urchin' to whom rape and violence are axiomatic has 'never heard / Of any world where promises were kept / Or one could weep because another wept' (57–9). These lines evoke the end of *Iliad* 24, the climactic conciliatory meeting of Priam and Achilles, where Achilles weeps 'because another wept'. Homer's Achilles weeps from recognition, since Priam reminds him of his own father (a restorative masculine influence, the *Iliad* suggests). Yet Auden is not merely lamenting the demise of universal human values in an imminent future, but also the disappearance of literature itself. . . . Auden's ragged urchin has *never heard of* any world where promises are kept. Auden is not just imagining a modern world where trust and sympathy are unknown, but also a world in which the stories that transmit those values have died from memory. In other words, he is imagining a world bereft of occasions for recognition provided by art.[69]

Pellicer moreover invokes the contrasting experience of Virgil's Aeneas who, inspecting the murals on the temple of Juno in Carthage, weeps precisely because he *does* recognize the occasion provided by that work of art. 'What Auden mourns, then', Pellicer writes, 'is not the loss of Trojan or Greek civilization, not the loss of the Homeric world, but the loss of Homer, the literary standard that Virgil inherited and passed on'.[70] In just this way, Auden mourns a world in which moderns have cut themselves off from the literary classics. Metre as mourning.

By the time he published 'Epistle to a Godson', it had been two decades since Auden had conceded that the classical inheritance that meant so much to him was already being lost: 'We have to accept as an accomplished fact', he wrote in 1948, 'that the educated man of today and tomorrow can read neither Latin nor Greek'.[71] He meant not only that Greece and Rome in general were being forgotten, but particularly the direct experience of classical literature in the Greek and Latin languages themselves, with all of their untranslatable contours. 'The untranslatable classics', as Frost put it. To vary Pellicer's terms slightly, it is not just that now people have 'never heard *of* the classics, but have never *heard* the classics, never heard the Greek or Latin itself, never heard the particular music of a sapphic or asclepiad – or an alcaic. Auden's chagrin is made clear in one of his alcaic poems, partly *because* it is an alcaic poem, a part of that increasingly unclaimed inheritance. In 'Ode to Terminus', Auden laments a latter-day disregard for the sacred and creative value of boundaries and limitations. Among these is one kind of boundary particularly relevant to our study: the boundary that is poetic metre itself.

> Venus and Mars are powers too natural
> to temper our outlandish extravagance:
>   You alone, Terminus the Mentor,
>   can teach us how to alter our gestures.
>
> God of walls, doors and reticence, nemesis
> overtakes the sacrilegious technocrat,
>   but blessed is the City that thanks you
>   for giving us games and grammar and metres.

As if it were not enough to emphasize the relationship of moral order to poetic metre, the very line 'for giving us games and grammar and metres' constitutes a momentary deviation from the rhythmless norm of syllabic verse. The (ironically extrametrical) line could be scanned like this: u / u u / u / u u / u – a pattern which, with its echoing choriambs, itself echoes the defining cadence of classical lyric, perhaps especially the alcaic decasyllabic. Here, for once, we can actually *hear* a kind of Horatian movement, even in a syllabic poem. The same effect comes through in one of Auden's last poems, the last alcaic he would ever write, 'Posthumous Letter to Gilbert White' (1973). In an acoustically themed stanza, Auden imagines that great naturalist meeting Henry David Thoreau, and the two men together

> noting
> the pitches owls hoot on, comparing
> the echo-response of dactyls and spondees.[72]

(18–20)

It happens that the cadence of the last five syllables of this stanza, 'dactyls and spondees' (/ u u / u) is also the adonic cadence of the sapphic stanza. The very words for metrical terms, 'dactyls and spondees', momentarily reproduce an ancient metrical cadence in a syllabic poem (where no particular cadences are expected). The accentual pattern of the preceding line, moreover, could be very plausibly scanned u / u / / / u / u. This very nearly replicates the pattern of a classical alcaic enneasyllabic line. 'Audible' remnants of the alcaic rhythm break out in this way surprisingly often in the third lines of Auden's stanzas, where the alcaic context justifies finding special meaning in the iambic rhythm and feminine endings: e.g., 'then on the tennis court one morning' ('To T. S. Eliot on His Sixtieth Birthday', 3), and 'beset by every creature comfort' ('Ode to the Medieval Poets', 11). In other words: in these rare instances when Auden's syllabic verses 'lapse' from unrhythmic syllabics into something like the rhythmical movement of accentual verse, they tend to echo the rhythms of the alcaic strophe.[73] In 'Posthumous Letter to Gilbert White', Auden confesses to his imaginary interlocutor that he is himself no naturalist, and could not be trusted to identify flora or fauna. 'How many / birds and plants can I spot? At most two dozen' (24–5). (This from the man who prided himself for being able to spot 'curious prosodic fauna like bacchics and choriambs'.) One of the implied subtexts of all of Auden's alcaic poems is a sort of melancholy that, in a time when educated people can no longer read the Greek and Latin languages, we are losing one of the hitherto most durable traces of civilization: not just the sight, but the sound, of ancient lyric metres.

In his introduction to an anthology of Greek literature in English translation, Auden praised the Greeks' unrivalled achievement but nevertheless issued this disconcerting qualification: that 'if Greek literature has to be read in translation, then the approach can no longer be an aesthetic one', since the aesthetic depends so much on features that inhere in the Greek language itself, as wielded by each individual artist: its sound, its syntax, its wordplay, its rhythms and metres.[74] It is something for an anthologist to declare to his own Greekless readers that whatever pleasures they are about to take from the literature on offer, aesthetic pleasure will not be one of them. It is a melancholy paradox that the same concession applies not only to translation from the classics themselves, but to the appreciation of Auden's own metrical receptions of the classics.

A decade before his remark on reading Greek in translation, Auden had composed *For the Time Being: A Christmas Oratorio*, which imagines the kinds of culture that threatened to supplant Greco-Roman and Judeo-Christian traditions:

> Instead of building temples, we build laboratories;
> Instead of offering sacrifices, we perform experiments;
> Instead of reciting prayers, we note pointer-readings;
> Our lives are no longer erratic but efficient.
>
> ('The Summons': III: 16–19)

This is the culture of the 'sacrilegious technocrat' about which Auden would later write in the alcaics of 'Ode to Terminus', and against which he would set the precious inheritance of 'grammar and metres'. Something similar is anticipated in the same passage of *For the Time Being*:

> Instead of inflexions and accents
> There are prepositions and word-order;
>
> (4–5)

This conception of moral decline is expressed – remarkably – in terms of linguistic devolution. Grammatical inflection is precisely the feature of Latin that makes possible the syntactical flexibility so characteristic of Horatian alcaics and other lyric metres. Because modern English has mostly shed inflections, it relies instead on 'prepositions and word-order'. This makes nearly impossible the kinds of Horatian displays of syntactic dislocation and metrical variety I demonstrated in Chapter 2. I have written elsewhere of Auden's attempts to recapture the effects of Latin 'inflections and accents' in a particularly complex alcaic poem, 'Streams'.[75] In it, Auden tries to suggest syntactical involutions and metrical nuances through a complex system of internal rhymes – a brilliant, but failed, attempt to compensate for the fact that English is now bound by the straightjacket of 'prepositions and word-order'. In Auden's notion of cultural disinheritance, the very features of morphology and syntax that distinguish Greek and Latin from modern languages represent the slide into the soullessness of modern technocracy. But without the experience of Latin or Greek, one cannot feel the moral force of Auden's analogy. Those who came of age, as Auden did, when classics were still *de rigueur* will understand what he means by the loss of 'inflexions and accents'. To everyone else the reference will be baffling – and that is precisely Auden's point.

For all that his alcaics represent a new beginning, opening new currents of his own imagination, and showing the way for later writers of English alcaics, Auden is nevertheless the last of a breed, and his alcaics are as such a sign of the end of an era. He belongs to the last generation of writers and readers brought up on the classics as a matter of course. His alcaics both resist and reflect the decline of classical culture. They are simultaneously a beginning (the first alcaics truly at home in English, and truly at one with the author's style) and an end (as emerging at the least propitious moment, when for the first time in five centuries, 'the educated man' or woman could 'read neither Latin nor Greek'). His alcaics are not arbitrary, as Clive James thought; neither are they technical curiosities. They are moral, in their determination to preserve and renew valuable traces of civilization, and the civilized values that those ancient poetic forms embody. After Auden, his admirers do indeed pick up the alcaic, and the stanza-form paradoxically flourishes as never before in English. The results, though, are not the same. The alcaic after Auden *begins* with belatedness, emerging in a post-classical world. The post-Auden alcaic is inherently *after*, and as such gets not a chapter but an Afterword.

Afterword
From Inheritance to Quarry

The Alcaic in Postmodernity

'I sing to display my Alcaics'

How conversant with classical metres could a poet in the last decade of the twentieth century expect readers to be? I doubt that even those who, in 1993, rushed out to buy Donald Hall's new volume of *The Museum of Clear Ideas* will have readily recognized the variety of Greek and Latin metres they will have found in it. Fully half the book is given over to a sequence (itself called 'The Museum of Clear Ideas') of 38 poems, each corresponding to one of the lyrics in Horace's first book of odes. Very pointedly – because the age did not demand it – the poems attempt metrical equivalence, with the result that the book brims with Auden-sponsored syllabic versions of sapphics, various asclepiad measures, two poems in the alcmanic metre, and ten poems written in English alcaics.

This last metre, though, comes in for special attention. Hall is so self-conscious of the alcaic as to name it, uniquely, in one of the poems, 'I Celebrate Myself':

I celebrate myself. It's intelligent
to compound one's natural ability
   by hard work and luck, don't all of us
      agree? I sing in praise of Horsecollar,

complacently, without fear of murderous
rivals. I sing to display my Alcaics
   and my nobility of spirit:
      I praise my friends in the same project

and implore the muses that have favored me
to set resplendent laurels on the heads of

Flaccus, Camilla and Arbogast:
  'Parnassus affords adequate housing.'[1]

                                                    (1–12)

'Horsecollar' is the poet's pseudonym: the conceit of the sequence is that Hall re-writes Horace's odes under the name of Horace Horsecollar, 'a minor character in Walt Disney comics'.[2] (The suggestion that culture in the West has become Disneyfied is among Hall's chief themes.) Under cover of Horace's *Odes*, Horace Horsecollar gets away with a good deal of ironical horseplay, much of it satirizing American culture as declining from late republic to late empire, proliferating in trendy new pseudo-religions, mired in hopeless wars with half-understood middle-eastern enemies, and, on the literary front, teeming with tin-ear poetasters and rife with petty literary in-fighting. 'I Celebrate Myself' takes up this last theme, travestying a phrase of Walt Whitman's ('I celebrate myself, and sing myself') in order to send up authorial narcissism and the professional feuds it generates. It is also, however, a travesty of Horace's *Odes* 1.26, where the Roman poet goes in for a bit of boasting himself:

> As a friend of the muses, I shall fling gloom and fear to the turbulent winds to carry them into the Cretan sea: I am singularly indifferent about what king of a frozen region under the Bear is causing alarm, and what it is that's frightening Tiridates. You, sweet lady of Pipla, who take pleasure in fresh springs, weave sunny flowers, weave them into a garland for my dear Lamia. Without you all my tributes are worthless. To sanctify Lamia with new strings and the quill of Lesbos: that is a fitting task for you and your sisters.[3]
>
>   (1–12)

There's plenty of ironic whimsy in Horace's profession of indifference to the wild world of international politics: it is a characteristic form of self-deprecation, and a familiar gesture of recusal. But his insistence on the power of his verse to immortalize the memory of his friend Lamia is perfectly serious and demonstrably true: this book is among the proofs. Above all, for our purposes, there is a particular kind of boast: Horace's power to honour Lamia not just with any poetry, but with a metrical innovation, 'new strings and the quill of Lesbos' ('hunc fidibus novis, / hunc Lesbio sacrare plectro', 10–11). Horace means that he is the first poet to write, in Latin, poetry in the lyric tradition of Lesbos, and in this particular case the alcaic strophe. One cautious but persistent scholarly view is that this ode may even be Horace's first attempt at the alcaic strophe: a snapshot of the moment when the alcaic entered the second phase of its existence by passing from Greek lyric into a Latin poem.[4]

There is ironic point, then, in Hall's re-writing of this ode. 'I sing to display my Alcaics / and my nobility of spirit' undermines, with satirical crudity, Horace's serious claim of metrical innovation. Hall's persona mocks himself with self-praise, professing indifference not, as in Horace's poem, to the threat of national enemies, but the threat of rival poets, to whom he condescends with oleaginous professions of inclusivity: 'Parnassus affords adequate housing'. All this, while nevertheless setting himself apart from the lesser breed of poets presumably unable to write in alcaics – a glib echo of another alcaic poem, *Odes* 3.1, in which Horace distinguishes himself and his readers from the 'profanum vulgus', the common herd. (Whitman, who programmatically addressed the common man and eschewed formal metre, is in this way brought into ironical relationship with Horace.) Horsecollar trumpets the term 'alcaics' with the smugness of a schoolboy who has just learnt a new word. He knows that his audience, with the rarest exceptions, will not recognize the verse-form without the label 'alcaics'. The parallel is a middle-class visitor to a museum who appreciates a painting as soon as the label informs him it is a Rembrandt. By the late twentieth century, the very word 'alcaic' could seem as strange as the stanza form itself.

And what do Hall's alcaics look like? Superficially, very much like Auden's. They exactly replicate the alcaic syllable-count (11-11-9-10) without attempting to imitate any other metrical features. Hall is, in this sense as in many others, a son of Auden, one of those poets who, in the late twentieth and early twenty-first centuries, followed Auden's example and turned to the alcaic, together creating, at long last, a flourishing of the form in English. But unlike Auden's, Hall's alcaics are ventriloquized, spoken through the comical persona of Horace Horsecollar. The resulting ironic distance yields some insight into the whole prospect of writing alcaics at the turn of the twenty-first century.

In 'The Museum of Clear Ideas', Hall transposes the thirty-eight poems of Horace's first book of odes into the milieu of 1990s America. Cultural transposition of this kind is of course a commonplace of classical reception in English, perhaps most conspicuously in eighteenth-century Britain, when a global empire, whose literate population was still largely brought up on the classics, meant that the Rome of Horace or Juvenal seemed contemporary. Hence Pope's confident re-writing of Horace's epistles, and Samuel Johnson's versions of Juvenal's satires, with London standing in naturally for Rome. American writers in the twentieth century, as if dutifully receiving an inheritance from the mother country, pursued the same rough equation. Robert Lowell, to take one conspicuous example, had made new versions of Horace and Juvenal that suggested a 1960s America distinctly anxious about the possibility of its republic descending into empire. Donald Hall's Horace Horsecollar is himself rather more Juvenalian than Horatian in tone. The sequence as a whole builds up a picture of a decadent American-led Western culture. Despite its Horatian frame, it recalls later imperial Roman literature rather than Augustan.

The first poem in the sequence, corresponding to Horace *Odes* 1.1, introduces a cast of recurring characters as a kind of rogues' gallery. This is a significant departure from Horace's opening poem, which identifies various generic walks of life (some people are meant to be athletes, others farmers, or merchants, or soldiers) and concludes with Horace's programmatic declaration that as for himself, the muses have marked him out as a poet. There is no suggestion that any of those avocations is dishonourable. Hall's re-writing of Horace's poem, by contrast, parades a series of dubious late twentieth-century types, many of them assigned various ironical Greco-Roman pseudonyms. The tone is of arch disapproval. A number of characters, after an initial appearance in the opening poem (1–18), surface and resurface as the addressees of the later odes, including one Decius, the poet's own literary agent, 'whose guileful agency sustains / and decimates me'. (Much of the sequence takes aim at the absurdities of the literary economy upon which Hall himself partly depends.) Among the many academics similarly exposed are a certain Tanaquil (who fritters away her day dozing in the pub) and 'her Chair, who won an all-expenses paid / weekend in Rome, Italy' – an undignified but perhaps not entirely inaccurate characterization of an institutionally funded academic conference. Significantly, he 'would have favored / Las Vegas'. Meanwhile, Marvin is a drunkard. Joan backpacks through Toledo (Spain? Ohio? who knows?). Kim 'helicopters into Iranian / deserts', and Flaccus – despite his name, not to be confused with Horace Horsecollar, the fictive author of these poems – 'shoots tame wild antelope / in a hired game preserve'. (I take this as a dig at self-delusional and vainglorious poets.) There is a corrupt Senator Hell, who will re-appear, in Hall's version of ode 1.37, cast in the role of the lately defeated Cleopatra. And there is Julia, who 'treks through jungles and over Himalayas, / adding to her collections of deities'.[5] That last line is meant to be unflattering: the proliferation of novel, and especially of eclectic, forms of worship is a frequent object of Hall's scorn, as self-centred, consumerist, and deracinating.

One figure in Hall's rogue's gallery is especially illuminating: somebody called Madonna, who 'continues / to writhe in public, doing what she wants'. Hall may or may not have had in mind the pop music icon, who in any case by 1993 had become a household name. Madonna the entertainer suits the particular atmosphere of the sequence precisely because in her case the term 'icon' is doubly applicable. 'Madonna' is no mere stage name (she was christened Madonna Louise Ciccone at birth), but she does trade on a profane relation to her namesake, an arrangement that calls for little further engagement theologically, historically, or otherwise.[6] Given pop's eclipse of most other forms of culture, it is not hard to imagine educated adults for whom mention of the name 'Madonna' in all but a strictly ecclesiastical context would (at least at first) call to mind the singer rather than the saint. It is not unknown for her fans, even in countries where Christianity is long established, to discover that the Madonna's name is actually derivative of a medieval Italian term for the mother of Jesus. (I cannot throw stones: I admit that for me 'dulce et decorum pro patria mori' was first a line of Wilfred Owen's, and only later the work of Horace. The preposterous principle works equally well in pop culture as in classical poetry.) At the level of internet algorithms, this inversion is not potential but actual: a Wikipedia search for 'Madonna' serves up the pop star first; to get to the Virgin Mary requires persevering though at least two further steps: 'For further uses, see *Madonna (disambiguation)*.' Hall was writing half a decade before the internet began to catch on, but in the world he describes, the *ambiguation* of 'Madonna' had already begun. It is a world in which the residual forms of a disappearing culture can be tossed around as curiosities by artists who may very imperfectly understand them.

As the pop icon Madonna is to literal Christian icons of *the* Madonna, so is (roughly) Las Vegas to Rome. In 1993, when Hall published his alcaics, a visitor to Las Vegas could spend the better part of a day exploring a vast (is far vaster now) ersatz revision of ancient Rome, the casino and hotel complex called Caesars Palace. A version of ancient Rome, yes, but the Rome of which historical period, exactly? To insist on such a question would be obtuse, as presuming a principled engagement with antiquity. The spirit of Caesars Palace is rather of principled disengagement, which enables a kind of eclectic abandon. The 'classical' architecture and trappings draw on various phases of mostly imperial, but sometimes Etruscan, sometimes late republican, sometimes Renaissance aesthetics. Still other elements are nothing to do with Rome. All these are thrown together without discrimination. Rome wasn't built in a day, 'but on the other hand, Las Vegas *was* built in a day', as that city's most illustrious architectural defenders have rejoined.[7] The irony goes exactly to the point. A generous interpretation might be that Caesars Palace catches, if accidentally, something of the heady multicultural syncretism of the ancient Mediterranean world from the Hellenistic period through late antiquity. A more sceptical response would find the overall effect of the casino-complex to be hyperactive, and its exuberance fatuous, as avoiding, rather than inviting, informed engagement with the ancient world. In any case, the atmosphere of Caesars Palace, with its ersatz relation to history and culture, pervades the world of 'The Museum of Clear Ideas'. Of all of Hall's characters, the last person we would have expected to succumb to its allure is the senior academic, the one whose trip to 'Rome, Italy' is fully funded but who 'would have favored Las Vegas'. There's no accounting for taste, maybe, but what does it mean when a professor (we're not told if he's a professor of classics) prefers a kitsch version of Rome to the real thing? With respect to alcaics and the other Horatian metres in which Hall is writing, one implication is this: that there may be something ersatz about those English versions of Horatian metres. Hall's alcaics invite consideration as metrical kitsch. Their meaning, their relation to their Horatian source, is rather like the relation of Las Vegas to Rome.

'Lacking Latin, he follows his master visually'

Among Hall's characters, even more significant than Madonna is his spiritual eclectic, 'Julia'. She reappears in the poem that corresponds to Horace's *Odes* 1.12.[8] Hall's version, composed in syllabic sapphics, begins: 'The times are propitious for fake religions.' Julia, 'founder / of the God-of-the-Month-club', is the presiding spirit of a world of indiscriminately syncretized New-Age Glastonbury mysticism, Californianized quasi-Buddhisms, Joseph-Campbell-style Jungian self-help therapy, alternative pharmacology, native American shamanism, and on and on. The catalogue of 'fake' religious fads proliferates dizzily:

> Now with her biorhythm calculator,
> organic vitamins, ouija boards, yoga
> exercises, mesmerism, Iroquois shells,
>   Obeah routines,
>
> Zen meditation, Tantric sex games, Shirley
> MacLaine, phrenology, Fletcherizing, I
> Ching, and crucifix, she's in total control.
>   Unless she isn't.[9]

(29–36)

In any case, 'hype springs eternal', and Julia persists in her grab-bag spiritual experimentation. Accordingly, there's something odd about Hall's sapphics: in this context, their relation to their ancient sources is as tenuous as Julia's relation to the ancient spiritual and religious traditions she updates and dilutes. In the very same poem, though, there's a telling link to literary culture:

> Our bewitching friend
> mumbles and invokes, imploring the oak trees
> to accept worship – or should we say workshop?
> It's literary.[10]

(17–20)

That slip from 'worship' to 'workshop' points to a particular notion of literary decadence that runs through the world of 'The Museum of Clear Ideas', and offers a useful prism through which to understand the meaning of alcaic stanzas at the turn of the twenty-first century. 'Workshop' of course means writing workshops, that foundational instrument of the 'creative writing' programmes that emerged in American university English departments in the mid-twentieth century and eventually spread, after some decent shows of resistance, to universities across the English-speaking world. (Full disclosure: my own job involves leading workshops in writing poetry.) Hall's disapproval of writing workshops and their levelling influence on literary culture is a major theme in 'The Museum of Clear Ideas'. Here is his version of *Odes* 1.38, the final poem in Horace's first book:

> I, too, dislike it – the mannerism of plain,
> natural, or idiomatic language
> McPoets go in for. Horsecollar prefers
>   chatting in Latin,
>
> "Iowa delenda est," par example.
> Squish the demotic underfoot, Arbogast.
> When you take up syntax and semicolons,
>   then show me your stuff.

'Iowa' stands for the Iowa Writers' Workshop, then as now the most famous of university creative writing programmes in the anglophone world. For Hall the word is metonymic for what he took to be the unseemly professionalization of poetic practice. Under the guidance of a securely tenured poet-professor (or an anxious untenured aspirant), budding poets develop by submitting their work-in-progress to the scrutiny of their student peers, who voice their critiques round a seminar table. The process must surely be helpful in many ways: egregiously bad writing, for instance, is likely to be spotted and addressed. But to the degree that workshops begin to operate like committees, they tend, Hall thinks, to encourage consensus and uniformity. Consensus in writing programmes has tended to reward 'plain, / natural, or idiomatic language'. As against the honourable instincts of (say) a Wordsworth, seeking to bring the language of poetry closer to actual spoken English, workshop culture fosters a specious demotic that is itself a 'mannerism'. A budding poet, taking her lead from Donne or Pope or Hopkins (or indeed Horace), might submit for workshopping a poem alive with unconventional syntax, or with a richly complex and innovative metre, only to find her ambition cut down to size with admonitions to purge such eccentricities in favour of 'authentic' plain speech. If poets and their teachers had known enough to recognize 'Iowa delenda est' as a travesty of Cato the Elder's call for the destruction of Carthage, they might also have appreciated and sought to emulate the metrical craft and syntactic inventiveness of Horace's lyric verse. Writing programmes, for Hall, generate sameness and formlessness on an industrial model: McPoets assembling McPoems. (In another poem, 'Let many bad poets', a version of *Odes* 1.7, Hall complains of the ubiquity of 'free verse' / without attention to / line breaks', the product of merely credentialled poets who 'program' their 'poem-processors'.)[11] Aspiring poets these days don't go in for 'chatting in Latin', and wouldn't recognize how, in the last line of the poem, Hall not only achieves the requisite five syllables that the sapphic metre calls for, but also replicates the metrical pattern (/ u u / u). The very sapphic form of Hall's own poem is a rebuke to the deracinated, unambitious, shapeless free verse he complains of. The poem's first four words (a quotation from Marianne Moore) are particularly germane. Moore's own intricate syllabic prosody, as we saw in Chapter 5, played a crucial role in Auden's development of the kind of syllabic-based classical stanzas in which Hall himself writes. It is a poem that acknowledges its metrical genealogy, and makes an issue out of the very project of writing poetry in classical lyric forms as the twentieth century grinds to an end. In such a context, Hall's alcaic stanzas could hardly stand out more as counter to the prevailing literary culture.

And yet in the context of the relentlessly de-centred and deracinated 'culture' of 'The Museum of Clear Ideas', the force of the alcaic is starved of historical and cultural resonance. Its force now derives from its oddness: the unlikeliness of so exacting and unfamiliar a metrical structure. It has to be announced by name, like an exotic curiosity at a circus (or at Circus Circus): 'I sing to declare my Alcaics'. In that sense the decision of Horace Horsecollar to follow the metrical pattern of his ancient namesake is not so different from Julia's decision to take up her own version of some ancient forms of spirituality – Iroquois shells, the *I Ching* – in combination with ouija boards and phrenology.

Unlike Owen's 'old Kemp' or John Hollander, Horace Horsecollar hasn't come late to Latin: he hasn't come to Latin at all. 'Lacking Latin,' Hall writes in a footnote, 'he follows his master visually, the number and shape of stanzas,'[12] which means that his alcaics communicate their character as alcaics chiefly as visual signs, by their shape. On this point they differ from Auden's, whose classical lyrics they superficially resemble. Auden's stanzas originate in his own first-hand acquaintance with the movement of Horace's lyric metres, and his memory of their movements informs the composition of the syllabic stanzas. We saw in Chapter 5 how, from time to time, as in 'Ode to Terminus' and 'Posthumus Letter to Gilbert White', an audible Horatian cadence or two breaks cover, as it were, from the otherwise rhythmless syllabic stanzas. The poem from 'The Museum of Clear Ideas' that corresponds to Horace *Odes* 1.32 finds Horace Horsecollar, Latinless, aiming instead for 'syllabic / exactitude', and achieving this by counting 'on his eleven fingers'. Eleven fingers, of course, because of the hendecasyllabic lines in both the alcaic and sapphic strophes.

There is nothing dishonourable composing alcaics as Horsecollar does, counting out the syllables on his eleven fingers. We can, though, distinguish one kind of English alcaic (syllabic stanzas, but composed by a poet who like Auden has heard the music of Horace's lyric meters) from those alcaics composed by poets working at a remove from an encounter with the Latin, poets who reconstruct a visual stanza from the syllable-count of an ancient form whose music they cannot hear. Horace Horsecollar and his ilk, poets who, as a result of Auden's example, can now 'display' their syllabic alcaics in English, are working not only at a remove from Horace but also even at a remove from Auden, who heard something they have never heard, which cannot be reflected in their stanzas. Such poets may write beautiful lyrics in syllabic alcaics, but aural and cultural continuities will be broken or attenuated, for better or for worse. They can approach the alcaic through counting fingers, but not through their ears. This increasing distance from Horace (and the classical inheritance more generally) is the major characteristic of twenty-first century alcaics.

The Auden tradition

A second phenomenon is the increasing association of alcaics with Auden rather than Horace. It can be noted even in those poets, now exceptional, who work squarely and consciously within the classical tradition. John Hollander offers a prime example, in the two English alcaic poems we met in Chapter 1: his rendering of Horace's Soracte ode (1.9), and 'To an Old Latin Teacher'. These are not the works of a poet ignorant of the classics. Their overt references to Horace could hardly be more specific. Both poems are written not in Audenesque syllabic stanzas, but in accentual-syllabics that come close to replicating, in English stressed-based measures, the ancient alcaic's pattern of longs and shorts, slightly modified. Hollander knows how the alcaic moves metrically: he does not need to count on his eleven fingers to reconstruct the stanza (though in fact he would need twelve fingers to number the syllables of his particular version of the alcaic). For all these Horatian qualities, though, we find Audenesque resonances in 'To an Old Latin Teacher'. One telling bit of evidence is in his handling of the first two lines of his alcaic strophe, which should strictly be masculine, but in Hollander are made feminine, as in so many of Auden's alcaics, and indeed in all of them from 1969 on. This detail would help to explain why, in praising Hollander's early work, Auden himself singled out for particular mention the younger poet's happy alternation of masculine and feminine line endings.[13] Hollander's alcaics bear the mark of Auden's later alcaic experiments. Auden is so outstandingly the main impetus of the twenty-first century proliferation of alcaics that even such a poet as Hollander, writing with a complete awareness of that metre as a Horatian inheritance, nevertheless writes alcaics within an emerging Audenesque tradition.

Other accomplished writers of English alcaics, though, appear to be working on the example of Auden without any discernible reference to Horace or any other ancient lyricist. One instance out of many would by Marilyn Hacker. She has written hundreds of alcaic strophes, but they descend chiefly from Auden rather than Horace. Sometimes she acknowledges this influence overtly. One of her major alcaic poems, 'Farewell to the Finland Woman', a long elegy to a Hungarian survivor of the Nazi death camps, tellingly uses for its epigraph lines from Auden's alcaic poem 'In Memory of Sigmund Freud'.[14] For another alcaic poem, 'Days of 1992',[15] she chose as an epigraph a line from fellow American Alfred Corn's 'Somerset Alcaics'; Corn himself is another disciple of Auden. Hacker's alcaics, like Auden's, are syllabic rather than accentual (as in Hollander). They are Audenesque, too, in a different way, which has more to do with pacing and tone, and opens up questions of metrical propriety. Auden's alcaic poems tend to be prolix and garrulous, especially the later examples, though a similar discursiveness is evident even in early examples such as the Freud ode. This aspect of the American Auden stands in contrast to the terser English Auden, and to the lapidary compression typical of Horatian odes which, even at their longest, are never chatty, as Auden's are. Rosanna Warren, picking up on this quality, has suggested the term 'talking ode' as a way of characterizing the way that Auden's alcaic poems, while formally invoking song, nevertheless rhetorically 'perform speech and argument'.[16] Another way of putting it would be to say that Auden's reinvention of the alcaic involves making it a vehicle for discursive rumination: he draws his rambling, essay-like musings through stanza after stanza of the ancient lyric metre, producing a counterpoint between two very different modes. Running Walt Whitman's rambling ruminations and catalogues through the template of Emily Dickinson's compact stanzas would produce a similar effect.

Hacker's alcaic poems pick up on the conversational prolixity of Auden's, as if, by the force of his example, the gabby rhetorical mode had somehow become linked to the ancient metrical form. In her long, expertly meandering poem 'Quai Saint-Bernard',[17] Hacker delivers a relaxed, rangy report of the various activities of humans and animals drawn, like her, to the banks of the Seine on a Sunday morning. The stanzas are alcaic, but the character of the poem is nothing like the formal compression of a Horatian ode. The leisurely pace, the urbane tone, the very gentle hint of satire, have more in common with the feel of Horatian *sermo* rather than his lyrics. Hacker runs against the grain of Horatian metrical propriety: one can imagine Horace writing about a stroll along the Tiber, but in hexameter, not in lyric measures. Contemporary writers of alcaics tend to imitate Auden's discursive style instead. It is the Anglo-American, not the classical, alcaic.

One even gets this conflation of lyric form and discursive mode in the elegant alcaics of the Canadian poet Daryl Hine, who took his undergraduate and advanced degrees in classics, and produced verse translations of Theocritus, the Homeric Hymns, and other classical works. He knows his Horace, and in his epigraph to his alcaic poem 'Choubouloutte', even calls it 'An Horatian Ode'. But again, the movement and tone are more relaxed, rangy and ruminative than is typical of Horatian lyric. The poet has visited a Caribbean island, of which he proceeds to give a chromatically vivid picture, while posing philosophical questions about Western colonialism.[18] His English alcaics are as accomplished as any: the sentences run limberly and variously through the metrical template, with minimal contortion. Readers with a good ear and a knowledge of the alcaic may even be able to pick up the rhythm. In spoken performance, a conscientious reader could plausibly realize the alcaic pattern in the ear by stressing the relevant accents without too much violence to ordinary English pronunciation. In terms of pacing and tone, though, Hine's poem is evidence that English alcaics have now been adopted to a discursive and ruminative rhetorical mode, which has more in common with Horace's satires and epistles than with his odes. It would make more sense to set Hine's alcaics alongside Auden's rambling alcaic verse-essays than it would to compare them with any of Horace's odes.

Where is this emerging tradition leading? To stanzas like the following, which comes near the end of a beautiful poem called 'Living' by the American poet (and accomplished translator from the Swedish) Bill Coyle. A frozen lake in a New England winter provokes the following reflection – a literal reflection:

> There is a dark below and a dark above;
> The fish are darting stars while the stars are schools
>   That drift so glacially their slightest
>   Movement plays out over generations.
>
>   (25–8)[19]

Much of the stanza's excellence is Coyle's alone. Some part of it, though, flows to him as an inheritance from Alcaeus to Horace and through Auden to Auden's mostly North American successors. Coyle's alcaics have travelled further from their classical sources than any we have yet seen. The success of Auden's followers has meant the alcaic strophe has at last become naturalized into the anglophone tradition, so that a skilful poet such as Coyle can take up the form confidently and elegantly, while writing in the tradition of Hollander and Hacker rather than Horace. It is now possible for alcaics to be written that have swum free of any classical context, as if modern writers of *terza rima* could expect their readers not to think of Dante. To write alcaics on such a blank cultural slate was impossible for Tennyson: even up through the middle of the twentieth century it was hardly possible. Neither Alcaeus, nor even Horace, is any longer necessarily a presence in English alcaics, even as the verse-form is at last flourishing.

A movement against free verse

One dimension of this state of things has to do with a late twentieth-century reaction against the ubiquity of free verse. By the 1970s it had become countercultural to compose formal metrical verse, and those practising and promoting it came to be known (though the name is misleading) as 'The New Formalists'.[20] Among its manifestations was a flourishing market for handbooks on formal poetic technique, introducing the principles of English prosody and supplying examples of its various fixed verse forms.[21] Aspiring poets curious about formal models could find examples of non-English forms, among them the classical metres, though usually illustrated only with English examples, such as Coleridge's mnemonic couplet demonstrating the classical elegaic in English, or a poem of Hardy's to illustrate the sapphic. The implicit assumption was that many readers will have been reared without a firm grasp even of traditional English prosody, let alone the classical metres. Sadly, the most common model in such handbooks for the alcaic is Tennyson's ode to Milton, meaning that this unattractive experiment, for many curious readers who consult metrical handbooks, will constitute their entire experience of the form. Study of classical metres was no longer connected to study of the classical languages and their literatures.[22]

The editors of one of the best such manuals, *An Exaltation of Forms* (2002), strive to avoid polemic, but one clear burden of their book is to offer some resistance to what one of the contributors calls the current 'hegemony of free verse'.[23] That contributor was none other than Marilyn Hacker, whose own alcaics, then, may be understood as part of a conscious resistance to the dominant verse-form of the turn of the twentieth-first century. Readers of *An Exaltation of Forms* are implicitly invited to resist that hegemony: the manual presents itself as, among other things, 'a text for a poetry writing class', and offers the budding poet examples of dozens of received verse forms, ancient and modern, as models. Poets casting about for alternatives to free verse (perhaps in one of those creative writing workshops that Donald Hall so dislikes) could turn to such a manual and, as it were, shop around for an intriguing form. A poet might in this way discover the alcaic in the abstract, bypassing any sustained encounter with the tradition of that form. I present this fact as critically neutral: picking up a metre casually from a manual, rather than coming to know it from the experience of reading actual poems attentively over time, may in some cases precipitate an excellent poem. I only mean that the New Formalist movement and its associated manuals of metrical forms made it particularly easy to encounter the alcaic without reading even Auden, let alone Auden's ancient forbears. There was also the risk of mistaking the alcaic (or any other metre) for a mere abstract scheme, as distinct from the actual poems shaped by responses of generation of poets writing in that metre across space and time.

'What the Loeb gives'

One way of pondering the curious dissociation of alcaics from their classical sources would be to write a scholarly monograph. Perhaps a more vivid way would be to write a satirical poem, and to compose it in alcaics. For just such a poem (and this will be the last alcaic poem I enlist for this book) we return to Donald Hall's 'Museum of Clear Ideas'. Horace Horsecollar's rendering of Horace *Odes* 1.37, the Cleopatra ode, transposes the complex Mediterranean scene into an American election year. Whereas Horace's poem celebrates, or purports to celebrate, Octavian's victory over Marc Antony (and Cleopatra) at Actium in 31 BCE, Hall's version gloats over last night's electoral defeat of the unsavoury Senator Hell, 'tobacco's senator' (21), bluff exponent of 'fund-raising, bigotry, merde, contempt for art' (18).[24] To re-imagine a military victory as a win at the polls is clever enough, but an asymmetry weakens the force of Hall's poem, or ironizes it: he writes from the relative security and ease of a free democratic republic. Senator Hell may be awful, but at least he is seen off without bloodshed, and in decent democratic fashion. In Horace's ode rather more is at stake. The Roman republic is on the verge of extinction; Octavian's victory seems to promise an end to decades of civil war, but at the price of enabling autocracy; and poor Horace, veteran of a Republican army not long ago crushed by Octavian himself, must now find a way of praising his former enemy's victory. These tensions, highlighted by a longstanding debate as to whether Horace depicts the defeated Cleopatra too sympathetically, are absent from the painless triumphalism of Hall's poem.

There's some compensating irony, though. Hall begins his version of the Cleopatra ode by quoting Horace's own opening words (one of those Horatian tags so familiar to Wilfred Owen and John Hollander) in the original Latin:

> Nunc est bibendum. To condescend the phrase
> into the preferred demotic – Latin that
>   plain folks talk, picking up Anglish from
>   the cowboy and High Dutch from the sergeant –
>
> we may translate the suggestion, "let's get burnt,"
> or choose the style of C. E. Bennet (Cornell
>   University, nineteen-fourteen):
>   'Now is the time to drain the flowing bowl.'
>
>   (1–8)

Here is a re-writing of Horace, composed in alcaics, that draws attention to the predicament of re-writing Horace in alcaics in modern America. The immediate problem is one of diction: what is a credible register in which to voice Horace in 1993? 'Let's get burnt' will not quite do, but neither will the elaborate translationese of the 1914 Loeb Classical Library version: 'Now is the time to drain the flowing bowl'. We are living in a world where the name 'Horace' no longer instantly conveys a world of associations, many of them rooted in childhood, as they did in 1914, the year of Bennet's translation, the very year when Wilfred Owen wrote home to report his astonishment that his friend Kemp was only learning his Latin at 24 years of age. The English alcaics of the young E. E. Cummings (briefly mentioned in the Preface) date from 1916; Wilfred Owen began 'Dulce Et Decorum Est' in 1917. Donald Hall is not only rendering a famous ode of Horace, but, in the very act, conspicuously drawing attention (Cornell / University, nineteen-fourteen') to the distance the culture has travelled, in less than a century, from a first-hand acquaintance with its classical sources.

The implication is not just that Horace Horsecollar, 'lacking Latin' like everybody else, has got to repair to the Loeb Classical Library, with its en-face translations, to get a sense of what Horace 'literally' said, by looking at Bennet's translation on the right-hand page. He also wants to get a sense of the shape of Horace's stanzas ('lacking Latin, he follows his master *visually* – the number and *shape* of his stanzas', my emphasis), and for this he turns to the Latin printed on the left-hand page. Whereupon he works out at least the syllable-count ('Horsecollar counts on his eleven fingers'), though no amount of eyeballing could deduce the rhythmic pattern of the quantitative Latin metre. Cut off from the aural dimension of the alcaic's prosody, he can mirror only the syllable-count. And voilà: English syllabic alcaics, deduced from studying the shape of Horace's mute stanzas on the page, without ever having heard the rhythm of those Latin stanzas, and as such conveying no audible metre in English. The paradoxical nature of the new kind of English alcaic is described in a poem itself written in this new kind of English alcaic.

The effect of Hall's meta-commentary may not be very funny, but it does achieve satiric point. The idea is that the whole classical inheritance is still there: mostly confined to old books, maybe, but at least available. It is no longer, though, so much an inheritance as a quarry to be raided. The classical part of the Western tradition, by the mid-twentieth century, was no longer getting efficiently passed on to the next generation as the common property of literate people. It was being stashed away in various kinds of silos. It is there to be found, but you must seek it out yourself. Classics faculties may have done their best to keep the tradition going, but many factors, including the decline of Latin teaching in schools, and a growing emphasis on professionalization and specialization in the universities,[25] meant that the classics had increasingly become a niche academic subject rather than a common inheritance. Classics departments were like silos where the classical inheritance was stowed.[26]

Another kind of silo is books, and here we return to Loeb Classical Library, out of which Donald Hall's Horace Horsecollar reconstructs his postmodern Horatian ode and his version of the alcaic metre. The first volumes of the Loeb series began to appear in 1913. Early reviews make clear that its first readers understood them chiefly as an aid to the amateur classicist seeking to refresh his rusty Greek or Latin. Or indeed *her* rusty Greek or Latin, since the most distinguished of those early reviewers, Virginia Woolf, described the Loebs as a 'gift' to those amateur 'lovers of Greek' who, having long ago studied the ancient language, now wanted to exercise their 'moribund faculties' so that their 'little stock of Greek became improved'.[27] We have already encountered, in Chapter 1, a less distinguished (but for that reason more representative) critic, John Henry Fowler, who, reviewing the new Loeb edition of Catullus, took for granted that its readers would be *reminded* of the Latin cadences they had already studied as schoolboys. The Loebs, then, first appeared in a literary culture where at least the memory of Latin was still broadly assumed as a common possession rather than a professional specialization.

Writing at the other end of the twentieth century, Donald Hall finds that the purpose of the Loeb Library radically changed. In his world, almost nobody knows Latin, not even his poetic persona, Horace Horsecollar, who, undaunted, composes a series of 38 Horatian odes. The Loebs are now more likely be the site of one's first encounter with the classics, rather than occasion for reminiscence and re-acquaintance. In 1993, almost nobody has a classical past to remember. Horace Horsecollar experiences Horace not as an inheritance, but as quarry, not as part of the living culture, but as an inert stock of literary material available to make use of, if you know where to find it. Horsecollar accordingly plunders the relevant Loeb. He gets out of it what he can, and that happens to include a version of the alcaic strophe. One can feel the difference between an inheritance and a plundering. To read *In Memoriam* is to feel, at the level of poetic metre and in every other way, Tennyson's transformation of a poetic tradition that had been a part of his mental and spiritual life from childhood, as part of the cultural air he breathed. To read Donald Hall's alcaics, or more properly Horace Horsecollar's, is to experience something else: a clever child raiding a trunk in the attic, pulling from among the cottonballs the costume of another day and age, trying it on, and – this is the point of Hall's ironic self-referentiality – admiring himself, half-comprehendingly, in the mirror. (I will return to this attic shortly.)

The volumes of the Loeb Library in that sense embody a paradox that casts light on the reception of alcaics in the twentieth-first century. They constitute a transitional moment in the gradual democratization of the classics, a process that, as I have written elsewhere, has been underway since at least the nineteenth century.[28] An aspiring middle class, together with working-class autodidacts, clamoured for access to the Greek and Latin masterpieces that their merely English education had denied them. A translation industry rose to meet the demand for workmanlike but serviceable renderings of classical literature. The result has been a blessing, but a mixed one. On the one hand: far better Thucydides in translation than no Thucydides at all. On the other hand, when 'democratization of the classics' entails the widespread abandonment of the study of Greek and Latin, the result is, perversely, to make access to the classics themselves even more exclusive. When it comes to the cadences of lyric verse, one might say there is no substitute for the actual Greek and Latin poems. The paradox of the Loebs is that they capture the tension between the untranslated classics and the popular reliance on translation. At the moment of their appearance, the Loebs were a manifestation of what was still even then – though not for much longer – the centrality of the classics. They allowed a broad class of readers to revisit their acquaintance with the ancient languages themselves.

Seamus Heaney used the Loebs in precisely that way. In his 2010 poem 'The Riverbank Field', among the most remarkable instances of his lifelong preoccupation with Virgil, Heaney produced a dizzyingly allusive re-writing of a passage from the sixth book of the *Aeneid*. He lets a river in his native Northern Ireland, the Moyola, stand in for the infernal River Lethe. Nothing unusual about that. What is unusual, though, is that Heaney cites the relevant volume of the Loeb Classical Library as both his point of departure and as his mediator between the ancient and modern worlds: 'Ask me to translate what the Loeb gives as / "In a retired vale ... a sequestered grove" / And I'll confound the Lethe in Moyola' (1–3).[29] Heaney goes on to quote from both Virgil's Latin and the Loeb translator's rendering, recreating the experience of a reader's eyes shuttling back and forth between the left- and right-hand pages, between the Latin and the English. The presence of a single, unqualified word – 'Loeb' – is all that Heaney needs to summon a universe of associations and feelings. The idea, for instance, of a received cultural standard, needing no introduction or justification. Virgil, as embodied in the Loeb edition, with both the half-remembered Latin and the English translation side-by-side, is understood as a common possession, part of the culture. The Loeb itself is a feature of memory. It is a shared baseline from which Heaney can then creatively elaborate, translating Virgil's Elysian Fields onto the topography of his Irish homeland. For Heaney, the Loeb edition of Virgil both assumes, and is itself part of, a cultural continuity, an inheritance.

Donald Hall casts a colder eye. In his poem, the Loeb is not what it is for Heaney, but the opposite: a reminder of cultural discontinuity. It is an artifact from the past – he emphasizes the distance in time with bibliographic detachment: 'C. E. Bennet (Cornell / University, *nineteen fourteen*)'. His translator-persona comes to that Loeb volume, with its outmoded translation, not as Heaney comes to his, but as a stranger to the ancient language and its alien metrical movements. It is not, as for Heaney, a revisiting, stirring up ghosts of childhood Latin which then, exquisitely, join with the shades of the underworld that Virgil conjures. Horace Horsecollar's encounter with his Roman namesake is a novelty, and the Loeb volume 'contains', as if in storage, a strange quantity labelled 'Horace'. Hall shows us what it looks like when a curious postmodern, with his own absurdly deracinated postmodern name, Horace Horsecollar, raids a Loeb, and in that way comes upon what he is unprepared to inherit. That is roughly what I mean by the title of this chapter. What might have been received as an inheritance has to be got, if at all, as quarry.

'Deracinated fragments of a globalized post-modernity'

I wrote in the Preface of this book that it springs from a chapter that I published in a 2009 collection of essays on Horatian reception. That chapter was a mere sketch of what I wanted to say: 'given in outline and no more'. Now that I have had an ampler say, I want to bring in two provocative responses to that earlier work from two distinguished classicists. Writing in *TLS* in reference to my chapter, Charles Martindale – to whom all of us who write about the classical tradition are deeply indebted – wrote that 'if the *Odes* are Horace's greatest work, there is no substitute for an encounter with the original Latin'. I agree. As for the twenty-first century alcaics I had briefly pointed to, Martindale went on to write that 'such deracinated fragments of a globalized post-modernity hardly represent a significant classical tradition in any worthwhile sense'.[30] This is a wonderfully trenchant claim. Do I agree? That is the question implicit in this Afterword. I share Martindale's doubt about the value of a classical 'tradition' of the kind that Horace Horsecollar's alcaics embody and ironically (in a world where such ironies exasperatingly never end) contributes to. The alcaic strophe survives in English, and in its odd way now prospers; but it is not at all clear to me what this survival means if (to borrow a biblical image) alcaics are cut off from the vine.

I have held in reserve one poem which supports Martindale's scepticism. It appeared in the remarkable 2002 translation-by-many-hands of Horace's *Odes* edited by J. D. McClatchy. It is a relaxed re-writing, by the American poet Robert Bly, of *Odes* 1.26 – the very poem with which, in Hall's version, I began this Afterword. Like Hall's 'I sing to display my Alcaics', Bly's poem explicitly (and eccentrically) refers to the metre of Horace's original. He addresses his muse with a gung-ho request: 'Let's do this in Alcaic meter' (10).[31] Despite the solecism ('in Alcaic meter'), Bly has done some homework, and discovered that Horace's poem is written in the poet's signature stanza. He may even have learnt that 1.26 is thought by some scholars to be Horace's very first alcaic poem, the alcaic's debut in Latin verse – in which case there would be some licence for naming the verse-form in the translation itself, though Horace in his own poem does not. Bly's translation consists of twelve metrically inert lines, grouped into quatrains to impart a specious sense of order on their formlessness. The contrast between Bly's own metrical sloppiness and the artfulness of the alcaic whose name he so insouciantly drops, but which he cannot himself 'do', is not flattering. To have written 'let's do this in Alcaic meter' awkwardly calls attention to Bly's failure to have done it. This may itself be pointedly ironic, but I find no evidence of self-consciousness. For its combination of glib cockiness combined with metrical indifference, Bly's poem represents a low point in my account of the alcaic presence in twenty-first century English verse. If this is the classical tradition, we have to wonder, with Martindale, whether it is worthwhile.

A more whimsical response to my earlier work comes from Richard Tarrant, in his 2020 study of Horace's *Odes*. Reflecting on my account of Latinless poets writing English alcaics without any knowledge of Horace, he conjured a personage out of Wonderland: 'Horace himself fades away like the Cheshire Cat, leaving his meter behind – not what he meant by *non omnis moriar* ("I shall not entirely die"), but a form of survival nonetheless.'[32] If I share Martindale's scepticism about the value of a post-modern, deracinated alcaic 'tradition', then Tarrant's image helps me articulate another dimension of my feeling. The 'survival' of the Cheshire Cat's smile is marvellous but also disconcerting and bemusing. You might say of a zombie that at least he isn't entirely dead, and if, with respect to the alcaic, 'non omnis moriar' has turned out to mean not quite as Horace had meant it, then maybe the thing to do is to shrug one's shoulders and be content with 'a form of survival'. One could argue, though, that the 'strophic vigor' that Hollander refers to in his own engaging English alcaics springs from their rootedness in their classical sources as a living tradition. I think of Mary Sidney, and the vividness with which her embrace of the classical tradition (which includes rich interrelations with Christian and Hebrew scripture and liturgy, ancient and modern) animates and gives meaning to the alcaics of her Psalm 120. Deracinated, post-modern alcaics, on the other hand, are more likely to suffer from a corresponding anaemia. They may be less remarkable on their own terms than as tokens of cultural disinheritance. The lingering grin of the faded Cheshire Cat? I find it disconcerting, and leave it lingering here as an apt image for this Afterword, as the Afterword itself is about to fade away.

A coda

So much for alcaics. In turning at last away from them I return to this book's introduction. It began not with alcaics but phalaecean hendecasyllabics. Here, as a bookend, is another English poem in that metre, this time (aptly) by W. H. Auden. In July of 1963, as part of a sequence of poems celebrating the various rooms of his house, he composed a little meditation on the domestic attic and called it 'Up There'. These are its first six lines:

> Men would never have come to need an attic.
> Keen collectors of glass or Roman coins build
> Special cabinets for them, dote on, index,
> Each new specimen: only women cling to
> Items out of their past they have no use for,
> Can't name now what they couldn't bear to part with.

If we needed an emblem to mediate between 'inheritance' and 'quarry', we might light upon the image of the attic. In the house you grew up in, or the house of a family member, what's in the attic may prove to be both an inheritance *and* a quarry. The time comes when (because of spring cleaning, or to fix a leaky roof, or on the death of a parent or grandparent, or just out of curiosity) you break into the attic and discover, or rediscover, what had been stowed there. You raid the attic. What you find, though, may prove more than just quarry: it may also be your inheritance, somebody else's past to which you yourself are connected. The sense of mere plunder decreases in proportion as one knows, understands, feels connection to, those who came before.

The attic of Western culture is crammed. What do you do with old stuff you find in it? Auden thought he could distinguish two responses to what may be recovered from our past. (He proposes, by the way, a distinction between men and women that nobody ought to be expected to assent to. For my own part I think he meant it to be taken whimsically rather than dogmatically.) In light of my preoccupations in this book, I could read Auden's poem like this. A certain kind of poet – such as Mary Sidney, or Tennyson, or Auden himself – resembles the 'keen collector' of Roman coins who self-consciously signals expertise in ancient artifacts by labelling them and building 'special cabinets' to showcase them. Such poets deploy the alcaic in English not casually, but with expert deliberation, conscious of the metre's allusive resonance, and inviting the ghosts of earlier practitioners, ancient and modern, to inhabit their verses. On the other hand, another kind of poet may handle alcaics in English skilfully but without an acute sense of Greek or Latin poetry itself, and with no special use in mind, and indeed may not know much more about the alcaic other than its name. That sort of poet is closer to Auden's indiscriminate hoarders who 'cling to / Items out of their past they have no use for, / Can't name now what they couldn't bear to part with.' The year was 1963: who, in 1963, would cling to an ancient form? Who would have a use for it? Yet here was an English poet writing in a classical metre, hoping it would catch the eye of whatever dream readers may still be left who could hear the phalaecean hendacsyllabic and spot the choriambs.

Notes

Preface

1 W. H. Auden, reply to a symposium on Auden's 'A Change of Air', *Kenyon Review* 26 (Winter 1964): 208.

2 Throughout this book I use particular symbols (– and u) to indicate the 'long' and 'short' syllables of classical quantitative prosody, based on the duration of syllables. A different set of symbols (/ and u) are used to indicate the 'stressed' and 'unstressed' syllables of English accentual prosody. These representations, though conventional, are crude: both systems are far more subtle than can be conveniently represented. For instance, any sensitive reading of English accentual verse registers also the quantity of a syllable, even though there is no conventional diacritical mark to indicate that dimension. What is more: English poets seeking to reproduce classical metres in English most often translate a classical 'long' into English as a stressed syllable, and a classical 'short' as an unstressed syllable. Even for Auden himself, though he was not at all deaf to English quantities, an English choriamb meant, more or less, two stressed syllables enclosing two unstressed syllables (/ u u /). This is not the same thing as a Greek or Latin choriamb (– u u –), two long syllables enclosing two shorts. The English accentual form is an analogy, not a replication, of the classical form, but it is a reasonable compromise, and after several centuries of use, poets – not to speak of critics – can sometimes seem cavalier about the distinction. I myself, throughout this book, toggle between discussions of classical quantitative and English stress metres, tending to minimize the differences, except in instances where the distinction becomes urgent.

3 John Haffenden, *W. H. Auden: The Critical Heritage* (Abingdon, UK: Routledge, 1983), 55.

4 W. H. Auden, *The Portable Greek Reader* (Harmondsworth, UK: Penguin, 1948), 3.

5 Throughout this book, I use the terms 'strophe' and 'stanza' interchangeably.

6 Robert Frost, *Collected Poems, Prose, and Plays*, ed. Richard Poirier and Mark Richardson (New York: Library of America, 1995), 208.

7 Stanley Burnshaw, *Robert Frost Himself* (New York: G. Braziller, 1986), 131.

8 Jeffrey S. Cramer, *Robert Frost Among His Poems* (Jefferson, NC: McFarland, 1995), 79.

9 Letter to George Whicher, 23 May 1919, now in the collections of Amherst College Library.

10 Frost, *Collected Poems, Prose, and Plays*, 776.

11 Timothy Steele, '"Across Spaces of the Footed Line": The Meter and Versification of Robert Frost', in *The Cambridge Companion to Robert Frost*, ed. Robert Faggen (Cambridge: Cambridge University Press, 2001), 133.

12 Frost, *Collected Poems, Prose, and Plays*, 670.

13 Ibid., 849.

14 Ibid., 469.

15 Lawrence Buell, 'Frost as a New England Poet', in Faggen, *The Cambridge Companion to Robert Frost*, 111.

16 Jay Parini, *Robert Frost, A Life* (New York: Henry Holt, 1999), 181.

17 Rueben Brower, *The Poetry of Robert Frost: Constellations of Intention* (New York: Oxford University Press, 1963), 136–9.

18 Steele, 'Across Spaces', 142.

19 A point made by the leading Catullan commentator contemporary with Frost: Robinson Ellis, *A Commentary on Catullus* (Oxford, Clarendon Press, 1889), xiv.

20 Frost, *Complete Poems, Prose, and Plays*, 852.

21 Ibid., 446, 451.

22 Quoted in Reginald Cook, *Robert Frost: A Living Voice* (Amherst, MA: The University of Massachusetts Press, 1974), 91.

23 David D. Cooper, s.v. 'For Once, Then, Something', in *The Robert Frost Encyclopedia*, ed. Lewis Tuten and John Zubizarreta (Westport, CT: Greenwood Press, 2001), 120.

24 *Times Literary Supplement* (10 April 1913), 155.

25 Norman Douglas, 'Poetry', *The English Review* 14 (1913): 505.

26 Lascelles Abercrombie, 'A New Voice', *The Nation* 15 (1914): 423.

27 George W. Nitchie, quoted in Donald J. Greiner, *Robert Frost: The Poet and His Critics* (Chicago: American Library Association, 1974), 224.

28 Cooper, 'For Once, Then, Something', 120.

29 Greiner, *Robert Frost: The Poet and His Critics*, 224.

30 In this line Frost expertly brings ictus and accent into tension: English prose sense requires stressing the word 'clear', which in the hendecasyllabic scheme coincides with an unstressed position. A disruption in the metre, then, just at the moment when the droplet of water disrupts the surface of the pool and removes the clarity.

31 Ellis, *A Commentary on Catullus*, 48.

32 D. F. S. Thomson, *Catullus* (Toronto: University of Toronto Press, 1997), 312.

33 Hans Peter Syndikus, *Catull: Eine Interpretation* (Darmstadt: Wissenschaftliche Buchgesellschaft, 1984) I, 6: 'Ein Teil der in Hendekasyllaben abgefassten Gedichte hat einen ausgesprochen jambischen Charakter, und Catull bezeichnet auch dieses Versmaß als Träger jambischen Angriffs.'

34 Kenneth Quinn, *Catullus: The Poems* (London: Macmillan, 1970), 144, appreciates the way that lines 1–2, which he takes as conveying a mere figure of speech, come, by the time they are repeated at the end of the poem, to acquire their 'literal, obscene meaning'.

35 For general accounts of Lesbian lyric monody, see Dimities Yatromanolakis, 'Alcaeus and Sappho', in *The Cambridge Companion to Greek Lyric*, ed. Felix Budelmann (Cambridge: Cambridge University Press, 2009), 204–26; A. P. Burnett, *Three Archaic Poets: Archilochus, Alcaeus, Sappho* (London: Duckworth, 1983); D. A. Campbell, *The Golden Lyre: The Themes of the Greek Lyric Poets* (London, Duckworth, 1983). The editors of the following editions supply useful general introductions: D. L. Page, *Sappho and Alcaeus* (Oxford, Oxford University Press, 1955; D. A. Campbell, *Greek Lyric*, vol. 1 (Cambridge, MA: Harvard University Press, 1982); G. O. Hutchinson, *Greek Lyric Poetry: A Commentary on Selected Larger Pieces* (Oxford: Oxford University Press, 2001); Felix Budelmann, *Greek Lyric: A Selection* (Cambridge: Cambridge University Press, 2018).

36 On the musical aspect, see M. L. West, *Ancient Greek Music* (Oxford: Oxford University Press, 1992).

37 See my discussion in '"The Principle of the Daguerreotype": Translation from the Classics', in *The Oxford History of Classical Reception in English Literature*, vol. 4, ed. Norman Vance and Jennifer Wallace (Oxford: Oxford University Press, 2015), 64–5. For Matthew Arnold's influential attempts to create a hexameter tradition in English, see Yopie Prins, 'Nineteenth Century Homers and the Hexameter Mania', in *Nation, Language, and the Ethics of Translation*, ed. Sandra Bermann and Michael Wood (Princeton: Princeton University Press, 2005), 229–56.

38 For a discussion, see Yatromanolakis, 'Alcaeus and Sappho', 204–6.

39 For Philip Sidney's sapphics, and those of his friends Edward Dyer and Fulke Greville, see Julie Crawford, 'Sidney's Sapphics and the Role of Interpretive Communities', *ELH* 69:4 (2002): 979–1007. John Buxton, *Sir Philip Sidney and the English Renaissance* (London: Palgrave Macmillan, 1987), 121, notes that Greville wrote sapphic verses in response to Sidney's. Crawford, 'Sydney's Sapphics', 998, suggests an exchange in the opposite direction.

40 Christopher Ricks, *The Poems of Tennyson* (Harlow, UK: Longman, 1987), II: 497.

41 'Thee Saphick, to my seeming, hath the prehemynencye', whereupon Stanyhurst introduces his version of Psalm 4, rendered in 'English Saphick verse.' Edward Arber, ed., Richard Stanyhurst, *Translation of the first Four Books of the Aeneis of P. Virgilius Maro: with other poetical Devices thereto annexed, 1582* (London: The English Scholar's Library, 1880), 131.

42 Hannibal Hamlin, Michael G. Brennan, Margaret P. Hannay, and Noel J. Kinnamon, *The Sidney Psalter: The Psalms of Sir Philip and Mary Sidney* (Oxford: Oxford University Press, 2009), xiv.

43 J. Alison Rosenblitt, *E. E. Cummings' Modernism and the Classics: Each Imperishable Stanza* (Oxford: Oxford University Press, 2016), 298.

44 George J. Firmage, *E. E. Cummings: Complete Poems, 1904–62* (New York: Liveright, 2016), 873.

45 For a brief discussion, and bibliography of both primary and secondary sources, see Chapter 2.

46 John Talbot, 'A Late Flowering of English Alcaics', in *Perceptions of Horace: A Roman Poet and His Readers*, ed. L. B. T. Houghton and Maria Wyke (Cambridge: Cambridge University Press, 2009), 305–23. I expand upon – and sometimes rethink – various points of that chapter throughout the present volume.

47 Charles Martindale, 'Roman Mosaic', *TLS* (8 October 2010): 12; Jonathan Wallace, *BMCR* 2011.04.54.

48 The alcaic verses of Hölderlin in particular attracted the attention of W. H. Auden: see Chapter 5, note 60. For the alcaic strophe in German verse, see W. Bennett, *German Verse in Classical Metres* (The Hague: Mouton & Co., 1963), 123–6. Alcaics figure prominently in the Italian verses of Giosue Carducci. For the influence of German alcaics on Carducci, see Giuseppe Basilone, *Guida allo Studio dell' Opera Letteraria di Carlucci* (Napoli: Casa Editrice Federico e Ardia, 1953), 54–5.

49 I am thinking of works such as Joseph Phelan, *The Music of Verse: Metrical Experimentation in Nineteenth-Century Poetry* (London: Palgrave Macmillan, 2012), Meredith Martin, *The Fall of Meter: Poetry and English National Culture, 1860–1930* (Princeton, NJ: Princeton University Press, 2012) and the various contributions to *Meter Matters: Verse Cultures of the Long Nineteenth-Century*, ed. Jason David Hall (Athens, OH: Ohio University Press, 2011).

50 Quoted in Brower, *The Poetry of Robert Frost*, 139.

51 The seminal expression of this idea, and still by far the most influential, is Charles Martindale, *Redeeming the Text: Latin Poetics and the Hermeneutics of Reception* (Cambridge: Cambridge University Press, 1993). Writing in a special issue devoted to that book's influence twenty years on, Martindale characterized the principle neatly: 'Milton's reception of Virgil then becomes potentially of as much significance for Virgilians as for Miltonists, as much a part of Classics as it is of English literature,' ('Reception: A new humanism? Receptivity, pedagogy, the transhistorical', *Classical Receptions Journal* 5.2 (2013):171). My broad sympathy with Martindale's conception of classical and English relations as reciprocal and dialogic, and his rejection of the crudest forms of literary historicism, informs the present book. For an eloquent exposition of this kind of reception aesthetics that nevertheless seeks to give due credit to the virtues of historicist approaches, see David Hopkins, *Conversing with Antiquity: English Poets and the Classics, From Shakespeare to Pope* (Oxford: Oxford University Press, 2010), 1–36. On the emerging field of classical receptions generally, see e.g. Charles Martindale and Richard F. Thomas, eds., *Classics and the Uses of Reception* (Oxford: Blackwell, 2006; Craig W. Kallendorf, ed., *A Companion to the Classical Tradition* (Oxford: Blackwell, 2007); Lorna Hardwick and Christopher Stray, eds., *A Companion to Classical Receptions* (Oxford: Blackwell, 2008).

52 W. H. Auden, *The Dyer's Hand* (London: Faber and Faber, 1963), 50.

53 Derek Attridge, *Moving Words: Forms of English Poetry* (Oxford: Oxford University Press, 2013), 9.

54 Attridge, *Moving Words*, 13.

55 Gillian Woods, *Shakespeare's Unreformed Fictions* (Oxford: Oxford University Press, 2013), 19.

56 Peter McDonald, *Sound Intentions: The Workings of Rhyme in Nineteenth Century Poetry* (Oxford: Oxford University Press, 2012), 319.

57 McDonald, *Sound Intentions*, 316.

58 Ross Wilson, 'Both Free and Bound', *TLS* (9 May, 2014): 28.

59 So Kenneth Haynes, 'Introduction', in D. S. Carne-Ross, *Classics and Translation: Essays by D. S. Carne-Ross*, ed. Kenneth Haynes (Lewisburg, PA: Bucknell University Press, 2010), 13.

60 Steiner classed Carne-Ross along with Coleridge, Heidegger, Benjamin, and others – including, presumably, himself. George Steiner, *A George Steiner Reader* (New York: Oxford University Press, 1984), 97.

Chapter 1

1 T. S. Eliot, *Collected Poems* (New York: Harcourt, Brace & Co., 1963), 62.

2 Oliver Goldsmith, *The Vicar of Wakefield*, ed. Arthur Friedman (Oxford: Oxford University Press, 2006), chapter XXIV.

3 Wilfred Owen, *The Complete Poems and Fragments*, 2 vols., ed. Jon Stallworthy (London: Norton, 1982), 1.140–1.

4 Translation here and *passim* is that of Niall Rudd, *Horace: Odes and Epodes* (Cambridge, MA, Harvard University Press, 2004).

5 For details, see the further discussion in Chapter 2.

6 This is the abstract scansion; a fuller reading would acknowledge the force of 'Lie' in creating a powerful spondaic substation in the second foot.

7 Harold Owen and John Bell, *Wilfred Owen: Collected Letters* (London: Oxford University Press, 1967), 595. Owen later protested, in a letter to his mother, that Graves had seen only a working draft of the poem, and that he himself was 'perfectly aware of all the solecisms' (Owen and Bell, *Collected Letters*, 501).

8 There is insufficient evidence to establish whether Owen had read Horace in the original. The quotation from Horace in itself proves nothing: the Latin tag was as well-known, and in the years just before and during Great War was very frequently quoted by polemicists and poets. Elizabeth Vandiver, *Stand in the Trench, Achilles: Classical Receptions in British Poetry of the Great War* (Oxford: Oxford University Press, 2010), 393–404, collects and discusses several instances of the tag 'dulce et decorum est pro patria mori' in contemporary verses. A judicious sifting of the evidence has led Vandiver to conclude that it is unlikely Owen had actually read

Horace's odes in the original (129). On the other hand, though, it is unlikely that
Owen was unacquainted with the alcaic strophe. He owned a 1908 edition of
R. F Brewer's handbook *Orthometry: The Art of Versification and the Technicalities of
Poetry* (Edinburgh: John Grant, 1908), which includes an explanation of the alcaic,
presents a schema of the strophe, and offers as an example a stanza from Tennyson's
alcaic poem to Milton (268). With his keen interest in both Latin and versification, it
is unlikely Owen would have overlooked Brewer's discussion of classical metres in
general, and the alcaic in particular. Whether he knew Horace's Latin at firsthand or
through such sources as Brewer, Owen's misquotation of Horace's metre produces
effects that are as striking as Eliot's misquotation of Goldsmith's metre.

9 Jessie Pope, *Jessie Pope's War Poems* (London: Grant Richards, 1915), 38.

10 Owen, *Complete Poems and Fragments*, 294, 296. See also W. G. Bebbington, 'Jessie
Pope and Wilfred Owen', *Ariel* 3.4 (1972): 82–93.

11 Characteristic of similar lectures and sermons are W. Shirley, *Moral: The Most
Important Factor in the War* (London: Greening, 1909), 3; and Arthur F. Winnington-
Ingram, *A Day of God: Being Five Addresses on the Subject of the Present War*
(London: Wells, Gardner, Darton, 1914), 4–5.

12 Whether Horace himself is among Owen's targets is far from clear. If Owen were
really repudiating mild-mannered, genial Horace who, in another poem (*Odes*
2.7.9–10) had practically congratulated himself for abandoning the field of battle in
a fit of cowardice, then that could be construed as a critique of one of the pillars of
Western culture. It is at least as likely that Owen takes umbrage not at Horace but at
the contemporary poetasters who have appropriated a famous line of Latin poetry in
support of their own kind of militarism. On such a reading Horace himself could be
seen as having been traduced by inferior writers.

13 E.g. Sven Bäckman, *Tradition Transformed: Studies in the Poetry of Wilfred Owen*
(Lund: C. W. K. Gleerup, 1979), who notes also Horace's satirical use of the Horatian
'beatus ille' in 'Insensibility' ('Happy are men who yet before they are killed / Can let
their veins run cold'); and Jennifer Breen, *Wilfred Owen: Selected Poetry and Prose*
(London and New York: Routledge, 1988), 171–5.

14 Though she is concerned with iambic pentameter, not the alcaic metre, there is
corroborative value in Meredith Martin's claim that the significant but 'latent
critique' implicit in Owen's verse was his disruptive handling of conventional English
metre, which expressed his suspicion of 'forms and orders that profess to protect'. *The
Rise and Fall of Meter: Poetry and English National Culture, 1860–1930* (Princeton,
NJ: Princeton University Press, 2012), 178.

15 Owen and Bell, *Collected Letters*, 254.

16 Owen and Bell, *Collected Letters*, 94, note 2.

17 Ibid., 254.

18 Ibid., 215.

19 Ibid., 140.

20 Vandiver, *Stand in the Trench*, 118, generously allows that this is the kind of mistake an intermediate Latin student might understandably make.

21 My treatment of this topic owes much to a brilliant article of Erik Gray, 'Nostalgia, the Classics, and the Intimations Ode: Wordsworth's Forgotten Education', *Philological Quarterly* 80:2 (2001): 187–203.

22 Thomas Babington Macaulay, 'Milton', in *Complete Writings* (Boston: Houghton Mifflin, 1899–1900), 11: 93–4.

23 In Owen's case, Macaulay's terms are particularly apt, since Macaulay himself was among Owen's memories of the classroom. Owen's own exercise books from Shrewsbury Technical School find him studying Macaulay's 'Horatius': see Jon Stallworthy, *Wilfred Owen* (Oxford: Oxford University Press, 1974), 40. At about the same time he was finishing 'Dulce et Decorum Est', in the first weeks of 1918, he also composed ten lines of verse, untitled and beginning with the line 'Having, with bold Horatius, stamped her feet'. 'She' is a teacher, schooling her charges in the patriotism of the republican Roman hero Horatius as presented in Macaulay's *Lays of Ancient Rome*. The teacher 'bleats' about 'the brave days of old', waving her hand with a 'swashing arabesque' before she 'Slapped her Macaulay back upon the desk' (2–5). Her composure is then tested by the unwelcome attention, through the window, of three soldiers. 'One was called 'Orace whom she would not greet' (10). Macaulay himself, so eloquent on the link between childhood and the classics, is one of Owen's own links to his schoolboy encounters with ancient Rome.

24 George Eliot, *The Mill on the Floss*, ed. Gordon S. Haight (Oxford: Clarendon Press, 1980), 22.

25 Gray, 'Nostalgia', 197.

26 C. A. Alington, *Eton Lyrics* (London: Ingleby, 1925) 95.

27 Owen's reaction to Alington's verses would have been more complicated: the Birkenhead Institute was no Eton, and his Latin training came to a premature end. Still, he would have understood the experience of childhood memories of Latin.

28 *TLS* (12 September 1912): 369.

29 Virginia Woolf, 'The Perfect Language', *TLS* (24 May 1917): 247.

30 John Henry Fowler, '*Three Roman Poets Translated*', *TLS* (15 May 1913): 208.

31 The more obvious senses of the word 'old' do still obtain: 'old' *ancient*, denoting the literal antiquity of Horace's Latin. And yes, too, 'old' *venerable*, in that Horace's phrase has hardened into a sort of monument, a classic formulation of patriotic fervour. But Owen elsewhere was alive to the sense 'old' *familiar, intimate*: e.g., 'Write my old girl, Jim, there's a dear' ('The Letter', line 22). Just so when Owen refers to his friend as 'old Kemp', where the power of 'old' lies not in emphasizing the seniority of a man a mere three years older than Owen, but in a potent mingling of affection and (crucially here) pity. 'Old', too, can conduce to affections that are other than affectionate. When

I remind you of 'my old troubles', I refer not only to the duration of my ailment, but to the sadly intimate terms on which I live with it (and perhaps perversely cherish it). Owen speaks of 'their old wounds', in 'Insensibility' line 22. For strong evocations of that contempt that is the more contemptuous for being also familiar, few good old English words are so unostentatiously effective as 'old': 'And that great dragon was cast out, that old serpent' (Rev. 12.9). Here 'old' catches not just a fact of chronology, Satan's literal antiquity, but also the Evangelist's exasperated familiarity, intimacy even, with the arch-fiend. Something like that revulsion is what makes Owen's phrase 'the old Lie' less of a factual statement than an emotional evocation. What the poem takes for granted with 'old' is long acquaintance with Horace that begins in childhood, and alone can produce the kind of familiarity and intimacy that Owen's poem has the power to poison.

32 Owen, *Complete Poems and Fragments*, 2: 297.

33 The text is that of Christopher Ricks, *The Poems of Tennyson*, second edition (London: Longman, 1987) II: 652–3.

34 See Martin Forrest, 'The Abolition of Compulsory Latin and Its Consequences', in *The Classical Association: The First Century 1903–2003*, ed. Christopher Stray (Oxford: Oxford University Press, 2003), 43–66. For a brisk account of the decline of Greek and Latin in both British and American universities in the twentieth century, see Isobel Hurst, 'Classics in Education after 1880' in *The Oxford History of Classical Reception in English Literature*, vol. 4, ed. Kenneth Haynes (Oxford: Oxford University Press, 2019). See too Bob Lister, 'Exclusively for Everyone', in *Learning Latin and Greek from Antiquity to the Present*, ed. Elizabeth P. Archibald, William Brockliss, and Jonathan Gnoza (Cambridge: Cambridge University Press, 2015), 184–6.

35 The text is that of John Leonard, *John Milton: The Complete Poems* (London: Penguin, 1988).

36 This is the eloquent formulation of Gray, 'Nostalgia', 189.

37 Ibid., 194.

38 John Hollander, *Picture Window* (New York: Alfred A. Knopf, 2005), 64–7.

39 Hollander, *Picture Window*, 63.

40 Note Hollander's demotion of 'Old lie' to 'old lie' – itself a new lie.

41 Hollander too, just as Eliot had done, takes another poet's line and breaks it on the word 'and', though this time the Latin word for 'and'.

42 It happens the first line of this Horatian ode may be an allusion to a line of Alcaeus: see G. O. Hutchinson, *Greek Lyric Poetry: A Commentary on Selected Larger Pieces* (Oxford: Oxford University Press, 2001), 205–6.

43 Eduard Fraenkel, *Horace* (Oxford: Clarendon Press, 1957), 184.

44 For crisp discussion of the humour, and the perils, of taking the first stanza seriously, see Roland Mayer, *Horace: Odes Book 1* (Cambridge: Cambridge University Press, 2012), 168–9.

45 Wilamowitz, *Süddeutsche Monatshefte* 28:1 (October, 1930), 45: '*Integer vitae* kann an einem Grabe nur singen, wer es nicht versteht,' quoted by Fraenkel, *Horace*, 184. For more on the tradition of setting the first stanza to 'mournful music', see R. G. M. Nisbett and M. Hubbard, *A Commentary on Horace: Odes Book 1* (Oxford: Clarendon Press, 1970), 262.

46 Richard Thomas, *Horace Odes IV and Carmen Saeculare* (Cambridge: Cambridge University Press, 2011), 118.

47 Fraenkel, *Horace*, 439.

Chapter 2

1 So D. L. Page, *Sappho and Alcaeus: An Introduction to the Study of Ancient Lesbian Poetry* (Oxford: Clarendon Press, 1955), 321, and adds this description of his schema: 'First two lines, *anceps*, cretic, *anceps*, element – u u – u – ; third line, *anceps*, cretic, *anceps*; fourth one, element – u u – u prolonged to – u u – u u – u –, *anceps*.' The pattern, though, has been variously analysed. A grammarian writing in the fourth century CE, for example, saw the first two lines as based on iambs and heroic dimeters; the third as based on epitrites; and the fourth as a heroic dimeter followed by a trochaic dimeter (Diomedes, *Ars Grammatica*, quoted in Ernst Diehl, *Anthologia Lyrica Graeca* (Leipzig: B. G. Teubner, 1925), 551). Heinrich Kiel, *Grammatici Latini*, 7 vols. (Leipzig: Teubner, 1855–1928), 6:66, 268, 629), records similar but slightly varying accounts from three other grammarians. Our understanding of the stanza as having four lines is the result of orthographical decisions of Alexandrian editors: before then, lines three and four were conceived as consisting in a single colon: see Luigi Rossi, 'Horace, a Greek Lyrist without Music', in *Horace: Odes and Epodes. Oxford Readings in Classical Studies*, ed. Michele Lowrie (Oxford: Oxford University Press, 2009), 375, n. 4.

2 L. P. Wilkinson, *Horace and his Lyric Poetry* (Cambridge: Cambridge University Press, 1945), 152.

3 Gilbert Murray, *The Classical Tradition in Poetry* (Cambridge, MA: Harvard University Press, 1927), 114.

4 Rosanna Warren, 'Pronouncing "Carpenter": Quantitative Meter in English', in *An Exaltation of Forms: Contemporary Poets Celebrate the Diversity of their Art*, ed. Annie Finch and Katherine Varnes (Ann Arbor: University of Michigan Press, 2003), 87.

5 Page, *Sappho and Alcaeus*, 321, 323–4; Richard Heinze, *Die lyrischen Verse des Horaz* (Amsterdam: Hakkert, 1959), 77–90; but perhaps most notably R. G. M. Nisbet and M. Hubbard, *A Commentary on Horace: Odes I* (Oxford: Oxford University Press, 1970), xxviii ff; xl–xliii.

6 E.g., the massive and influential study of Eduard Fraenkel, *Horace* (Oxford: Clarendon Press, 1957), and the extensive commentary of H. P. Syndikus, *Die Lyric des Horaz* (Darmstadt: 1972–3).

7 Notably Brooks Otis, 'The Relevance of Horace', *Arion* 9:2–3 (1970): 146–74.

8 Beginning most notably with Steele Commager, *The Odes of Horace: A Critical Study* (New Haven, CT: Yale University Press, 1962), and Kenneth Reckford, *Horace* (New York: Twayne, 1969).

9 D. A. Campbell, 'Alcaeus', in *The Cambridge History of Classical Literature*, vol. I, ed. P. E. Easterling and E. J. Kenney (Cambridge: Cambridge University Press, 1985), II: 211.

10 Text and translation of Horace *passim* are those of Niall Rudd, *Horace: Odes and Epodes* (Cambridge, MA: Harvard University Press, 2004).

11 Heinze, *Die lyrischen Verse*, 79–80.

12 D. L. West, *Horace, Odes II: Vatis amici* (Oxford: Oxford University Press, 1998), xx, picking up on L. P. Wilkinson, *Golden Latin Artistry* (Cambridge: Cambridge University Press, 1963), 111. Armando Salvatore, *Prosodia e metrica Latina* (Rome: Jouvance, 1983), 85, registers a feeling of conturbation or excitement (*concitazione*) in the third line. Most recently Llewelyn Morgan, *Musa Pedestris: Metre and Meaning in Roman Verse* (Oxford: Oxford University Press, 2010), 9, has contributed to the consensus: 'the heart and focus of every alcaic stanza tends to be in its third line'.

13 Rosanna Warren, 'Alcaics in Exile: W. H. Auden's "In Memory of Sigmund Freud"', *Philosophy and Literature* 20:1 (1996): 111: 121.

14 Andrew S. Becker, 'Rhythm in a Sinuous Stanza: The Anatomy and Acoustic Contour of the Latin Alcaic', *American Journal of Philology* 133:1 (2012): 117–52.

15 Morgan, *Musa Pedestris*, 382.

16 Ibid., 382.

17 Morgan notes that whereas the shortest line in the sapphic stanza – the adonic fourth line – is also its rapidest, the shortest line in the alcaic (its enneasyllablic third line) is its slowest (217). His chief argument about the alcaic is to refute the notion that the alcaic's structure is inherently suited to grave themes: instead, the alcaic's association with 'serious' poetry is a matter of historical convention (215–18). Here again, the observation about alcaics is subordinate to larger claims about Morgan's chief topic, the metrical propriety of the sapphic.

18 Morgan, *Musa Pedestris*, 16.

19 Sappho is known to have used the form, but only one surviving fragment can be securely identified as alcaics (Campbell 137; see Page, *Sappho and Alcaeus*, 104–9). It has elicited various interpretations, ancient and modern, but at only five lines it yields no insights into the metre as such.

20 Campbell, 'Alcaeus', 208. All translations and texts of Alcaeus here and *passim* are those of D. A. Campbell, *Greek Lyric I* (Cambridge, MA: Harvard University Press, 1982).

21 Campbell, 'Alcaeus', 211.

22 On the distinction, see West, *Horace Odes II*, 47–50, and Rossi, 'Horace, a Greek Lyrist', 2009.

23 Horace, *Odes* 3.30.13–14: 'princeps Aeolium carmen ad Italos / deduxisse modos'. Horace boasts specifically of his adaptation of alcaic lyric in *Epistles* 1.19.32–3: 'Hunc ego, non alio dictum prius ore, Latinus / volgavi fidicen' (Him [Alcaeus], never before sung by other lips, I, the lyrist of Latium, have made known). The text and translation of the epistles is that of H. Rushton Fairclough, *Horace: Satires. Epistles. The Art of Poetry* (Cambridge, MA: Harvard University Press, 1926).

24 Rossi, 'Horace, A Greek Lyrist', argues that a more regular metre suits reading on the page better than singing.

25 Christopher Ricks, *The Poems of Tennyson* (Harlow, UK: Longman, 1987), II: 652.

26 Wilkinson, *Golden Latin Artistry*, 111.

27 Ibid., 111–12.

28 For the cultural implications of the types of wine, see Nisbet and Hubbard, *A Commentary on Horace Odes I*, 412, 415.

29 Nisbet and Hubbard, *A Commentary on Horace Odes I*, 351.

30 K. M. Coleman, *Statius Silvae IV* (Oxford: Oxford University Press, 1998), xxi.

31 Note, for instance, the paucity of references to alcaics even in such massive and standard works as F. Brunhöze, *Geschichte der Lateinischen Literatur des Mittelalters* (Munich: Wilhelm Fink Verlag, 1992).

32 F. J. Nichols, *An Anthology of Neo-Latin Poetry* (New Haven, CT: Yale University Press, 1979), 14–15.

33 Victoria Moul, 'Introduction', in *A Guide to Neo-Latin Literature*, ed. Victoria Moul (Cambridge: Cambridge University Press, 2017), 3.

34 Harvard University Press in 2001 initiated the I Tatti Renaissance Library, which is making available neo-Latin works with English translations on the facing page, on the model of the Loeb Classical Library. Meanwhile some venerable anthologies remain useful, including Alessandro Perosa and John Sparrow, *Renaissance Latin Verse: An Anthology* (Chapel Hill: University of North Carolina Press, 1979), and Nichols, *Anthology of Neo-Latin Poetry*. Two major collections of essays, Sarah Knight and Stefan Tilg, *The Oxford Handbook of Neo-Latin* (Oxford: Oxford University Press, 2015), and Moul, *Guide to Neo-Latin Literature*, provide a sense of the emerging vigour of the field, consolidate many of its findings, and imply avenues of further research. Specifically, British neo-Latin poetry is treated in Leicester Bradner, *Musae Anglicanae: A History of Anglo-Latin Poetry, 1500–1925* (New York: Modern Language Association of America, 1940), a topic that is receiving more rigorous attention in recent works such as L. B. T. Houghton and Gesine Manuwald, *Neo-Latin Poetry in the British Isles* (London: Bristol Classical Press, 2012). The collection of essays edited by J. W. Bins, *The Latin Poetry of English Authors* (Abingdon, UK: Routledge, 2015) has lately been reissued, more than forty years after its first publication. The most significant single contribution to this field is Victoria Moul, *A Literary History of Latin & English Poetry: Bilingual Verse Culture in Early Modern England* (Cambridge: Cambridge University Press: 2022).

35 Victoria Moul, 'Lyric Poetry', in *The Oxford Handbook of Neo-Latin*, 54.

36 See W. Hilton Kelliher, 'The Latin Poetry of George Herbert' in Bins, *Latin Poetry of English Authors* 26–57; and Victoria Moul's comments on and translations of Herbert's Latin verse in John Drury and Victoria Moul, *George Herbert: The Complete Poetry* (Harmondsworth, UK: Penguin, 2015).

37 Douglas Bush, *A Variorum Commentary on The Poems of John Milton, Volume I: The Latin and Greek Poems* (London: Routledge, 1970), 4.

38 Bradner, *Musae Anglicanae*, 252–3.

39 For the notion that Johnson's Latin verses are 'romantic' (as against his supposedly 'classical' English poetry), see D. Nichol Smith, 'Johnson's Poems', in *New Light on Dr. Johnson* (New Haven, CT: Yale University Press, 1950), 13.

40 Bradner, *Musae Anglicanae*, 326.

41 Ibid., 238.

42 Ibid., 236.

43 Ibid., 313.

Chapter 3

1 Hallet Smith, 'English Metrical Psalms in the Sixteenth Century and Their Literary Significance', *Huntington Library Quarterly* 9 (1946): 269.

2 Victoria Moul, *A Literary History of Latin & English Poetry: Bilingual Verse Culture in Early Modern England* (Cambridge: Cambridge University Press, 2024), 68.

3 Ibid., ch. 2.

4 Ibid., ch. 2.

5 Ibid., ch. 2.

6 Ibid., ch. 3.

7 Jerome, 'Preface to Eusebius' *Chronicles*', quoted in James Kugel, *The Idea of Biblical Poetry: Parallelism and its History* (New Haven, CT: Yale University Press, 1981), 152.

8 For the differing interpretations of Beza and John Calvin, see Hannibal Hamlin, Michael G. Brennan, Margaret P. Hannay, and Noel J. Kinnamon, *The Sidney Psalter: The Psalms of Sir Philip and Mary Sidney* (Oxford: Oxford University Press, 2009), 328–9.

9 For accounts of the attempts to establish an English version of quantitative prosody, see Derek Attridge, *Well-Weighed Syllables: Elizabethan Verse in Classical Metres* (London: Cambridge University Press, 1974), and Susanne Woods, *Natural Emphasis: English versification from Chaucer to Dryden* (San Marino, CA: The Huntington Library, 1984).

10 Moul, *A Literary History*, 114.

11 Rosanna Warren, 'Alcaics in Exile: W. H. Auden's "In Memory of Sigmund Freud"', *Philosophy and Literature* 20:1 (1996): 111–21, finds in Alcaeus' political vicissitudes

reason for associating his stanza-form with themes of exile or dispossession. Hannibal Hamlin, *Psalm Culture and Early Modern English Literature* (Oxford: Oxford University Press, 2012), 98, proposes that Beza's interpretation of the 'songs of degrees' as celebrating the return of Israel from Babylonian exile is here 'transposed to the context of the (English, Protestant) Renaissance return from cultural exile.'

12 In this extraordinary line, the first six syllables could all be read as stressed.

13 E.g., Horace *Odes* 1.2, 1.37, and especially the panegyric odes that figure so prominently in the last book of odes: 4.4, 4.5, 4.14., and 4.15.

14 Moul, *A Literary History*, ch. 4, argues convincingly that Marvell's ode, and other contemporary English panegyric lyric, descends chiefly from an 'essentially post-classical and primarily neo-Latin lyric tradition' (141).

15 William Simeone, 'A Probable Antecedent of Marvell's Horatian Ode', *Notes & Queries* 197 (1952): 316–18 argues that a manuscript likely to be Fanshaw's shows him writing in the metre of Marvell's ode roughly two decades earlier. See also Barbara Everett, 'The Shooting of the Bears: Poetry and Politics in Andrew Marvell', in *Andrew Marvell: Essays on the Tercentenary of his Death*, ed. R. L. Brett (Oxford: Oxford University Press for the University of Hull, 1979), 77, who calls it an 'anglicised Horatian metre'.

16 The text is that of Nigel Smith, *The Poems of Andrew Marvell* (London: Longman, 2003), 273–9.

17 Or it may not: the date of Milton's translation is famously uncertain.

18 The text is that of John Leonard, *John Milton: The Complete Poems* (London: Penguin, 1998).

19 H. W. Garrod, *Collins* (Oxford: Clarendon Press, 1928), 71–2.

20 Richard Wendorf and Charles Ryscamp, *The Works of William Collins* (Oxford: Clarendon Press,1979), 44–5.

21 Rachel Hadas, 'Ode 1.24', in *Horace: The Odes: New Translations by Contemporary Poets*, ed. J. D. McClatchy (Princeton, NJ: Princeton University Press, 2002), 73.

22 For an account of how acrimonious, how stubborn, and how various were the debates about even the fundamentals of poetic metre in the last half of the nineteenth century and beyond, see Meredith Martin's *The Rise and Fall of Meter: Poetry and English National Culture, 1860–1930* (Princeton, NJ: Princeton University Press, 2012). Clough comes too early to be included in her account, but his concerns anticipate some of those controversies.

23 Joseph Patrick Phelan, 'Radical Metre: The English Hexameter in Clough's Bothie of Toper-na-Fuosich', *Review of English Studies* 50: 198 (1999): 172.

24 Ibid., 169. For a broader view of Clough's relationship to the classics, see Isobel Hurst, 'Arthur Hugh Clough', in *The Oxford History of Classical Reception in English Literature,* vol. 4, ed. Norman Vance and Jennifer Wallace (Oxford: Oxford University Press, 2015), 495–508.

25 F. L. Mulhauser, *The Poems of Arthur Hugh Clough* (Oxford: Clarendon Press, 1974), 35.

26 Tennyson may well have known these alcaics: Hallam Tennyson, *Alfred Lord Tennyson: A Memoir by His Son* (London: Macmillan, 1911), II: 11, records his father's admiration of Clough's verse.

27 Christopher Ricks, *The Poems of Tennyson* (Harlow, UK: Longman, 1987), II: 494.

28 These juvenilia were first published by Arthur Pollard, 'Three Horace Translations by Tennyson', *Tennyson Research Bulletin* 4:1 (1982): 16–14.

29 For the dating, see Susan Shatto and Marion Shaw, *Tennyson: In Memoriam* (Oxford: Clarendon Press, 1982), 172–3.

30 'anne lacus tantos? te, Lari maxime, teque / fluctibus et fremitu adsurgens, Benace marino.' (Or tell of her mighty lakes? Of you, Larius, the greatest, or you, Benacus, who swell with a sea's surge and roar?) The text and translation are those of H. Rushton Fairclough, revised by G. P Goold, *Virgil: Eclogues, Georgics, Aeneid I-VI* (Cambridge, MA: Harvard University Press, 1999).

31 E.g., Catullus c. 41; Horace *Odes* 1.4, 1.17.

32 E.g., Catullus' characterization of Britain as lying at the very end of the earth (c. 11.11–12), or the boast of the British warrior Calgacus of his island's remoteness from the corruption of Rome in Tacitus, *Agricola* 30.

33 Ricks, *Poems of Tennyson*, II: 497.

34 Hallam Tennyson, *Memoir*, I: 430–1.

35 Ricks, *Poems of Tennyson*, II: 497, finds this view expressed in 'Despair', 26, and 'Faith', 7–8.

36 Text and translation of Horace *passim* are those of Niall Rudd, *Horace: Odes and Epodes* (Cambridge, MA: Harvard University Press, 2004).

37 See Ronald Syme, *The Roman Revolution* (Oxford: Oxford University Press, 1939, rev. edn. 1960), 409.

38 For details on the distinction between wines cheap and posh, and on their social implications in the poem, see R. G. M. Nisbet and M. Hubbard, *A Commentary on Horace: Odes I* (Oxford: Oxford University Press, 1970), 244–52.

39 Text and translation are those of H. Rushton Fairclough, *Horace: Satires, Epistles, Ars Poetica* (Cambridge, MA: Harvard University Press, 1929).

40 The text is that of John Leonard, *John Milton: The Complete Poems* (London: Penguin, 1998).

41 D. S. Carne-Ross and Kenneth Haynes, *Horace in English* (Harmondsworth, UK: Penguin, 1996).

42 Charles Stuart Calverley, *Literary Remains of Charles Stuart Calverley* (London: George Bell, 1855), 182.

43 Ricks, *Poems of Tennyson*, II: 652.

44 Pollard, 'Three Horace Translations', 17.

45 A. A. Markley, *Stateliest Measures: Tennyson and the Literature of Greece and Rome* (Toronto: University of Toronto Press, 2004), 97.

46 Ricks, *Poems of Tennyson*, III: 163.

47 Ibid., III: 162.

48 Ibid., III: 163.

49 Ricks, *Poems of Tennyson*, III: 162.

50 Cf. *In Memoriam* 61.11, 'Who roll'd the psalm to wintry skies'.

51 Ricks, *Poems of Tennyson*, III: 220.

52 Anon. *Notes & Queries* (19 July 1851): 14.

Chapter 4

1 For the sake of clarity, all citations of *In Memoriam* in this chapter follow the example of Susan Shatto and Marion Shaw, *Tennyson: In Memoriam* (Oxford: Oxford University Press, 1983) in substituting Arabic numbers for the Tennyson's original Roman numerals. Some of the ideas in this chapter I first proposed to a graduate student, Ryan Stewart, and gave him permission to take them up in a masters thesis I supervised with him. He has in turn kindly given me permission to revisit here some of my ideas I proposed to him then. Despite his modest protestations, I gratefully acknowledge his contribution to many hours of conversation on *In Memoriam*.

2 It would be decades later – 1882 – that Tennyson would write that it was Virgil who wielded 'the stateliest measure ever moulded by the lips of man' ('To Virgil, Written at the Request of the Mantuans for the Nineteenth Centenary of Virgil's Death'). But Virgil's metre was the dactylic hexameter, not a lyric meter at all. As such his commendation of the hexameter does not cancel the force of his praise for the alcaic. And is there something in the later judgment that can be explained by pressure to satisfy the citizens of Mantua who had requested Tennyson's encomium?

3 E.g., the sonnet sequences 'Lacrymae' and 'An Apology for the Revival of Christian Architecture in England' in Geoffrey Hill, *Tenebrae* (London: André Deutsch,1979).

4 All quotations are from Edward FitzGerald, *Rubáiyát of Omar Khayyám, the Astronomer-Poet of Persia* (London: Bernard Quaritch, 1859).

5 Translations here and *passim* are those of Niall Rudd, *Horace: Odes and Epodes* (Cambridge, MA: Harvard University Press, 2004).

6 Alfred McKinley Terhune and Annabelle Burdick Terhune, *The Letters of Edward FitzGerald, vol. 4, 1877–83* (Princeton, NJ: Princeton University Press, 1980), 245–6.

7 FitzGerald, *Rubáiyát*, xi–xii.

8 Stephen Gwynn, *Tennyson: A Critical Study* (London: Blackie & Son, 1899), 218.

9 Ricks, *Poems of Tennyson*, II: 497.

10 C. S. Calverley, *The Complete Works of C. S. Calverley* (London: George Bell and Sons, 1901), 443–4. This edition mistakenly prints 'CVI' for 'CVII'.

11 Ibid., 509.

12 Ibid., 249; 254–66.

13 Christopher Ricks, *Tennyson* (London and Berkeley: Macmillan and University of California Press, 1989), 216.

14 Ibid., 216.

15 John Conington, *The Odes and Carmen Saeculare of Horace* (London: Bell, 1892), xvii.

16 Ibid., xvii.

17 Ibid., xvii. As late as 1925, A. E. Housman, even as he commended Calverley's as 'the most poetical versions of Horace', nevertheless thought them still 'too Tennysonian': Archie Burnett, *The Letters of A. E. Housman* (Oxford: Oxford University Press, 2007), 520.

18 Conington, *Odes*, xvii.

19 Anonymous, 'Horace and His Translators', *The Quarterly Review* 180 (January–April 1895): 131.

20 Anonymous, 'Recent Translations of Horace', *The Christian Remembrancer* 56 (July–October 1868): 24.

21 Anonymous, 'Some Translations from the Classics', *The Academy* 32 (July–December 1887): 52.

22 Burnett, *The Letters of A. E. Housman*, 520.

23 For evidence of the dating, see Christopher Ricks, *The Poems of Tennyson* (Harlow, UK: Longman, 1987), II: 310, 327, and Shatto and Shaw, *Tennyson: In Memoriam*, 172–3.

24 Shatto and Shaw, *Tennyson: In Memoriam*, 172.

25 As early as A. C. Bradley, *A Commentary on Tennyson's In Memoriam* (London: Macmillan, 1902), 91, and recently as Shatto and Shaw, *Tennyson: In Memoriam*, 172.

26 Ricks, *Tennyson*, 213.

27 62.6 'But half my life I leave behind', closely followed by 69.3: 'My bosom friend and half of life', referring ironically to Grief.

28 Cf. other instances of a spondaic substitution in line 3 producing the effect of a peak or pivot: 16.11, 34.7 (linked to 36.15 by use of the word 'wild'), 34.16, 49.15, 54.15, 78.7, 87.7, 90.15, 91.11, 100.3.

29 Even if 'full' is given the value of a stressed syllable, it is clearly weaker than 'wings'.

30 E.g., 17.16; 22.12; 23.20; 84.112; 92.4; 99.6.

31 Conington, *Odes*, xi.

32 E.g., 13.7–8, 60.15–16, 68.11.12.

33 E.g., 1.20, 2.7, 2.17, 3.29.

34 E.g., 1.4, 2.14, 4.7.

35 Tennyson had written on this theme in 'The Lotos Eaters', 115–31.

36 This precis is Hallam Tennyson's.

37 All translations and texts of Alcaeus here and *passim* are those of D. A. Campbell, *Greek Lyric I* (Cambridge, MA: Harvard University Press, 1982).

38 The edition is that of Kenneth Haynes, *Algernon Charles Swinburne: Poems and Ballads and Atalanta in Calydon* (London: Penguin, 2000). Haynes is useful not only on the sapphic stanza (365–6) but on Swinburne's adaptation of classical metres in general.

39 D. S. Carne-Ross, 'Jocasta's Divine Head: English with a Foreign Accent', in *Classics and Translation: Essays by D. S. Carne-Ross*, ed. Kenneth Haynes (Lewisburg, PA: Bucknell University Press, 2010), 40.

40 Yopie Prins, *Victorian Sappho* (Princeton, NJ: Princeton University Press, 1999), 112–73.

41 Ibid., 114.

42 Ibid.,142.

43 Ibid.,145.

44 Ibid., 145.

45 Ibid., 114.

46 Ibid.,146.

47 Ibid., 120.

48 E.g., *IM* 41. For an elegant discussion, see Erik Gray, *Alfred, Lord Tennyson: In Memoriam* (New York: W. W. Norton, 2004), xvi–xxi.

Chapter 5

1 W. H. Auden, *The Dyer's Hand* (London: Faber and Faber, 1963), 47.

2 Samuel Johnson, *Lives of the English Poets*, 3 vols., ed. George Birkbeck Hill (New York: Octagon Books, 1967), I: 192–3.

3 Christopher Ricks, *The Force of Poetry* (Oxford: Clarendon Press, 1984), 94.

4 Robert Bridges, *Milton's Prosody: An Examination of the Rules of the Blank Verse in Milton's Later Poems, with an Account of the Versification of Samson Agonistes, and General Notes* (Oxford: Clarendon Press, 1894), 32.

5 Ibid., 32.

6 Newbolt, Henry, 'The Future of English Verse', *International Quarterly* 9 (1904): 376.

7 Ibid., 379. Newbolt's essay finds him participating in larger late-Victorian and Edwardian debates about the nature, limits, and potential of English prosody. Meredith Martin, *The Rise and Fall of Meter: Poetry and English National Culture, 1880–1930* (Princeton, NJ: Princeton University Press), 109–44, finds Newbolt pushing a fixed and simplified notion of English accentual prosody (with nationalistic aims), as against Bridges's preference for a plurality of English metrical traditions.

8 Robert Bridges and R. C. Trevelyan, *XXI Letters: a correspondence between Robert Bridges and R. C. Trevelyan on 'New Verse' and 'The Testament of Beauty'* (Stanford Dingley: The Mill House Press, 1955), 11.

9 Ibid., 12.

10 T. S. Eliot, 'Ezra Pound: His Metric and His Poetry', in *Selected Prose of T. S. Eliot*, edited by Frank Kermode (London: Faber and Faber, 1975), 150.

11 Ben Glaser, *Modernism's Metronome: Meter and Twentieth Century Poetics* (Baltimore: Johns Hopkins University Press, 2020), 18.

12 Robert Bridges, *Milton's Prosody, with a Chapter on Accentual Verse & Notes* (Oxford: Clarendon Press, 1921), 111.

13 Ibid., 99.

14 George Saintsbury, *History of Prosody from the Twelfth Century to the Present Day,* (London: Macmillan, 1910), I: 182. For a robust and perceptive appreciation of Saintsbury's methods and values, see Michael Hurley, 'George Saintsbury's *History of English Prosody', Essays in Criticism* 60:4 (October 2010), 336–60.

15 Derek Attridge, *Well-Weighed Syllables: Elizabethan Verse in Classical Metres* (Cambridge: Cambridge University Press, 1974), 68.

16 Ibid., 92.

17 Ibid., 92.

18 George Gascoigne, *Certayne Notes of Instruction Concerning the Making of Verse or Ryme in English, Written at the Request of Master Edouardo Donati*, in *Elizabethan Critical Essays*, 2 vols., ed. G. Gregory Smith (Oxford: Clarendon Press, 1904), I: 50.

19 Attridge, *Well-Weighed Syllables*, 93.

20 See the discussion in Attridge, *Well-Weighed Syllables*, 166–9.

21 D. S. Carne-Ross: 'Jocasta's Divine Head: English with a Foreign Accent', in D. S. Carne-Ross, *Classics and Translation*, ed. Kenneth Haynes (Lewisburg, PA: Bucknell University Press, 2010), 40.

22 Attridge, *Well-Weighed Syllables*, 89.

23 Robert Bridges and William Johnson Stone, *Milton's Prosody by Robert Bridges & Classical Metres in English Verse by William Johnson Stone* (Oxford: Clarendon Press, 1901), 8.

24 Ibid., 12.

25 Ibid., 12.

26 Ibid., 116.

27 Ibid., 116.

28 Ibid., 12.

29 Ibid., iv.

30 Ibid., iv.

31 Ibid., v.

32 Ibid., v. Prior to publication, Bridges had expressed a slightly more sanguine view in a letter to Henry Newbolt, 1 May 1900: 'He [Stone] thinks that classical metres could be written. I don't quite agree with him …' Nevertheless, 'some extraordinary results

come from its application.' Donald E. Stanford, *The Selected Letters of Robert Bridges, vol. 2* (Newark, DE: University of Delaware Press, 1984), 368–9.

33 Robert Bridges, *Poetical Works of Robert Bridges, Excluding the Eight Dramas* (Oxford: Oxford University Press, 1912), 410.

34 Ibid., 410.

35 Ibid., 410.

36 Ibid., 410.

37 Bridges, *Poetical Works*, 439.

38 Robert Bridges and William Stone Johnson, *Milton's Prosody*, 135.

39 Ibid., 28.

40 John Hollander, who had little patience for attempts to impose classical systems of prosody on English, dismissed the supposedly quantitative element of Tennyson's alcaics to Milton in terms that are equally applicable to Bridges's 'Peace Ode': 'the quantitative coding is rather like a door prize'. *Vision and Resonance: Two Sense of Poetic Form* (New Haven, CT: Yale University Press, 1986), 69.

41 Ibid., 156.

42 Robert Bridges, *New Verse Written in 1921 by Robert Bridges, Poet Laureate, With Other Poems of That Year and A Few Earlier Pieces* (Oxford: Clarendon Press, 1925), v.

43 Robert Beum, 'Syllabic Verse in English', *Prairie Schooner* 31:3 (1957): 274.

44 Ibid., 274.

45 Ibid., 274.

46 W. H. Auden, *A Certain World: A Commonplace Book* (New York: Viking, 1974) 372.

47 Christopher Isherwood, 'Postscript', in *W. H. Auden: A Tribute*, ed. Stephen Spender (New York: Macmillan, 1975), 79.

48 Auden, *A Certain World*, 375–6.

49 Robert Bridges, *Poetical Works of Robert Bridges, with 'The Testament of Beauty' but Excluding the Eight Dramas* (London: Oxford University Press, 1953), 507.

50 Robert Bridges, *New Verse*, v.

51 Auden, *The Dyer's Hand*, 297.

52 Ibid., 297.

53 See Beum, 'Syllabic Verse in English', 259–75.

54 Quoted in Elizabeth Gregory, *The Critical Response to Marianne Moore* (Westport, CT: Praeger, 2003), 137.

55 Ibid., 49.

56 The text of Auden's poems is that of W. H. Auden, *Collected Poems,* ed. Edward Mendelson (New York: Vintage, 1991).

57 John Fuller, *W. H. Auden: A Commentary* (London: Faber and Faber, 1998), 269.

58 'It is tactful, when making an obscure reference, to arrange that the verse shall be intelligible even when the reference is not understood.' Christopher Ricks, *Allusion to the Poets* (Oxford: Oxford University Press, 2002), 2.

59 Auden's earliest classical metres pre-date a mid-century vogue for translating Horace's odes in accentual-syllabic English equivalents. J. B. Lieshman, *Translating Horace: Thirty Odes Translated into the Original Metres with the Latin Text and an Introductory and Critical Essay* (Oxford: Bruno Cassirer, 1956), nowhere acknowledges, and may be unaware of, Auden's English versions of English Horatian lyric metres. Seven years later, James Mitchie, *The Odes of Horace* (Harmondsworth, UK: Penguin, 1967), followed suit by preserving the classical syllable-count of thirteen odes, eleven of them alcaics, acknowledging that Lieshman's example had persuaded him that 'Alcaics could be strictly and successfully naturalised' into English (xv). Like Lieshman, Mitchie makes no reference to Auden's alcaics.

60 John Hollander, *Vision and Resonance*, 276, calls the Freud elegy 'Hölderlin-shaped', aptly connecting it to the German tradition of the reception of the alcaic strophe. Fuller, *W. H. Auden: A Commentary*, 295, notes that Auden 'probably first read' Hölderlin in 1936.

61 It is an irksome fact that there is no consensus over the names for the various asclepiad metres. I use 'fourth asclepiad' here to correspond to the terminology adopted by Rudd in his Loeb edition of Horace's *Odes*.

62 Fuller, *W. H. Auden: A Commentary*, 413.

63 Edward Callan, *Auden: A Carnival of Intellect: Auden and His Work, 1923–73* (Oxford: Oxford University Press, 1983), 222.

64 Fuller, *W. H. Auden: A Commentary*, 513.

65 Auden, 'A Thanksgiving', *Collected Poems*, 671.

66 Clive James, 'A Testament to Self-Control', *TLS* (12 January 1973): 25.

67 Edward Callan, 'W. H. Auden', *TLS* (16 March 1973): 296.

68 John Hollander, *Vision and Resonance*, xii, wrote of Auden that his 'ear for prosody was like a moral sense'. Among many ways of construing that claim is that a concern for, and a cultivated capacity to perceive and appreciate, poetic form involves the morality of helping to preserve 'traces of civilisation' and the civilized values they exemplify.

69 Juan Christian Pellicer, *Preposterous Virgil* (London: Bloomsbury, 2022), ch. 2.

70 Ibid., ch. 2.

71 W. H. Auden, *The Portable Greek Reader* (Harmondsworth, UK: Penguin, 1948), 3.

72 In Auden's prosody, 'the' and 'echo' elide, and so constitute two rather than three syllables.

73 On the question of whether the emergence of a conventional rhythm within a syllabic form constitutes a 'lapse', John Hollander's criticism is exemplary, and particularly germane to the present discussion, since his points of reference are none other than Bridges, Moore, and Auden. On the one hand, he finds it a kind of failure that Bridges's famous syllabic poem 'Cheddar Pinks' begins with two lines that already could be construed as having an iambic rhythm (*Vision and Resonance*, 274).

On the other, he notes that one feature – not a bug – of the syllabic verses of Moore and Auden is their ability to allow conventional rhythms from time to time to surface and submerge. With respect to Auden, Hollander's view is reflected in the judgment of Richard Hillyer, *Auden's Syllabic Verse* (Lanham, MD: Lexington Books, 2020), xxi: 'Auden's own practice reveals how syllabic verse can create expressive effects without forsaking its identity when making use of phrases intelligible in terms of traditional foot-scansions associated with accentual syllabic metres; effectiveness here requires that these brief ventures into more familiar territory stand out against their backdrop.'

74 Auden, *Portable Greek Reader*, 4.

75 See John Talbot, 'Auden's Horatian Mosaic,' *Classical and Modern Literature* 25.2 (2005): 9–28. In 'Streams,' Auden's alcaics imply a reference to the little stream of Bandusia that Horace celebrates in *Odes* 3.13. What makes 'Streams' stand out among Auden's alcaics is grafting into the alcaics an extraordinarily complex system of internal rhymes that suggest, sonically, the grammatical 'rhymes' created by syntactical hyperbaton in Horace's odes. The result is the most elaborate and most Horatian of all of Auden's alcaic verses, but the sound-effects cannot quite compensate for the elaborate syntactical and metrical effects of a Horatian ode.

Afterword

1 Donald Hall, *The Museum of Clear Ideas* (New York: Tichnor and Fields, 1993), 82.

2 Hall, *Museum of Clear Ideas*, 120.

3 Translations of Horace are those of Niall Rudd, *Horace: Odes and Epodes* (Cambridge, MA: Harvard University Press, 2004).

4 See R. G. M. Nisbett and M. Hubbard, *A Commentary on Horace Odes: Book I* (Oxford: Clarendon Press, 1970), 302.

5 Hall, *Museum of Clear Ideas*, 43–4.

6 A breakthrough and signature song is 'Like a Virgin' (1984). 'How could I be anything else but what I am, having been named Madonna? I would either have ended up a nun or this.' Mary Cross, *Madonna: A Biography* (Westport, CT: Greenwood, 2007), 1.

7 Robert Venturi, Denise Scott Brown and Steven Izenour, *Learning from Las Vegas: The Forgotten Symbolism of Architectural Form* (Cambridge, MA: The MIT Press, 1977), 18. After a half decade, this is still the freshest and most gamesome analysis of Caesars Palace's relation to Roman culture. The authors relish the wanton eclecticism (see especially 51), find in Roman triumphal arches an antecedent of massive Vegas billboards (53), and – who knows whether with conscious irony or not? – link the semantic clutter of the Strip to 'the complex architectural accumulations of the Roman Forum' (116).

8 Hall, *Museum of Clear Ideas*, 60–2.

9 Ibid., 61.

10 Ibid., 60.

11 Ibid., 54.

12 Ibid., 120.

13 Auden's praise is recorded in his introduction to John Hollander, *A Crackling of Thorns* (New Haven, CT: Yale University Press, 1958), x–xi, which he had chosen for the Yale Younger Poets prize.

14 Marilyn Hacker, *Desesperanto: Poems 1999–2002* (New York: W.W. Norton) 2003, 32–5.

15 Marilyn Hacker, *Winter Numbers* (New York: W. W. Norton, 1995), 71–2.

16 Rosanna Warren, 'Pronouncing "Carpenter": Quantitative Meter in English', in *An Exaltation of Forms: Contemporary Poets Celebrate the Diversity of their Art*, ed. Annie Finch and Katherine Varnes (Ann Arbor: University of Michigan Press, 2002), 90–1.

17 Hacker, *Winter Numbers*, 41.

18 Daryl Hine, *Resident Alien* (New York: Atheneum, 1975), 32–2.

19 Bill Coyle, *The God of This World to His Prophet* (Chicago: Ivan R. Dee, 2006), 9.

20 'The New Formalism' is a misleading and contentious term, often repudiated by those to whom it has been applied. But it has in any case now come to stand very generally for a small but significant movement, chiefly among North American poets, calling for renewed emphasis on formal technique, especially attention to traditional metre and rhyme. For a book-length account of the revolution in taste that resulted in the domination of free verse and the supposed marginalization of traditional forms, written from the point of view of a prominent New Formalist, see Timothy Steele, *Missing Measures: Modern Poetry and the Revolt against Meter* (Fayetteville: University of Arkansas Press, 1990).

21 E.g., Alfred Corn, *The Poem's Heartbeat: A Manual of Prosody* (Brownsville, OR: Story Line Press, 1997), who cautions neophytes that merely replicating classical metrical templates may produce poems whose pattern cannot actually be *heard*, 113; Lewis Turco, *The New Book of Forms* (Lebanon, NH: University Press of New England, second edition, 1986; third edition, 2000); John Hollander, *Rhyme's Reason: A Guide to English Verse* (New Haven, CT: Yale University Press, 1981); Robin Skelton, *The Shapes of our Singing: A Comprehensive Guide to Verse Forms and Meters from Around the World* (Spokane, WA: Eastern Washington University Press, 2002); Timothy Steele, *All the Fun's in How You Say a Thing* (Athens, OH: Ohio University Press, 1999), significant, for our purposes, in part because its author's reputation stands in part upon his success in writing English versions of the sapphic strophe).

22 Contrast the historically rooted character of nineteenth-century manuals surveyed in chapter 3 of Meredith Martin, *The Rise and Fall of Metre: Poetry and English National Culture, 1860–1930* (Princeton, NJ: Princeton University Press, 2012.

23 Marilyn Hacker, 'The Sonnet', in *An Exaltation of Forms: Contemporary Poets Celebrate the Diversity of their Art*, edited by Annie Finch and Kathrine Varnes (Ann Arbor: The University of Michigan Press, 2002), 297.

24 Hall, *Museum of Clear Ideas*, 97.

25 I give an account in John Talbot, '"The Principle of the Daguerreotype": Translation from the Classics', in *The Oxford History of Classical Reception in English Literature*, vol. 4, edited by Norman Vance and Jennifer Wallace (Oxford: Oxford University Press, 2015), 57–78.

26 At the time of writing in 2021, increased hostility to the very idea of 'Classics departments', and the perception of requiring students to learn Greek and Latin as socially harmful, is acting as a further barrier to encountering the classics themselves, rather than via anglicized mediation.

27 Virginia Woolf, 'The Perfect Language', *Times Literary Supplement* (14 May 1917), 247.

28 See Talbot, 'The Principle of the Daguerreotype', 58–62.

29 Seamus Heaney, *The Human Chain* (London: Faber and Faber, 2010), 46.

30 Charles Martindale, 'Roman Mosaic', *TLS* (8 October 2010): 12.

31 Robert Bly, 'I.26', in *Horace: The Odes: New Translations by Contemporary Poets*, ed. J. D. McClatchy (Princeton, NJ: Princeton University Press, 2002), 77.

32 Richard Tarrant, *Horace's Odes* (Oxford: Oxford University Press, 2020), 213.

Works Cited

Abercrombie, Lascelles. 'A New Voice'. *The Nation* 15 (1914): 423.

Allington, C. A. *Eton Lyric*. London: Ingleby, 1925.

Anon. *Notes & Queries* (19 July 1851): 14.

Anon. 'Horace and His Translators'. *The Quarterly Review* 180 (January–April 1895): 111–37.

Anon. 'Recent Translations of Horace'. *The Christian Remembrancer* 56 (July–October 1868): 19–34.

Anon. 'Some Translations from the Classics'. *The Academy* 32:794 (July–December 1887): 52–3.

Arber, Edward. *Richard Stanyhurst, Translation of the first Four Books of the Aeneis of P. Virgilius Maro: With Other Poetic Devices Thereto Annexed 1582*. London: The English Scholar's Library, 1880.

Attridge, Derek. *Well-Weighed Syllables: Elizabethan Verse in Classical Metres*. Cambridge: Cambridge University Press, 1974.

Attridge, Derek. *Moving Words: Forms of English Poetry*, Oxford: Oxford University Press, 2013.

Auden, W. H. *The Portable Greek Reader*. Harmondsworth, UK: Penguin, 1948.

Auden, W. H. *The Dyer's Hand*. London: Faber and Faber, 1963.

Auden, W. H. Reply to Auden's 'A Change of Air'. *Kenyon Review* 26 (Winter, 1964): 190–208.

Auden, W. H. *A Certain World: A Commonplace Book*. New York: Viking, 1970.

Auden, W. H. 'New Poems'. In *The Critical Response to Marianne Moore*, edited by Elizabeth Gregory, 136–8. Westport, CT: Praeger, 2003.

Bäckman, Sven. *Tradition Transformed: Studies in the Poetry of Wilfred Owen*. Lund: C. W. K. Gleerup, 1979.

Basilone, Giuseppe. *Guida allo Studio dell' Opera Letteraria di Carducci*. Napoli: Casa Editrice Federico e Ardia, 1953.

Bebbington, W. G. 'Jessie Pope and Wilfred Owen'. *Ariel* 3.4 (1972): 82–93.

Becker, Andrew S. 'The Rhythm in a Sinuous Stanza: The Anatomy and Acoustic Contour of the Latin Alcaic'. *American Journal of Philology* 133:1 (2012): 117–52.

Bennett, W. *German Verse in Classical Metres*. The Hague: Mouton & Co., 1963.

Beum, Robert. 'Syllabic Verse in English'. *Prairie Schooner* 31:3 (1957): 259–75.

Bins, J. W. *The Latin Poetry of English Authors*. Abingdon, UK: Routledge, 1974, 2015.

Bly, Robert. '1.26'. In *Horace: The Odes: New Translations by Contemporary Poets*, edited by J. D. McClatchy, 77. Princeton, UK: Princeton University Press, 2002.

Bradley, A. C. *A Commentary on Tennyson's In Memoriam.* London: Macmillan, 1902.

Bradner, Leicester. *Musae Anglicanae: A History of Anglo-Latin Poetry, 1500-1925.* New York: Modern Language Association of America, 1940.

Breen, Jennifer. *Wilfred Owen: Selected Poetry and Prose.* London: Routledge, 1988.

Brewer, R. F. *Orthometry: The Art of Versification and the Technicalities of Poetry.* Edinburgh: John Grant, 1908.

Bridges, Robert. *Milton's Prosody: An Examination of the Rules of the Blank Verse in Milton's Later Poems, with an Account of the Versification of Samson Agonistes, and General Notes.* Oxford: Clarendon Press, 1894.

Bridges, Robert and William Johnson Stone. *Milton's Prosody by Robert Bridges & Classical Metres in English Verse by William Johnson Stone.* Oxford: Clarendon Press, 1901.

Bridges, Robert. *Poetical Works of Robert Bridges.* Oxford: Oxford University Press, 1912.

Bridges, Robert. *Milton's Prosody, with a Chapter on Accentual Verse & Notes.* Oxford: Clarendon Press, 1921.

Bridges, Robert. *New Verse Written in 1921 by Robert Bridges, Poet Laureate, With Other Poems of That Year and A Few Earlier Pieces.* Oxford, Clarendon Press, 1925.

Bridges, Robert. *Poetical Works of Robert Bridges, with 'The Testament of Beauty' but Excluding the Eight Dramas.* London: Oxford University Press, 1953.

Bridges, Robert and R. C. Treveylan. *XXI Letters: A correspondence between Robert Bridges and R. C. Trevelyan on 'New Verse' and 'The Testament of Beauty'.* Stanford Dingley: The Mill House Press, 1955.

Brower, Rueben. *The Poetry of Robert Frost: Constellations of Intention.* New York: Oxford University Press, 1963.

Brunhöze, F. *Geschichte der Lateinischen Literatur des Mittelalters.* Munich: Wilhelm Fink Verlag, 1992.

Budelmann, Felix. *Greek Lyric: A Selection.* Cambridge: Cambridge University Press, 2018.

Buell, Lawrence. 'Frost as a New England Poet'. In *The Cambridge Companion to Robert Frost,* edited by Robert Faggen, 101–22. Cambridge: Cambridge University Press, 2001.

Burnett, Anne Pippin. *Three Archaic Poets: Archilochus, Alcaeus, Sappho.* London: Duckworth, 1983.

Burnett, Archie. *The Letters of A. E. Housman.* Oxford: Oxford University Press, 2007.

Burnshaw, Stanley. *Robert Frost Himself.* New York: G. Braziller, 1986.

Buxton, John. *Sir Philp Sidney and the English Renaissance.* London: Palgrave Macmillan, 1978.

Callan, Edward. 'W. H. Auden'. *TLS* (16 March 1973): 295–6.

Callan, Edward. *Auden: A Carnival of Intellect: Auden and His Work, 1923-1973.* Oxford: Oxford University Press, 1983.

Calverley, Charles Stuart. *Literary Remains of Charles Stuart Calverley.* London: George Bell, 1885.

Calverley, C. S. *The Complete Works of C. S. Calverley.* London: George Bell, 1901.

Campbell, D. A. *Greek Lyric I.* Cambridge, MA: Harvard University Press, 1982.

Campbell, D. A. *The Golden Lyre: The Themes of the Greek Lyric Poets.* London: Duckworth, 1983.

Campbell, D. A. 'Alcaeus'. In *The Cambridge History of Classical Literature*, vol. 1, edited by P. E. Easterling and E. J. Kenney, 209–14. Cambridge: Cambridge University Press, 1985.

Carne-Ross, D. S. 'Jocasta's Divine Head: English With a Foreign Accent'. In *Classics and Translation: Essays by D. S. Carne-Ross*, edited by Kenneth Haynes, 19–48. Lewisburg, PA: Bucknell University Press, 2010.

Carne-Ross and Kenneth Haynes. *Horace in English.* Harmondsworth, UK: Penguin, 1996.

Coleman, K. A. *Statius Silvae IV.* Oxford: Oxford University Press, 1998.

Commager, Steele. *The Odes of Horace: A Critical Study.* New Haven, CT: Yale University Press, 1962.

Cook, Reginald. *Robert Frost: A Living Voice.* Amherst, MA: The University of Massachusetts Press, 1974.

Commager, Steele. *The Odes of Horace: A Critical Study.* New Haven, CT: Yale University Press, 1962.

Conington, John. *The Odes and Carmen Saeculare of Horace.* London: Bell, 1892.

Cooper, David D. 'For Once, Then, Something'. In *The Robert Frost Encyclopedia*, edited by Lewis Tuten and John Zubizarreta, 120. Westport, CT: Greenwood Press.

Corn, Alfred. *The Poem's Heartbeat: A Manual of Prosody.* Brownsville, OR: Story Line Press, 1997.

Coyle, Bill. *The God of This World to His Prophet.* Chicago: Ivan R. Dee, 2006.

Cramer, Jefferey S. *Robert Frost Among His Poems.* Jefferson, NC: McFarland, 1996.

Crawford, Julie. 'Sidney's Sapphics and the Role of Interpretive Communities'. *English Literary History* 69:4 (2002): 979–1007.

Cross, Mary. *Madonna: A Biography.* Westport, CT: Greenwood, 2007.

Diehl, Ernst. *Anthologia Lyrica Graeca.* Leipzig: B. G. Teubner, 1925.

Douglas, Norman. 'Poetry'. *The English Review* 14 (1913): 505.

Drury, John and Victoria Moul. *George Herbert: The Complete Poetry.* Harmondsworth, UK: Penguin, 2015.

Eliot, George. *The Mill on the Floss*, edited by Gordon S. Haight. Oxford: Clarendon Press, 1980.

Eliot, T. S. *Collected Poems.* New York: Harcourt, Brace & Co., 1963.

Eliot, T. S. 'Ezra Pound: His Metric and Poetry'. In *Selected Prose of T. S. Eliot*, edited by Frank Kermode, 149–50. London: Faber and Faber, 1975.

Ellis, Robinson. *A Commentary on Catullus.* Oxford, Clarendon Press, 1889.

Everett, Barbara. 'The Shooting of the Bears: Poetry and Politics in Andrew Marvell'. In *Andrew Marvell: Essays on the Tercentenery of his Death*, edited by R. L Brett, 62–103. Oxford: Oxford University Press for the University of Hull, 1979.

Fairclough, H. Rushton. *Horace: Satires. Epistles. The Art of Poetry.* Cambridge, MA: Harvard University Press, 1926.

Fairclough, H. Rushton, revised by G. P. Goold. *Virgil: Eclogues, Georgics, Aeneid I-VI.* Cambridge, MA: Harvard Univrsity Press, 1996.

Firmage, George J. *E. E. Cummings: Complete Poems, 1904-1962.* New York: Liveright, 2016.

FitzGerald, Edward. *Rubáiyát of Omar Khayyám, the Astronomer-Poet of Persia.* London: Bernard Quaritch, 1859.

Fowler, John Henry. 'Three Roman Poets Translated'. *TLS* (15 May 1913): 208.

Forrest, Martin. 'The Abolition of Compulsory Latin and Its Consequences'. In *The Classical Association: The First Century 1903-2003*, edited by Christopher Stray. Oxford: Oxford University Press, 2004.

Fraenkel, Edward. *Horace.* Oxford: Clarendon Press, 1957.

Frost, Robert. *Collected Poems, Prose, and Plays*, edited by Richard Poirier and Mark Richardson. New York: Library of America, 1995.

Fuller, John. *W. H. Auden: A Commentary.* London: Faber and Faber, 1998.

Garrod, H. W. *Collins.* Oxford: Clarendon Press, 1928.

Gascoigne, George. *Certayne Notes of Instruction Concerning the Making of Verse or Ryme in English, Written at the Request of Master Edouardo Donati.* In *Elizabethan Critical Essays*, edited by G. Gregory Smith, 46–57. Oxford: Clarendon Press, 1904.

Glaser, Ben. *Modernism's Metronome: Meter and Twentieth Century Poetics.* Baltimore: Johns Hopkins University Press, 2020.

Godman, Peter. *Poetry of the Carolingian Renaissance.* Norman: University of Oklahoma Press, 1985.

Goldsmith, Oliver. *The Vicar of Wakefield*, edited by Arthur Friedman. Oxford: Oxford University Press, 2006.

Gray, Erik. 'Nostalgia, the Classics, and the Intimations Ode: Wordsworth's Forgotten Education'. *Philological Quarterly* 80:2 (2001): 186–203.

Gray, Erik. *Alfred, Lord Tennyson: In Memoriam.* New York: W. W. Norton, 2004.

Gregory, Elizabeth. *The Critical Response to Marianne Moore.* Westport, CT: Praeger, 2003.

Greiner, Donald J. *Robert Frost: The Poet and His Critics.* Chicago: American Library Association, 1974.

Gwynn, Stephen. *Tennyson: A Critical Study.* London, 1899.

Hacker, Marilyn. *Winter Numbers.* New York: W. W. Norton, 1995.

Hacker, Marilyn. 'The Sonnet'. In *An Exaltation of Forms: Contemporary Poets Celebrate the Diversity of their Art*, edited by Annie Finch and Kathrine Varnes, 297–307. Ann Arbor: University of Michigan Press, 2002.

Hacker, Marilyn. *Desesperanto: Poems 1999–2002.* New York: W. W. Norton, 2003.

Hadas, Rachel. '1.24'. In *Horace: The Odes: New Translations by Contemporary Poets*, edited by J. D. McClatchy, 73. Princeton, NJ: Princeton University Press, 2002.

Haffenden, John. *W. H. Auden: The Critical Heritage.* Abingdon, UK: Routledge, 1983.

Hall, Donald. *The Museum of Clear Ideas.* New York: Tichnor and Fields, 1993.

Hall, Jordan David, ed. *Meter Matters: Verse Cultures of the Long Nineteenth-Century.* Athens, OH: Ohio University Press, 2011.

Hamlin, Hannibal. *Psalm Culture and Early Modern English Literature.* Cambridge: Cambridge University Press, 2004.

Hamlin, Hannibal, Michael G. Brennan, Margaret P. Hannaway, and Noel J. Kinnamon. *The Sidney Psalter: The Psalms of Sir Philip and Mary Sidney.* Oxford: Oxford University Press, 2009.

Hardwick, Lorna and Christopher Stray, eds. *A Companion to Classical Receptions.* Oxford: Blackwell, 2008.

Heinze, Richard. *Die lyrischen Verse des Horaz.* Amsterdam: Hakkert, 1959.

Heaney, Seamus. *The Human Chain.* London: Faber and Faber, 2010.

Hill, Geoffrey. *Tenebrae.* London: André Deutsch, 1979.

Hillyer, Richard. *Auden's Syllabic Verse.* Lanham, MD: Lexington Books, 2020.

Hine, Daryl. *Resident Alien.* New York: Atheneum, 1975.

Hollander, John. *A Crackling of Thorns.* New Haven, CT: Yale University Press, 1958.

Hollander, John. *Rhyme's Reason: A Guide to English Verse.* New Haven, CT: Yale University Press, 1981.

Hollander, John. *Vision and Resonance: Two Senses of Poetic Form.* New Haven, CT: Yale University Press, 1986.

Hollander, John. *Picture Window.* New York: Alfred A. Knopf, 2005.

Hopkins, David. *Conversing with Antiquity: English Poets and the Classics, from Shakespeare to Pope.* Oxford: Oxford University Press, 2010.

Houghton, L. B. T. and Gesine Manuwald. *Neo-Latin Poetry in the British Isles.* London: Bristol Classical Press, 2012.

Hurley, Michael. 'George Saintsbury's *History of English Prosody*'. *Essays in Criticism* 60:4 (October 2010): 336–60.

Hurst, Isobel. 'Arthur Hugh Clough'. In *The Oxford History of Classical Reception in English Literature*, vol. 4, edited by Norman Vance and Jennifer Wallace, 495–508. Oxford: Oxford University Press, 2015.

Hurst, Isobel. 'Classics in Education after 1880'. In *The Oxford History of Classical Reception in English Literature*, vol. 5, edited by Kenneth Haynes, 23–41. Oxford: Oxford University Press, 2019.

Hutchinson, G. O. *Greek Lyric Poetry: A Commentary on Selected Larger Pieces.* Oxford: Oxford University Press, 2001.

Isherwood, Christopher. 'Postscript'. In *W. H. Auden: A Tribute*, edited by Stephen Spender, 78–9. New York: Macmillan, 1975.

James, Clive. 'A Testament to Self-Control'. *TLS* (12 January 1973): 25–6.

Johnson, Samuel. *Lives of the English Poets*, edited by George Birkbeck Hill. New York: Octogon Books, 1967.

Kallendorf, Craig W. *A Companion to the Classical Tradition.* Oxford: Blackwell, 2007.

Kelliher, W. Hilton. 'The Latin Poetry of George Herbert', In *The Latin Poetry of English Authors*, edited by J. W. Binns, 26–57. Abingdon, UK: Routledge, 1974, 2015.

Kiel, Heinrich. *Grammatici Latini*. 7 vols. Leipzig: Teubner, 1855–1928.

Knight, Sarah and Stefan Tilg. *The Oxford Handbook of Neo-Latin*. Oxford: Oxford University Press, 2015.

Kugel, James. *The Idea of Biblical Poetry*. New Haven, CT: Yale University Press, 1981.

Leishman, J. B. *Translating Horace: Thirty Odes Translated into the Original Metres with the Latin Text and an Introductory and Critical Essay*. Oxford: Bruno Cassirer, 1956.

Leonard, John. *John Milton: The Complete Poems*. London: Penguin, 1988.

Lister, Bob. 'Exclusively for Everyone'. In *Learning Latin and Greek from Antiquity to the Present*, edited by Elizabeth P. Archibald, William Brockliss, and Jonathan Gnoza, 184–97. Cambridge: Cambridge University Press, 2015.

Macaulay, Thomas Babington. 'Milton'. In *Complete Writings*, vol. 11. Boston: Houghton Mifflin, 1899–1900.

Markley, A. A. *Stateliest Measures: Tennyson and the Literature of Greece and Rome*. Toronto: University of Toronto Press, 2004.

Martin, Meredith. *The Rise and Fall of Meter: Poetry and English National Culture, 1860–1930*. Princeton, NJ: Princeton University Press, 2012.

Martindale, Charles. *Redeeming the Text: Latin Poetics and the Hermeneutics of Reception*. Cambridge: Cambridge University Press, 1993.

Martindale, Charles and Richard F. Thomas, ed. *Classics and the Uses of Reception*. Oxford: Blackwell, 2006.

Martindale, Charles. 'Roman Mosaic'. *TLS* (8 October 2010): 12.

Martindale, Charles. 'Reception: A New Humanism? Receptivity, Pedagogy, the Transhistorical'. *Classical Receptions Journal* 5.2 (2013): 169–83.

Mayer, Roland. *Horace: Odes Book 1*. Cambridge: Cambridge University Press, 2012.

McDonald, Peter. *Sound Intentions: The Workings of Rhyme in Nineteenth Century Poetry*. Oxford: Oxford University Press, 2012.

Mitchie, James. *The Odes of Horace*. Harmondsworth, UK: Penguin, 1967.

Morgan, Llewelyn. *Musa Pedestris: Metre and Meaning in Roman Verse*. Oxford: Oxford University Press, 2010.

Moul, Victoria. 'Lyric Poetry'. In *The Oxford Handbook of Neo-Latin*, edited by Sarah Knight and Stephan Tilg, 41–56. Oxford: Oxford University Press, 2015.

Moul, Victoria. 'Introduction'. In *A Guide to Neo-Latin Literature*, edited by Victoria Moul, 1–13. Cambridge: Cambridge University Press, 2017.

Moul, Victoria. *A Literary History of Latin & English Poetry: Bilingual Verse in Early Modern England*. Cambridge: Cambridge University Press, 2022.

Mulhauser, F. L. *The Poems of Arthur Hugh Clough*. Oxford: Clarendon Press, 1974.

Murray, Gilbert. *The Classical Tradition in Poetry*. Cambridge, MA: Harvard University Press, 1927.

Newbolt, Henry. 'The Future of English Verse'. *International Quarterly* 9 (1904): 366–81.

Nichols, F. J. *An Anthology of Neo-Latin Poetry*. New Haven, CT: Yale University Press, 1979.

Nisbet, R. G. M. and M. Hubbard. *A Commentary on Horace: Odes I*. Oxford: Oxford University Press, 1970.

Otis, Brooks. 'The Relevance of Horace'. *Arion* 9:2–3 (1970): 146–74.

Owen, Harold and John Bell. *Wilfred Owen: Collected Letters*. London: Oxford University Press, 1967.

Owen, Wilfred. *The Complete Poems and Fragments*. 2 vols, edited by Jon Stallworthy. London: Norton, 1983.

Page, D. L. *Sappho and Alcaeus*. Oxford: Oxford University Press, 1955.

Parini, Jay. *Robert Frost, A Life*. New York: Henry Holt, 1999.

Pellicer, Juan Christian. *Preposterous Virgil: Reading Through Stoppard, Auden, Wordsworth, Heaney*. London: Bloomsbury, 2022.

Perosa, Alessandro and John Sparrow. *Renaissance Latin Verse: An Anthology*. Chapel Hill: University of North Carolina Press, 1979.

Phelan, Joseph Patrick. 'Radical Metre: The English Hexameter in Clough's "Bothie of Toper-na-Fuosich"'. *Review of English Studies* 50:198 (1999), 166–87.

Phelan, Joseph. *The Music of Verse: Metrical Experimentation in Nineteenth-Century Poetry*. London: Palgrave Macmillan, 2012.

Pollard, Arthur. 'Three Horace Translations by Tennyson'. *Tennyson Research Bulletin* 4:1 (1982): 16–24.

Pope, Jessie. *Jessie Pope's War Poems*. London: Grant Richards, 1915.

Prins, Yopie. *Victorian Sappho*. Princeton, NJ: Princeton University Press, 1999.

Prins, Yopie. 'Nineteenth Century Homers and the Hexameter Mania'. In *Nation, Language, and the Ethics of Translation*, edited by Sandra Bermann and Michael Wood, 229–56. Princeton: Princeton University Press, 2005.

Quinn, Kenneth. *Catullus: The Poems*. London: Macmillan, 1970.

Reckford, Kenneth. *Horace*. New York: Twayne, 1969.

Ricks, Christopher. *The Force of Poetry*. Oxford: Clarendon Press, 1984.

Ricks, Christopher. *The Poems of Tennyson*, 3 vols. Harlow, UK: Longman, 1987.

Ricks, Christopher. *Tennyson*. London and Berkeley: Macmillan and University of California Press, 1989.

Rosenblitt, J. Alison. *E. E. Cummings' Modernism and the Classics: Each Imperishable Stanza*. Oxford: Oxford University Press, 2016.

Rossi, Luigi. 'Horace, a Greek Lyrist without Music'. In *Horace: Odes and Epodes. Oxford Readings in Classical Studies*, edited by Michele Lowrie, 356–77. Oxford: Oxford University Press, 2009.

Rudd, Niall. *Horace: Odes and Epodes*. Cambridge, MA: Harvard University Press, 2004.

Saintsbury, George. *A History of English Prosody from the Twelfth Century to the Present Day*. 3 vols. London: Macmillan, 1910.

Salvatore, Armando. *Prosodia e metrica Latina*. Rome: Jouvance, 1983.

Shatto, Susan and Marion Shaw. *Tennyson: In Memoriam*. Oxford: Oxford University Press, 1992.

Shirley, W. *Moral: The Most Important Factor in the War*. London: Greening, 1909.

Simeone, William. 'A Probable Antecedent of Marvell's Horatian Ode'. *Notes & Queries* 197 (1952): 316–18.

Skelton Robin, *The Shapes of our Singing: A Comprehensive Guide to Verse Forms and Meters from Around the World*. Spokane, WA: Eastern Washington University Press, 2002.

Smith, G. Gregory. *Elizabethan Critical Essays*. 2 vols. Oxford: Clarendon Press, 1904.

Smith, Hallet. 'English Metrical Psalms in the Sixteenth Century and Their Literary Significance'. *Huntington Library Quarterly* 9 (1946): 249–71.

Smith, D. Nichol. 'Johnson's Poems'. In *New Light on Dr. Johnson*. New Haven, CT: Yale University Press, 1950.

Smith, Nigel. *The Poems of Andrew Marvell*. London: Longman, 2003.

Stallworthy, Jon. *Wilfred Owen*. Oxford: Oxford University Press, 1974.

Stanford, Donald E. *The Selected Letters of Robert Bridges*, vol. 2. Newark, DE: University of Delaware Press, 1984.

Steele, Timothy. *Missing Measures: Modern Poetry and the Revolt Against Meter*. Fayetteville: University of Arkansas Press, 1990.

Steele, Timothy. *Sapphics and Uncertainties*. 1995.

Steele, Timothy. *All the Fun's in How You Say a Thing*. Athens, OH: The Ohio University Press, 1999.

Steele, Timothy. '"Across Spaces of the Footed Line": the Meter and Versification of Robert Frost'. In *The Cambridge Companion to Robert Frost*, edited by Robert Faggen, 123–53. Cambridge: Cambridge University Press, 2001.

Steiner, George. *George Steiner: A Reader*. New York: Oxford University Press, 1984.

Stray, Christopher. *The Classical Association: The First Century 1903–2003*. Oxford: Oxford University Press, 2004.

Swinburne, Charles Algernon. 'Sappho'. *The Saturday Review* (21 February 1914): 679.

Syndikus, Hans Peter. *Catull: Eine Interpretation*, vol. 1. Darmstadt: Wissenshalftliche Buchgesellschaft, 1984.

Syme, Ronald. *The Roman Revolution*. Oxford: Oxford University Press, 1939, 1960.

Talbot, John. 'Auden's Horatian Mosaic'. *Classical and Modern Literature* 25.2 (2005): 9–28.

Talbot, John. 'A Late Flowering of English Alcaics'. In *Perceptions of Horace: A Roman Poet and His Readers*, edited by L. B. T. Houghton and Maria Wyke, 304–22. Cambridge: Cambridge University Press, 2009.

Talbot, John. '"The Principle of the Daguerreotype": Translation from the Classics'. In *The Oxford History of Classical Reception in English Literature*, vol. 4., edited by Norman Vance and Jennifer Wallace, 57–78. Oxford: Oxford University Press, 2015.

Tarrant, Richard. *Horace's Odes*. Oxford: Oxford University Press, 2020.

Tennyson, Hallam. *Alfred Lord Tennyson: A Memoir by His Son.* 3 vols. London: Macmillan, 1911.

Terhune, Alfred McKinley and Annabelle Burdick Terhune. *The Letters of Edward FitzGerald, Volume 4, 1877–1883.* Princeton, NJ: Princeton University Press, 2016.

Thomas, Richard. *Horace Odes IV and Carmen Saeculare.* Cambridge: Cambridge University Press, 2011.

Thomson, D. F. S. *Catullus.* Toronto: University of Toronto Press, 1997.

Traugott, Elizabeth Closs. 'Auden's Streams: A Verbal Rite Fittingly Done'. *Indian Journal of Applied Linguistics* 10:1–2 (1984): 29–49.

Turco, Lewis. *The New Book of Forms.* Lebanon, NH: University Press of New England, 2000.

Vandiver, Elizabeth. *Stand in the Trench, Achilles: Classical Receptions in British Poetry of the Great War.* Oxford: Oxford University Press, 2010.

Venturi, Robert, Denise Scott Brown and Steven Izenour. *Learning from Las Vegas: The Forgotten Symbolism of Architectural Form.* Cambridge, MA: The MIT Press, 1977.

Warren, Rosanna. 'Alcaics in Exile: W. H. Auden's "In Memory of Sigmund Freud"'. *Philosophy and Literature* 20:1 (1996): 111–21.

Warren, Rosanna. 'Pronouncing "Carpenter": Quantitative Meter in English'. In *An Exaltation of Forms: Contemporary Poets Celebrate the Diversity of their Art*, edited by Annie Finch and Katherine Varnes, 86–94. Ann Arbor: University of Michigan Press, 2002.

Wells, Arthur F. *A Day of God: Being Five Addresses on the Subject of the Present War.* London: Wells, Gardner, Darton: 1914.

Wendorf, Richard and Charles Ryscamp. *The Works of William Collins.* Oxford: Clarendon Press, 1979.

West, M. L. *Ancient Greek Music.* Oxford: Oxford University Press, 1992.

West, D. L. *Horace, Odes II: Vatis amici.* Oxford: Oxford University Press, 1998.

Wilkinson, L. P. *Horace and his Lyric Poetry.* Cambridge: Cambridge University Press, 1952.

Wilkinson, L. P. *Golden Latin Artistry.* Cambridge: Cambridge University Press, 1963.

Williams, Gwyn. *An Introduction to Welsh Poetry from the Beginnings to the Sixteenth Century.* Freeport, NY: Books for Libraries Press, 1954, 1970.

Wilson, Ross. 'Both Free and Bound'. *TLS* (9 May 2014): 28.

Woods, Gillian. *Shakespeare's Unreformed Fictions.* Oxford: Oxford University Press, 2013.

Woolf, Virginia. 'The Perfect Language'. *TLS* (24 May 1917): 247.

Yatromanolakis, Dimities. 'Alcaeus and Sappho'. In *The Cambridge Companion to Greek Lyric*, edited by Felix Budelmann. Cambridge: Cambridge University Press, 2009.

Index